THE LIFE

OF

WILLIAM PENN,

THE

SETTLER OF PENNSYLVANIA,

THE

FOUNDER OF PHILADELPHIA, AND ONE OF THE FIRST LAWGIVERS IN THE COLONIES, NOW UNITED STATES, IN 1682.

CONTAINING ALSO,

HIS CELEBRATED TREATY WITH THE INDIANS—HIS PURCHASE OF THEIR COUNTRY—VALUABLE ANECDOTES OF ADMIRAL PENN—ALSO OF KING CHARLES II., KING JAMES II., KING WILLIAM, AND QUEEN ANNE, IN WHOSE REIGNS WILLIAM PENN LIVED—CURIOUS CIRCUMSTANCES THAT LED HIM TO BECOME A QUAKER—WITH A VIEW OF THE ADMIRABLE TRAITS IN THE CHARACTER OF THE PEOPLE CALLED FRIENDS OR QUAKERS, WHO HAVE DONE SO MUCH TO MELIORATE THE CONDITION OF SUFFERING HUMANITY.

BY M. L. WEEMS,
Author of the Life of Washington, &c.

Character of William Penn, by Montesquieu.

"William Penn is a real Lycurgus. And though the former made PEACE his principal aim, as the latter did WAR: yet they resemble one another in the singular way of living to which they reduced their people—in the astonishing ascendant they gained over freemen; and in the strong passions which they subdued."

Character of William Penn, by Edmund Burke.

"William Penn, as a legislator, deserves immortal thanks from the whole world. 'Tis pleasing to do honour to those *great men* whose *virtues* and *generosity* have contributed to the peopling of the earth, and to the *Freedom* and *Happiness* of *mankind;* and who have preferred the interest of a remote posterity and times unknown, to their own fortune, and to the quiet and security of their own lives."

PHILADELPHIA:
URIAH HUNT & SON,
No. 44 North Fourth Street.
AND FOR SALE BY BOOKSELLERS GENERALLY THROUGHOUT THE UNITED STATES.
1852.

THE LIFE

OF

WILLIAM PENN.

CHAPTER I.

> If, by your ancestors, yourself you rate;
> Count me those only who were GOOD and GREAT.

If ever a son of Adam and of Eve had cause to glory in the flesh, that son was HONEST, BROAD-BRIMM'D William Penn. "A generation there is," says Solomon, "O how they can lift up their eyebrows, and how they can roll their eyes;" swelling and strutting like the star-tail'd birds of the dunghill, because their fathers before them were *knights* or *baronets!* though all beyond were shoe-blacks or rat-catchers. But not so the noble founder of Pennsylvania. He was of the "*well born*," in the worthiest sense of the word. For fifteen generations, the best and bravest blood in England had flowed in the veins of his family, unstained by a single act that history should blush to record. No scoundrel sycophants were made *drunk* at their tables, while the poor tenant's children cried for bread; nor the needy hireling pined for his pay, while their proud drawing-rooms were filled with costly carpets and sideboards. No unsuspecting stranger, after sharing their splendid hospitalities, was fleeced of his purse by their *gambling* arts, and then turned out of doors, to curse the polished robbers. No! Such stains of pride and villany were never known to sully the Penn coat of arms. For, on the contrary, the flood-tide of wealth, won by their high-toned virtues, was constantly turned into such active channels of private and public usefulness, that they were the boast and blessing of all the country. And to this day, often, as the traveller through Buckinghamshire, charmed with the stately mansions, shining amidst clovered meadows and fields of golden grain, inquires, "*what lovely farms are these?*" the honest rustic, with joy brightening on his sun-burnt face, replies, "why, sir, *this* is PENN'S DALE! or PENN'S HOUSE! *that, is* PENN'S WOOD! or PENN'S LAND!

As like generally begets like; and the ring-dove that saddens the grove with his cooings, is never sprung from the fire-ey'd falcon: so many have supposed that our gentle William Penn must have descended from a long succession of Quaker ancestors. But this is altogether a mistake; for he was the first of that sect ever heard of in his numerous family. Indeed, so far from having been a meekly looking FRIEND, his father was a fierce iron-faced admiral in the British navy: and not as in these halcyon days neither, when British captains, like ladies' lap-dogs, can sleep on velvet cushions, and move about in clouds of sweet-scented bergamot and lavender. But he was a sea captain in the bloody days of Van Tromp, and the Duke of York, when the great rival republics of England and Holland were rushing forth, in all their thunders and lightnings, striving for the rule of the watery world. And it is but justice to record of him that, so many were the proofs which he had given of an extraordinary valour and skill, he was appointed to the command of a man of war, at the green age of twenty-one. And he continued gallantly fighting, and rapidly rising, till after passing all the degrees of admiralship, such as rear-admiral, vice-admiral, admiral of the blue, admiral of the red, &c. he had the highest honour of all, conferred on him; the honour to be next in command to the brave Duke of York in the Dutch war of 1665. And the triumph of the British flag in the great and terrible sea-fight in that year was so largely due, under God, to his courage and seamanship, that he was created a knight; and was always received at court with the utmost cordiality. Though then but in the middle of his days, (45) yet his constitution was so wrecked by hard services, that he left the sea, and set himself in good earnest, to prepare for his last great voyage—to heaven. And it is generally thought that he is safely moored there too: for he was a man, in many respects, of a noble heart: and, for a sailor, uncommonly devout; as would appear, among many other still better proofs, from the following epitaph, written by himself, on one of his unfortunate sailors, who, drowned with many others on the coast of Deal, was picked up and buried in the church-yard near that place:—

The boist'rous winds and raging seas,
Have tost me to and fro;
But spite of these, by God's decrees,
I harbour here below—

Where safe at anchor I do ride
With many of our fleet;
In hope one day, again to weigh,
GREAT ADMIRAL CHRIST to meet.

From what has been said of him, most of my readers are, I suppose, so well pleased with our honest admiral as to be ready to pray that, if ever he had a son, that son proved to him a Barnabas, a "son of consolation."

Well, glory to him whose goodness often prepares the richest answer to prayer, even before it is formed in the generous breast!

And still greater glory to him who has made us capable of that amiable philanthropy whereby we can send back our sympathies to the generations that are past, and take a lively interest in the joys of those who lived long before our day. By virtue of this 'tis pleasing to learn of our good admiral that he married—married *early*—and begat a son: but not in his own image. For, while the *father* lived only to represent the miseries of that IRON AGE spoken of by the prophet, when wretched men, blinded by their passions, could rush into bloody fight for *filthy lucre*, the *son* lived to give some blessed signal of that golden age to come, when filled with all the sweetness of divine love, men should deem it "*glory to suffer the spoiling of their goods for conscience sake.*" This child of honour was born to the admiral in the year 1644.

When the incarnate God descended on the earth, the temples of horrid war were shut that selfsame year; and silver-tongued angels were heard to chaunt their anthems of "*Glory to God for coming in the flesh to restore the golden age of peace and good will among men.*" It is not pretended that any testimonials of this high character were given at the birth of this true disciple of the BENEVOLENT SAVIOUR: but it appears, from the unanimous testimony of his historians, that the dove-like spirit of meekness descended upon him even in the cradle.

And here I cannot but relate an anecdote of little William, which will serve to show how soon the ideas of moral right, if not *innate*, may be *planted* in our nature. According to that famous historian, Xenophon, the schoolmasters among the ancient Persians, took much less pains to teach their children the knowledge of *letters* than to inspire them with the love of *Justice*, because, in their opinion, "Honest dealing among men is far more important to happiness than all human learning." They neglected no opportunity to inculcate this on the youthful mind. If, for example, they saw a little man with a big coat, and a big man with a little coat, they would straight fall to catechising the child as to what ought to be done in that case. If the child said, *exchange the coats;* they answered *no:* that might be convenience, but not justice. For if the little man, by his virtues, had got himself a big coat, would it be justice to take it away from him and give it to a big man whose idleness had brought him to rags?

That the Admiral had taken pains to educate his son in this sublime style, may, I think, very fairly be inferred from the following story of little William when only seven years old. Among his father's tenants was a poor man named Thomas Pearce, just such an honest good natured soul as every body loves. The Penn family set great store by him, and especially little William, whom honest Thomas had so often carried in his arms, and returning from the Fair, had brought him many a cake and apple. On some sudden emergence, the Admiral had got Tom with his cart to assist him. After looking, with an air of much sympathy on the poor man, where he wrought till the sweat in big drops trickled down his pallid face, little William came to the Admiral, and said "*father an't you going to pay poor Tom Pearce for working for you so?*"

What makes you ask that, William, replied the Admiral.

Why, because, father, I think you ought to pay him.

Why so, my son?

Why, because, father, I don't see why he should work so hard for you for nothing.

Well, I dare say, William, I shall pay him.

But, father, if you don't pay him money, I'll tell you what you ought to do.

What, my son?

Why, father, when poor Tom comes to want any work done, you should send your wagon to help him.

My *cart*, you mean, William, for you see I have only his cart.

Yes, father, but your wagon is not so much bigger than his cart as you are richer than poor Tom."

God bless my son, cried the Admiral, embracing him, I hope you'll be a BRAVE, HONEST-HEARTED ENGLISHMAN, as long as you live."

From a child, William was given to be sedate and thoughtful, which contributed much towards his improvement of those many providences, such as sickness, whether of himself or his parents, death of relations, frightful dreams, thunder-gusts, and so on—which, like "*line on line, and precept on precept*," are meant of God to lead even children to wisdom. His mother, of whom he was doatingly fond, often seized such providences to make good impressions on his mind. And these impressions were still more deepened by the dismal scenes which his father, sitting by the family fire-side, would often describe, when maddening nations "*go down in ships on the mighty waters*," to mix in bloody fight, among roaring winds and waves. Sometimes he would tell of the great ships of war—how, pierced by a thousand bullets in the dreadful fight, they suddenly disappear with all their shrieking crews, going down swift into their watery graves, while the dark mountain billows, closing over their hapless heads, leave no sign that there any ship had ever sailed before. At other times he would paint the hostile navies, in close and furious combat, hid in clouds of smoke and flame, when, all at once, their magazines taking fire, they blow up with the sound of a thousand thunders, while hundreds of ill-fated seamen, torn limb from limb, by the horrid blast, are thrown miles into the air, nor they nor ships ever seen again.

The earnestness with which little William would listen, and his changeful looks, often bathed in tears, strongly bespoke his kindred feelings, and how truly he mourned the wretched victims of war. But among the many things which the Admiral would tell, to improve the heart of his son, the following seems well worthy of remembrance, as it marks that constantly superintending providence which directs the affairs of men.

On board of the Admiral's ship was a young officer of the name of Fenton, the only son of his mother, and she a widow. Fenton was giddy and dissipated in a high degree, which cost his mother many a tear. One day, as drowned in sorrow, she took leave of him going on ship-board to fight the enemy, she repeated all her former good advice, giving him, at the same time, a beautiful little Bible, which she put into a side pocket made by her own hands, over his left breast. The two fleets met, and a most bloody conflict ensued. The ships grappled each other; and the eager crews, quitting their cannon, fought hand to hand, with pistols and cutlasses, as on dry ground. In the mortal fray, the decks all covered with the dying and the dead, Fenton was attacked by a stout Dutchman, who, presenting his pistol to his heart, drew the trigger. The ball struck. Feeling the shock, Fenton concluded he was mortally wounded, but being naturally brave, he continued to fight on with great fury, though not without secretly wondering that he did not fall. On the ceasing of the battle, which terminated in favour of the British, he began to search for his wound. But not a scratch could he find, nor even a drop of blood. This, no doubt, was great good news to him who had given himself up for dead. He then thought of his Bible, and drawing it from his side pocket, found it miserably torn by the ball, which, but for that strange stop, would have been buried in his heart. The thoughts of heaven and of his mother rushed on his mind. And, for the first time in his life, he fell on his knees and adored a God. Carefully opening his Bible, he found that the ball, after penetrating one half of the sacred volume, had stopped exactly at that famous verse—"Rejoice, O young man, in thy youth and let thy heart cheer thee in the days of thy youth; and walk in the ways of thy heart and in the sight of thine eyes; but know thou, that for all these things God shall bring thee into judgment!" Fenton was so struck with this, as a call from heaven, that he immediately altered his life; and from a worthless reprobate became a GOOD CHRISTIAN—that is, A REAL GENTLEMAN.

CHAPTER II.

As a man must ask his *wife*, whether he is to be a rich man or a beggar; so, a child must ask his *mother*, whether he is to be a wise man or a fool, a saint or a demon for ever. It was in *her* warm bowels that he first received his "*substance, yet being imperfect;*" and his first pulse of life from her throbbing heart. It was in her fond arms that he found his dearest cradle, and his sweetest pillow on her snowy orbs. There were the first eager drawings of his thirsty lips; and there the wanton pattings of his fingers, as filled with the fragrant nectar and gladdened through all his frame, he fell back on her arms, and laughed and jumped and crowed to her strong kissings and chirpings. And still with the rolling years, this tender attachment to his mother continued, "growing with his growth, and strengthening with his strength," because her banners over him were LOVE. Is he frightened? he runs to her for safety. Is he aggrieved? he carries all his complaints to her dear bosom. And while his father, that hardier parent, can turn away from him and sleep and snore insensible to his moans, he feels his mother's arms still pressing him closer and closer to her heart, or hears her tender sighs, as, bathing him with tears, she kisses his feverish lips, and answers him groan for groan.

O happy the child, whose mother, after thus winning his love, seeks to improve it as a ladder, whereby he may ascend to Heaven on the pleasant steps of early piety and virtue. This was the favoured lot of young William Penn. From concurrent testimony of all historians of that day, his mother was a daughter of wisdom. Far different from the credulous million, who, how often soever deceived by the world, will yet go on, like passionate lovers, to woo and woo again the same perfidious mistress. And though sent home chagrined and sad from many a joyless ball and rout, will still hope better things from some subsequent adventure.—*Aye! that will do—another suit of diamonds and of silks!—A new and richer coach and still more flaming harness.*" Thus fond of being led on, like children, by the butterfly attractions of hope. Not so the wiser Mrs. Penn. Disappointments served but to startle her into thought—and to spring suspicions of this world's vanity. As a delicate bird of the skies, accidentally lighting on a *barren*, and defrauded of the *nectarine* food she seeks, instantly lifts the ivory beak and pensive eye of disappointment, then, spurning the inhospitable soil, she spreads her golden plumes and with chirping joy springs towards her native element. Just so it was with the mother of young William Penn. Born for a better, she soon discovered that this world was not the place of her rest.—" A land of shadows, where hardly any thing is real but trouble; and nothing certain but death." Instantly she gave her heart to God. She sought an equal happiness for her son. How could a mother of her sensibility, behold his soft flaxen locks and tender cheeks of youth without tears of solicitude that he might have the Lord for his God?

Such were the views of Mrs. Penn with regard to her son. And correspondent was the education which she gave him. Oh how different from that which many an unfortunate child, now-a-days, receives from an ignorant mother, who at the first step leaves out God and Heaven with all the present and eternal advantages of piety! "*Come, make haste son,*" says she, "*and learn your books*, and *you shall be a great man by and by.*" By *learning his book*, she means, at most, nothing beyond a showy, college education, which, though it may increase his pride and arrogance, seldom adds any thing to his DIVINE and SOCIAL AFFECTIONS, which alone render young men amiable and happy. And by being a *great* man she means only a great *scholar;* a great *physician;* a great *lawyer;* making a great deal of money; building great houses and so on—and after all, the dupe of his passions, and as miserable as pride, envy, hate, intemperance, and duelling can render him! The mother of William Penn did not thus direct his immortal affections to mortal goods, thereby filling up his life with feverish hopes and anguish fears; and all for vanities which he might never win, or soon must lose for ever. Nor did she imitate that other class of mothers, who, if they do, at times, show as though they would lead their children to piety, do not seem to understand wherein it consists. Many a mother for example, just as her little son is dying for sleep, will pull him to her knee, and say "Come, darling, your bed is ready: now say your prayers first. Well, darling, who made you?

Half asleep he drawls out—GOD.

Well, who redeemed you?

JESUS CHRIST.

Well, who sanctified you?

The HOLY GHOST.

What did God make you for?

To serve him.

How are you to serve him?

In spirit and truth.

WELL SAID, DARLING! continues the mother; and praises him for a *good boy;* though what the poor thing has been saying about "*Redeemed*"—"*Sanctified*"—

"*Holy Ghost*," and "*Spirit and Truth*," he no more understands than the parrot does when he prates poor Poll! poor Poll! Now what is this but a delusion of Satan lulling the silly mother into the fatal conceit that she is making a great Christian of her son, while she is actually keeping him in that ignorance of God which is the true cause of all vice and misery. But Mrs. Penn did not thus catechize her son on the *mysteries* of Revelation while as yet he was ignorant of the first truths of natural religion. No! she well knew that before he could "*come to God, he must believe that he is*"—and that before he could "*love him with all his heart*" he must "*know him*" to be that infinitely GREAT and GOOD being who alone is *worthy* of all love. It was her belief that the works of God in the creation were purposely set off in such a style of grandeur and beauty, and convenience in order to startle all, even the young, into a sense of the perfections of the Creator. Hence, Paul argues that—"*the invisible things of God, even his eternal power and Godhead, are clearly seen by the things that are made, insomuch that if men do not adore him as God, they are without excuse.*" And hence it is that David so vehemently calls upon all men to "*give thanks unto the Lord.*" Why? why "*because he is good and his mercy endureth for ever.*"—"*To him who by wisdom created the Heavens; for his goodness endureth for ever.*" "To him who made the sun to rule the day, and the moon and stars to rule the night; for his goodness endureth for ever"—"to him who stretched forth the green earth above the mighty waters; for his goodness endureth for ever"—"to him who created man but a little lower than the angels; for his goodness endureth for ever." And indeed it was in these his wondrous works, as in a glass, that the pious in all ages have employed themselves seeing and conversing with the Creator and singing him ceaseless hymns of praise. "*We ought,*" says Socrates, "*to sing a hymn of praise to God when we are ploughing the sweet scent-*

ed earth."—"*We ought to sing a hymn of praise to God, when we behold the waving harvest; or the orchards laden with delicious fruits."*—"*We ought to sing a hymn of praise to God, when we look around upon the beauties of the fields or survey the glories of the heavens."* So much for Socrates, David, and Paul, the three brightest ornaments of the three grand dispensations of religion—Socrates for the *Light of Nature*, David for the Law by Moses, and Paul for the Gospel by Jesus Christ—all of whom clearly and harmoniously teach us that in educating a dear child for heaven, parents should never think of contenting themselves with a few shallow notions and shibboleths, but should "*dig deep*" and lay an immovable foundation in the glorious being and attributes of God, as so easily and sweetly discoverable in his wonderful works around us. What parent then, or what child but must read with the liveliest pleasure and interest, the following curious dialogue between little William Penn and his mother?

CHAPTER IV.

William, a fine, plump, fleshy boy, five or six years old, standing at his mother's knees, waiting for her to talk with him; while she, after pressing him to her bosom, thus, in a sprightly voice, addresses him—"Well, William, I want to see if you can answer mother one *great question.*"

"Well, mother," replied William, his eyes sparkling, "come tell me what it is."

Well, William, said she, can you tell mother who *made* you?

Yes, to be sure, mother, that I can, easy enough. God did make me, didn't he?

How do you know that, my son?

Heigh, mother, didn't you tell me so a matter of a hundred times and more?

But suppose, William, I had not told you that God made you, do you think you could have found it out?

Here William paused—at length replied, indeed mother I don't know.

Why not, my son, it seems very easy.

Well then, mother, come tell me.

Well now, my son, you see that stone that lies there at your feet, don't you?

Yes, mother, to be sure I do. And what of that stone, mother?

That stone is *something*, isn't it my son?

Yes, to be sure, it is something.

But how do you know it is *something*, William?

Heigh, mother, don't I *see* it; and don't I *feel* it that it is *something;* and a mighty *hard* and *big* and *heavy* something too.—Here good reader, let us pause and note how soon the divine light of reason darts on the minds of children! What master of the mathematics could give a better definition of *matter*, or as the text has it, of *something*, than little William here does "Don't I *see* it, mother," says he; don't I *feel* it that it is *something*, and a mighty *hard* and *big* and *heavy something too!*

Well, but, William, continued his mother, how *came* it to be this *something?*

Indeed, mother, I don't know.

Well, but does it not strike you, my son, that since it *is* something, it must have been *made* so, or, it must have *made itself so?* William paused, as if quite at a loss, but at length said: I don't see, mother, how it could have made *itself.*

Why not, my son?

What, this stone made itself! replied he, like one suddenly struck, as at the idea of something quite absurd and ridiculous; this stone made itself! why, dear me, mother, 'tis such a *dead* thing! it can't *see;* it can't *hear;* it can't *stir.* I don't see any *sense* it had to make itself a stone, or any thing else.

No indeed, William, nor can the greatest philosopher of them all see it neither: for in that case it must have had a great deal of *sense*, which I am sure it has not. Well, now, William, since it is plain that this stone did not make itself, who do you think could have made it?

Indeed, mother, I don't know, unless it was father. As he sails the great ships, perhaps he did make it. When he comes home we will ask him mother, won't we?

Oh no, said Mrs. Penn, shaking her head and smiling; oh no, William, your father did not make it, my son; nor could all the men in the world, put together make it, nor even a single grain of sand.

William appeared much at a loss at this. But after some silence he went on again with his questions—"Well then, mother, who did make that stone?"

Why, my son, answered Mrs. Penn, since it is plain that it had *no sense* to make itself; and since all the men in the world put together could not have made it, it follows that it must have *been made* by some mighty one who had wisdom and power to make all things.

Aye, that's *God*, isn't it mother?

Why yes, to be sure, my son, it is God. It is he made this stone, and all the stones, and all the trees, and all the cattle, and the birds, and the fishes, and all the people, and the mountains, and the skies, and every thing.

And did not God make *me too*, mother, asked William?

Yes, to be sure he did, my son.

But yet, mother, I'm your little boy, an't I?

Yes, that you are, William, and a dear little boy too, but still God did make you for all that. Since all the men in the world, as I said just now, could not make one grain of sand, then O how could I make such a beautiful little boy like you.

And so don't you know any thing, mother, how I came to be made?

No indeed, my son, no more than that stone there. When I married your dear father, I did not know any better than that stone, whether I was to have you or not. Or whether you were to be a little *boy* or not; or whether you were to have fine black eyes or not. I make you, indeed, William! when I cannot make even "one hair of your head white or black." And O how could I have made so fearful and wonderful a frame as yours, when even now that it is made, it is all a perfect mystery to me. See! I place my hand upon my son's heart, and I feel it beating against my fingers; but still I know nothing about how it beats. I put my hand upon his sweet bosom, and feel it heaving as he breathes, but still I am ignorant of it all. And when I look at him every morning, as he breakfasts on his little basin of milk and bread, Oh I'm lost! I'm lost! I'm lost!

Heigh, for what, mother? cried William, surprised.

Why for wonder how his milk and bread, white as snow, should be turned into blood red as crimson; and how that blood soft as milk should be turned, some into sweet little teeth, white and hard as ivory; and some into soft flowing hair like silk; some into sweet polished cheeks like rose buds; and some into bright shining eyes like diamonds! Could I have made you, William, after this wonderful manner? Oh no my son, no—not all the men on earth, nor all the angels in heaven, could have done it. No, none but the great God could have made you.

As good Mrs. Penn uttered these words, which she did with great emphasis, William appeared lost in thought; however, after some silence, and with a deep sigh, he looked up to his mother, and thus went on with his questions again.

Well, mother, what did God make me for?

Why, for his goodness' sake, my son, which loved you so, he wanted to make you happy.

How do I know, mother, that God loves me so; I did never do any thing for him?

Well, son, and what did you ever do for me, and yet I have always loved you very dearly, havn't I.

Yes, mother, but I always see you; but I did never see God.

True William, nor did you ever see your grand-father Pennwood; but still you know that he loved you, don't you?

Yes, mother, that I do know that grandfather Pennwood loves me, for he is always sending me such pretty things. He sent me, you know, mother, my pretty tame rabbits, and my pretty little horse, and a great many other pretty things.

Well then my son, if God gives you a great many more pretty things than grandfather Pennwood ever did, won't you say that he loves you too?

Yes, that I will, mother.

Done! 'tis a bargain, William. And now, my son, brighten up your thoughts and tell your mother who gives you every thing. Who gave you these beautiful eyes? Who gave you these sweet rosy cheeks? Who gave you this lovely forehead? Who gave you these dear ivory teeth? And these nimble little feet for you to run about—and these pretty fingers to handle every thing? And who gave you all the sweet apples, and pears, and cherries, for you to eat? And the birds to sing, and the bees to make honey-comb for you? And this beautiful earth with all the sweet flowers, and corn, and trees? And then who gave you these bright heavens away up yonder, and the sun, the moon, and the stars, all, all to shine so bright for you—O my dear,

dear son, did grandfather Pennwood ever give you any thing like all this?

Here, William, his bosom labouring as with sighs of wonder, replied, O mother, did God give me all these things?

O yes, to be sure, William, all these things; and ten thousand thousand times more than you can ever count.

Well then, mother, God must love me very much indeed, to give me all these things. But mother, what does God want from me that he gives me so many beautiful things?

Why, William, all that he wants of you, my son, is that you should love him very much.

Well but, mother, what good will that do to God though I should love him very much; I am only a little boy, I can't reach up to the skies to give him any thing?

True, William, but still God wants you to love him very much; not that you may give him any thing, but that he may give you a great deal more.

How, mother?

Why, son, because he knows that if you love him very much, you will be sure to be a good boy.

How so, mother?

Why, my son, don't you know that if you love any body very much, it will be sweet to you to do what will please them?

Yes, mother, that is sweet. And don't I always run to do what will please you? When you told me just now to run down into the garden to bring you up some roses, didn't I set off and run away, like my little buck that grand-pa' Pennwood gave me?

Yes, that's what my son did run like a little buck, I could hardly see his feet, he did run so fast. And when he came back, O how beautiful did he look? Not all the roses in the garden could blush like his cheeks—not all the morning sloes could shine like his eyes—

not all the buds of pinks could smell so sweet as his quick panting breath when, with his arms round her neck, and his flaxen locks floating on her bosom, he did hug and kiss his mother.

Well then, come mother, let me hug and kiss you again.

God bless my sweet little son for ever, cried Mrs Penn, pressing him to her snowy bosom, and smothering him with kisses. Soon as the delicious transport was over, little William, with cheeks and eyes glowing with vermilion and diamonds, called out, well, mother, now tell me what I must do for you again, and see how I will run and do it.

There now, William, cried Mrs. Penn, there now! didn't I tell you so? Did'nt I tell you that if you love any body very much, you will be so happy to do every thing for them? Then, O my son, how readily will you do every thing to *please* God, if you do but love him?

What will I do to please him, mother?

Why, my son, you will be *good*, and that's the way to please him.

But what is it that makes any body good, mother?

Why, to be always *praising* God, my son, to be always *praising* God, that's the first and great thing, to be good, to be always *praising* God. And there's nothing in the world my son, but God, who deserves to be praised. He alone, William, is GREAT, and therefore he alone is to be praised. He alone is GOOD, and therefore he alone is to be praised. He alone is from EVERLASTING to EVERLASTING, and therefore he alone is *to be praised.* He alone made all the worlds, and all the people, with all the riches, and beauties, and glories that are in them, and therefore he alone is to be praised.

Here, little William, sensibly affected with his mother's eloquence on this great subject, made a pause;

at length he said to her, But, mother, is *praising God*, all that is to make me good?

O no, my son, there's another blessed thing you must do—you must not only *praise* God for all the great things he has done for you, but you must also every day *pray* to him that he will give you a continual sense of this; so that you may feel such gratitude and love for him as always to do what you know will please him. And from constantly doing this, my dear son, you will feel such a joy and sweetness in your heart as will make you love every body. And then, William, you will be sure never to do them any harm —you will never tell stories upon them—never take any thing from them—never quarrel nor fight with them, but will always do them good as God is always doing *you* good.

Well, mother, replied William, looking at her with great tenderness, "and will God love me then, and be always good to me like you?"

O yes, my dear child, that he will love you like me; and ten thousand thousand times better. And then, though father and mother die and leave you, yet God will never die and leave you, but will be with you all your days long, to bless you in every thing. And when the time comes for you to die, he will send his Great Angels to bring you to himself in his own glorious heaven, where you will see all the millions of beautiful angels. And there perhaps, my son, you may see me, your mother—but, I hope, not as now, pale, and sickly, and often shedding tears for you—but ten thousand times beyond what I could ever deserve; even like one of his own angels, the first to embrace and welcome you to that happy place.

As the Parent Eagle calling her young to his native skies, when she sees the breaking forth of the sun over all his golden clouds, thus did this tender mother improve the precious hours of the nursery to sow the seeds of religion in the soul of her son. The reader will see in due season that this, her labour of love was not in vain. The seed fell on good ground. The dews of heaven came down: and the happy mother lived to feast on fruits, the richest that God can bestow on a parent this side of eternity, the sweet fruits of a dear child's virtues.

CHAPTER V.

Little William going to school.

MANY a tender mother, after having reared her son to be the sweet companion of her solitude, looks forward, with an aching heart, to the day when he is to be taken from her to go to school. "How can she live without him, whose love-glistening eyes were always dearer to her soul than the rising-sun, and his gay prattling tongue than the song of morning birds." Not so our wiser Mrs. Penn. With her, the blossom had all its charm: but still her thoughts were on the richer fruit. William, 'tis true, was lovely as a child; but she longed to see him glorious as a man—she longed to see him brilliant in conversation—noble in action—and always approached by his friends with that mingled affection and respect so gratifying to a parent's feelings. Soon therefore, as he had attained his ninth year, he was sent to a grammar school at Chigwell. The preference was given to this academy, not so much because it was somewhat convenient to one of the admiral's estates, but because of the teacher, a worthy CLERGYMAN, who had the reputation of taking great pains with his pupils to raise the fair fabrick of their education on the solid basis of PIETY and morals. Prayers, morning and evening, with reading a chapter from the gospels, with short and affectionate comments, was the constant practice in his school. This was a great recommendation with Mrs. Penn, who had seen so many promising young men suddenly lost to all virtue and character in life, merely for lack of religious principles. But though Mrs. Penn had herself chosen this situation for her son, yet when the time came to make preparations for his leaving her, she could not help feeling a tender melancholy. Nor could William, notwithstanding the sprightliness of youth, entirely escape the soft infection. For several days before he was to go away, it was observed that he seemed to have lost his spirits. In the midst of his play, he would break off and come and sit by her side, in silence, reposing his cheeks on her bosom. And often, when he lifted his eyes to look at his mother, they were seen watery and sad. But, stifling her own sighs, she would press him to her breast, and kissing away his tears, would say, "*never mind, my son, never mind;* our parting is unpleasant, but it is for good, for great good both of your honour and my joy. But still I am pleased to see you so sad at parting from your mother. It shows that you remember how much I have loved you. But though we part, William, it is only in the body; which is but small cause of grief. The mind is all, my son, the mind is all; and we can be together in the mind. And so, though I shall not see you, every day, with these bodily eyes, I shall see you with my mind's eye, which is a great deal better. And, O, how often, and how sweetly shall I see my son; every morning coming out from his chamber in dress so neat and clean—and with such sweetness of countenance saluting his school-mates—and so respectfully approaching his teacher! And then the looks of his teacher so bright with pleasure and approbation of his graceful manners and rapid progress in his studies!—and the eyes of all the boys shining upon him with such brotherly affection!"

Here William looked at his mother and heaved a sigh, as if he secretly feared he should hardly attain such honours; when Mrs. Penn, in a livelier tone, thus went on:—" Yes, William, it is often delightful to my thoughts to see my son in such company: but I often see him in higher company still. I see him every morning and evening on his knees, with placid countenance and meekly beaming eyes, lifted in devotio to his Creator."

Marking William's looks, as with redoubled attention he hung upon her words, she still went on:

" Aye, William, there's the true grandeur and glory of all! O, to think that I should ever have a son to CONVERSE WITH GOD!"

" Well, mother," said William, " Don't I always pray with you night and morning, as you taught me?"

" Yes," replied Mrs. Penn, " that you do, William; and that gives me good hope you will continue that pious practice at school. But lest the company of so many boys, and some of them perhaps *giddy*, should divert you from it, I want to make a bargain with you, my son."

" What's that, mother?" said William, eagerly.

" Why, here's a handsome watch, William," said she, taking one from her bosom; " that I have bought for you. It keeps good time, just like my own. Now, William, I give you this watch, that at a particular hour of the day, no matter what company or business is before you, you will retire to your chamber, and there spend one quarter of an hour in devotion. I will also, at the same moment, retire to my closet, for the same important purpose. And O, what joy will it be to my heart to think that while I am in the act of adoring God, my son is adoring him also; that while others are making their court to dying worms, my son is bowing before the Eternal King, and seeking those honours that will last for ever."

William took the watch from his mother, giving her at the same time the most solemn promise that he would meet her every day at the appointed hour of devotion; and assuring her, too, what pleasure it would give him to think he was worshipping God at the same moment with his dear mother.

Having discharged this high duty to her son, and the hour being come for his departure, Mrs. Penn took leave of her little William with that dignified kind of sorrow which alone can reach the heart of real piety. While William, having on this, as on all other occasions, such good cause to glory in his mother as his dear guardian angel, took leave of her with a joy mingled with his tears that made them delicious.

CHAPTER VI.

WILLIAM, now in his ninth year, is at Chigwell school, among a crowd of strangers. But though innocence like his feels not the bitterness of grief, yet the separation, and for the first time too, from a mother so dear, must wring some drops from his youthful heart. it is visible to every eye, nor least of all to his worthy preceptor. And if this amiable man, at first sight, felt such respect for him, as the son of the brave admiral Penn, that respect was mellowed into the kindest sympathy, when he saw his cheeks of youth shrouded with sorrow. This melancholy was of advantage to William. It caused him to think so dearly of his mother's last command, that every day, punctually as the appointed hour arrived, he would retire to his chamber to pray. But although, as he himself candidly acknowledged, this pious act was at first performed principally on account of his mother's request and his own promise; yet he soon began to find a delight in it. He soon found, on entering his chamber, a crowd of precious ideas pressing upon his mind.—He felt that "he was acting the dutiful child to a beloved mother—that beloved mother was at the same moment in her chamber to meet him—and both of them engaged in the most ennobling of all services—the worship of God."

Christ has said, "Suffer the little children to come unto me." And some are of opinion that, in uncorrupted minds, like those of children, it requires nothing but a little consideration to bring them to be religious and that if young people, who are yet tolerably innocent, would but retire awhile, every day, into some secret place, and indulge a few serious thoughts, such as—*how they came into existence*—where they *are now*—and where they *soon must be*—they could not but be startled into a solemn conviction of the being and attributes of God; their dependence on him; and the great wisdom of devotion. This appears to have been remarkably verified in the case of young Penn. It appears from all his biographers, that he had not been long engaged in this pious work of daily retiring by himself, like the youthful Samuel, to meditate and pray, before he was met, like that holy child, with a wonderful answer. One day, while alone in his chamber, he was suddenly surprised by a light of a most extraordinary lustre, which he called "AN EXTERNAL GLORY." And at the same time he experienced in his heart a LIGHTSOMENESS and JOY which he had never felt before. And though he could not define either this *internal* or *external* something; yet to his dying day, he spoke of it as "A VISITATION FROM GOD," who had thus lovingly condescended to invite him to the "HONOURS of a PIOUS LIFE."

Some gentlemen, and those too so modest as to think themselves the only wits in the world, will probably laugh at this as a mere childish weakness in young William Penn. But such persons ought to remember that William Penn is not the first nor the last who has been affected in this way in their devotions. Thousands and millions of souls, especially at first turning their backs on a false and wicked world, and coming to God in tender upright prayer, have felt the same "LIGHTSOMENESS AT HEART," which he speaks of as a "*visitation from God*," a call to the "HONOURS of a PIOUS LIFE." And where is the wonder of all this? Is man, for whom God created, and has so long sustained these heavens and this earth, is man of so little value, that his Maker will not *visit* him with smiles of approbation for doing what will exalt him to the great end of all, i. e. temporal and eternal happiness? Besides, is not every man and woman on earth daily receiving *visitations* from God, and calls to the honours of a pious life? What is every transport which the soul feels on obtaining the victory over lust, but a visitation from God? What is every secret blush of shame, or palpitation of heart from guilt, but a visitation from God, and a strong call to a good life? After this extraordinary affair at Chigwell, we hear nothing of young William worth relating, until his fifteenth year, when we meet him again at Oxford college. From a very important occurrence there, we have good reason to conclude that if he had not doubled his talents, (his *religious impressions*) at Chigwell, he had not buried them in the earth. Hearing that a strange sort of preacher, by some called a Quaker, was about to preach in Oxford, William thought he would go and hear him. The appearance of the preacher, who had neither reverend, nor right-reverend tacked to his name, but simple Thomas Loe, excited his surprise. He had been accustomed, both in the London and Oxford churches, to see divinity dressed up in great state of velvet cushions and embroidered pulpit cloths, and its ministers pompously habited in rich gowns and cassocks of silk and crape, with surplices and sashes of many a various hue and emblem. Guess then what he must have felt, when, at the rising of Thomas Loe to speak, he beheld a plain, fleshy, round-faced man, in a broad-brimmed hat and drab coat of the humblest cloth and cut, and a close snug neckcloth, all shining clean and neat. Nor was he less surprised at friend Loe's preaching, which struck him as entirely different from that of all the London and Oxford preachers he had ever heard. These latter were, all of them, GREAT SCHOLARS ; and for fear their hearers should forget this, they kept them constantly on the stare at their *high flown language.* And to complete their delirium of wonder, they would every now and then throw them a scrap of Latin or Greek, selected with ostentation and most pompously pronounced. But, far on the contrary, soon as friend Loe had got up and taken the beaver from his head, he began to address his hearers in the simple and affectionate manner that a father would use with his children whom he knew to be disorderly and unhappy. We regret that we cannot set before our readers an exact copy of the famous sermon that first set the great William Penn to seek eternal life. But it was the aim of the orator to affect his hearers with a pungent sense of the miseries of man in this life, while separate from God by sin; also that "*joy unspeakable*," which springs up in his soul from "*repentance and faith working by love.*" The looks and tones of friend Loe, while reasoning on this high subject, must have been of the highest style of sacred eloquence. Flowing from a fountain of the strongest light and love in his own soul, they penetrated the soul of young William Penn, and excited his deepest aspirations after a happiness which he heard so feelingly described, but which he did not know how to obtain. After bearing this burden for three days, he went to the principal of the college, who, according to the polite language of the day, was a LEARNED DIVINE , and told him his uneasiness. The principal inquired the cause ; and, on learning that he had been at a "*quaker sermon*," he laughed all his feelings to scorn, as mere fanaticism and nonsense , and advised him to " keep to the good old church, hear sermons, and take the sacrament, and all would soon be well again." William went to church—as indeed he ever had done—but he found not there the comfort which his soul longed after. Cold read prayers; cold read sermons; noisy organs, with crowds of gay ones and great, professing to worship God, but evidently idolizing themselves and one another.

Oh how illy did such vanities suit the seriousness of a mind like his! No wonder that he turned from them disgusted, and went away as restless and unsatisfied as he came.

CHAPTER VII.

William Penn does not inform us how long he continued under this cloud. Probably not long. He who asks nothing but the salvation of his offending children, is not hard to be intreated when he sees the contrite heart, and honest wish, for the blessedness of reconciliation with their heavenly father. O, would mourners but remember that "God is Love," and that "there is joy in heaven over one sinner that repenteth," they would not mope and mourn as many do, yea, and for great part of their lives. Our Saviour has given us the true pattern in the case of the prodigal son. There does not appear to have been much time lost betwixt the conviction and conversion of that young man. "Soon as he came to himself," for you see that while going on in sin, he is represented as one *quite out of his head*,—"soon as he came to himself," and found at what a mad rate he had been driving on—what a princely fortune he had squandered—and into what a woful condition he had brought himself—and also remembered what a wealthy and loving father he still had left him, he instantly resolved to face about and pack off home again. The moment he took up this resolution, the blessed work was all but done. For, "while he was yet a great way off, his father saw him; and had compassion on him, and ran and fell upon his neck and kissed him." The young man began to make a *speech*, but the father stopped him short. He saw that his poor self-ruined child was a *penitent*. And that was all he wanted. Besides, true love "will have mercy and not sacrifice." his son is naked and cold, and hungry and wretched. This is no time, the father thinks, to hear fine speeches. With all the vehemence of parental love yearning over his own flesh and blood a suffering, he cries aloud to the servants, "bring hither the best robe and put it upon him! and kill the fatted calf!" O how does the divine goodness break forth in this language! not simply the *robe* but the BEST robe; not merely the *calf* but the FATTED calf. And all this, good as it is, is not half good enough yet. The rich robe on his shoulders must be accompanied with glittering "rings on his fingers;" and the fatted calf must be diluted with precious *wine*. And then *music* too must come—music with all her soul-enchanting strains, to proclaim the happy father's joy, that "his son, who was dead, is alive; he was lost, but is found." Now Christ holding out such love and forgiveness, what are we to think of those who can be so long "seeking peace and not finding it?" Is there not ground for suspicion that they are not honest, like the prodigal, to return home to their heavenly Father, but must still stick to some of their "*husks* and *swine*" of sin, which God abhors. Their grum looks indeed, and godly groanings would pass them, already for saints; and the preacher often wonders why brother Longface "doesn't find peace." But put on your spectacles, thou purblind preacher, and try brother Longface's spirit, whether he has any marks of that "LOVE," which must always go before "peace and joy in the Holy Ghost." 'Tis true "he disfigures his face and seems to men to fast;" but still see how he "grinds the face of the poor," and "devours widows' houses." He uses *long prayers* in his family; but see how harsh and unloving he is in his manners towards them. He will *spruce up* and go fifty miles to a "CONFERENCE;" to an "ASSOCIATION;" to a "CONVENTION;" to a "PRESBYTERY;" to hear great sermons and to take a sacrament. But, how far will he go out of his way to pay a just debt? He builds "Cathedrals for the Lord of Hosts;" but oh! what wretched huts for his own servants! He "*makes feasts* for *the rich*," but alas how are his poor negroes fed! His own sons and daughters wear "soft raiment as in kings' houses," but his slaves are in rags! And is it to be wondered at, that God, the FRIEND OF THE POOR, does not lift up the light of his countenance on such a hypocrite?

Happily for William Penn he had none of these hindrances in his way to religion and its comforts. Through the promised blessing on a pious mother's instructions he had been early brought to relish the pleasures of moral goodness. Soon therefore as that good spirit which spoke to Socrates, which spoke to Cornelius, and which speaks to all, whispered to William Penn, and said "*this is the road; walk therein,*" he was ready to obey.

Fortunately recollecting, that while friend Loe was preaching, several of the youth of the college, his acquaintance, had appeared much affected, he went to their chambers, and after some search found out seven or eight; among whom was Robert, afterwards lord Spencer, and John Locke, the writer of the famous "TREATISE ON THE HUMAN UNDERSTANDING," and who, 'tis said, was in principle a FRIEND all his life. Drawn together by kindred sentiments, these favoured youth immediately formed themselves into a society, that by reading the scriptures, with free and mutual interchange of their feelings, and by prayer, they might preserve and improve their pious impressions. Finding more of the spirit and sweets of devotion in these warm little exercises with one another, than in the cold formalities at the established church, they began to absent themselves, and to spend their sabbaths together in the aforesaid excellent way. This their secession from the church was soon noticed by the professors of the college, and with much pain, on account indeed of them all, but chiefly of William Penn, partly because of his father, a favourite officer with the nation, but still more for himself, whose extraordinary talents at the green age of fifteen, had advanced him to the first honours of the University, and whose singular sweetness of spirit and many manly virtues had rendered him the object of general partiality. "A youth of such amiableness and promise, was not to be lost." He was of course sent for by the principal, who, with an air of parental tenderness, began with him by expressing his regret, that he had not followed the advice he lately gave him. He also expressed his astonishment that a young man of his rank and genius should so dishonour both, by exchanging the rational and dignified service of the *church*, for a worship so insipid and childish as that of the quakers.

William replied, with great modesty, that Christ himself had invited the little children to come unto him; for that his kingdom, or church, was composed of such. He added, "that however the great ones of this world, when waited on by their inferiors, might look for pomp and parade; yet to the Almighty all this was abomination in comparison of that approach of the soul to him in the meek and docile spirit of a child."

The principal branded all this as mere *delusion*, and entreated him, by all that he owed his parents, to whom he might afford a long life of comfort—by all that he owed his country, to which he might be a bright ornament—and by all that he owed the *church*, to whose glory such talents and early piety as his would greatly conduce, to give up his *fanatical notions*, and return to the faith he was born and brought up in.

William replied, that all this was very flattering, and far beyond any thing he could think himself entitled to; but that if it were ten times greater, he could not *grieve the Spirit* and darken the *Light within him.*

This latter phrase appeared to hurt the principal; for knitting his brow, he said, he hoped Mr. Penn would not compel him to use *severe measures.*

William asked what he meant by that.

"Why, sir, I shall be obliged to indict you for *non-conformity.*"

"That is, in plain English, you mean to *persecute* me; to *drive* me to your church contrary to my own reason and conscience. And what good can you expect to do me by that?"

"It is to keep you, sir, from the crying sin of *schism.* There cannot be a greater sin, sir, than for Christians to separate from one another."

"I see no ground, sir," said William, "for such a fear. I do not see how Christians can possibly separate from one another in a *bad sense* of the word. The lambs of the fold never separate, yea, though they may differ in the colours of their fleeces, some white and some black, yet still being all the same in innocence and gentleness, they do not separate, but cleave to one another by a natural affection. Even so, and indeed much more must Christians cleave to one another. I am sure they have infinitely sweeter and dearer ties to bind them together. For what is it, sir, that makes real Christians but '*perfect love* out of a PURE HEART;' and how can they who possess it themselves, but be charmed in others with that blessed spirit which is to do away all fraud and violence from the earth, and fill it with all the precious fruits of universal righteousness?"

"Well then, sir," said the principal, how can *you separate* from the good Christians of our church, and that too the very church your were born and brought up in?"

William replied, with the trepidation of one who feared he should give offence, that he had retired from the church he was born and brought up in, because he had not found in it what he prized above all things—the sweet society of loving *Christians.*

To this the principal returned with warmth, that it was great *presumption* in one so young as he was, to pass such a sentence on any church, and especially on the venerable mother church of the nation.

"I was afraid, sir," replied William, "that you would be offended. I did not wish it: but as you talked of persecuting and *fining* me for *non-conformity*, I felt it a duty to tell you my reasons. And now, sir, let me add, that, though I do not pretend to know their *hearts*, yet while I see among the members of the church, so little of the spirit of Christ, so little love for their brethren, or so little delight in doing them good; and, on the other hand, so much pride, and hate, and revenge, and flesh-pleasing of all sorts, how can I think them loving Christians?"

A profound silence ensued; when the principal, calling him "*an incorrigible young man*," took up his hat; and, as he turned to go away, advised him *to look sharp*, and be *constant at church*, or he should soon hear from him again.

But to cut short this shameful story, I will just first inform the reader, that William Penn and his religious young friends, *for "assembling themselves together to worship God, contrary to law*," were summoned before the HIGHER POWERS, and severely fined!!

CHAPTER VII.

As soon as it was known in college that he had turned Quaker, that he had been cited before the principal, and fined for non-conformity, the looks and manners of his acquaintance were sadly altered towards him; and he had the mortification to find that those who had caressed and courted him, because of his talents and high standing, now squinted at him as though he had just come out of the pillory.

That William Penn, by bravely combining the wisdom of the serpent with the harmlessness of the dove, might ultimately have borne down this prejudice, and turned his enemies into friends, there can be no doubt. People may laugh at the Quakers if they please, but laughing cannot alter the nature of things. Born to be happy, men naturally love happiness, and hate misery. And as virtue naturally makes men happy, and vice naturally makes them miserable, this natural loveliness of the one and hatefulness of the other, will force themselves upon us in spite of all the nicknames we can give 'em. And this conviction will daily grow stronger, as we grow wiser to understand the curses of the one and the blessings of the other. The young man who, by lies, keeps his acquaintance in hot water—or picks their pockets by his gambling—or cuts their throats in duels,—will quickly be abhorred, no matter how much he is cried up as a *Churchman*. While the youth who is uniformly virtuous and good humoured, will soon become the esteem and love of all, even though fools should at first laugh at him as a *Quaker*. That young Penn and his friends, by dint of persevering prudence and affection, would have gained this triumph, is unquestionable. But oh the weakness of poor human nature! how prone to error, and by excess of folly to throw "*dead flies into the apothecary's sweetest ointment.*" These same young men, viz.

Wm. Penn & Co. who but a few days before had been smartly taxed for not conforming to other people's notions, were ready now to tax others for not conforming to their notions; and having given up all variety of dress themselves, they thought that others ought to do so too, and even to be compelled to do it. This is confirmed by their own act; for meeting some of their young college acquaintance in dresses that to them seemed highly *fantastical* and *unchristian*, they began to remonstrate with them against such levity: and because the young fellows laughed at them as "*fanatics*," they fell upon them outright, and by main force rent their clothes from their shoulders!! This most impudent act was to William Penn like the uncorking of the vial of the seventh angel. It was followed by such floods and storms of trouble, that had not his mind been stayed on the "rock of ages," he must have been utterly swept away. He was instantly cited before the Professors and Trustees of the College, in the presence of the assembled students, and after having his conduct arraigned of such hypocrisy and folly as were sufficient to burn his cheeks to cinders, he was *formally expelled!*

This, though a most severe trial to an ingenuous youth like William Penn, was but a trifle in comparison of what he yet saw before him—the red fiery tempest of his father's face when he should be told of his *expulsion* from college, and the cause of it! and, worse still, the sudden paleness of his dear mother's cheeks, and her starting tears, on hearing of his disgrace. Willing, long as possible to delay giving them this pain, he purposely declined writing to his parents, preferring to be the bearer himself. Accordingly he set out for Penn's Dale, where his sudden appearance struck them with surprise. "Hallo William!" cried his father with joy, giving him his hand; "why, what, my son! returned to port already! I hope you hav'nt met with foul weather!" His mother, roused by the sudden music of William's name, turned around with her face all flushed with joy, and flying to embrace him, exclaimed, "High, my dear William! what brought you home so soon?" Alarmed at the sudden paleness on his cheeks, they both at once eagerly inquired *what was the matter!* With his characteristic firmness he replied—"*I'm expelled from the University!*" Pale as a blighted lily, poor Mrs. Penn stood a statue of speechless consternation; while the Admiral, clasping his hands and rolling his eyes, as if he had suddenly beheld half his fleet blown up by the Dutch, exclaimed—

"Expelled from the University!"

"Yes, sir, they have expelled me," replied William.

"Expelled you, do you still say, child," continued the Admiral, wild, and blowing like a frightened porpoise, "a child of mine expelled from an English University! why!—why!—what! in the name of God, could have been the cause?"—"Why, sir," answered William, "it was because I tore their dresses from off the shoulders of some of the students."—Here, the Admiral, with his cheeks puckered up, and a whistle, shrill as the boatswain's call of a man of war missing stays on a lee shore, exclaimed—"You tore the dresses from off the shoulders of some of the students! why, God's mercy on my soul! what had you to do with *their* dresses?"

"Why, father," answered William, "their dresses were so *fantastical* and *unbecoming* the dignity of Englishmen and the sobriety of Christians, that I felt it a duty to my country and conscience to bear my testimony against them. And moreover, I was assisted in it by Robert Spencer, and John Locke, and other discreet youths of the college."

Here, the death pale on Mrs. Penn's cheeks, brightening into the vermilion of joy, she exclaimed—"Well thank God! thank God, 'tis no worse."

"You ar. thankful for small favours, madam," said the admiral, peevishly; I don't see what could be worse.

Why, my dear, replied she, had William been expelled for drunkenness, gambling, duelling, or any other such detestable vices, would not that have been ten thousand times worse?

Why—why—yes; answered the admiral rather reluctantly, that—that would have been worse I confess. But this is bad enough, and too bad too. A son of mine to be expelled from college!—Such a thing was never heard of in my family before.

But still, my dear, we have great reason to be glad the cause of it was a pardonable error and not infamous vice, and that instead of attaching to our son the abhorrence due to crime, we should rather augment our respect for him as having done what he thought right.

Right, madam! what right had he to pass judgment on the dresses of others, and particularly of such grand institutions as Universities?

Why, father, replied William, my mind has been exceedingly *exercised* since I saw you.

Exercised! What do you mean by that?

Why, father, it has been given me here of late to see many things in a new light.

Zounds, sir, I hope it has not been given you to see things in the light of a blockhead. A child, like you, to talk of your *new lights!* 'Tis all nonsense.

I mean, father, replied William, that it has been given me to see many things very wrong which I once thought innocent.

The admiral wanted to know what he was to understand by that.

Why, certainly, father, answered William, every wise man should be consistent; and especially that wisest of all men the real Christian. If therefore we are simple within we should be all simplicity without

And he who inwardly in his heart is seeking the smiles of God, should not outwardly, by his dress, be courting the world.

Here good Mrs. Penn, her eyes sparkling on William, looked very much like an angel. But the Admiral turning to her said, rather ironically, why the boy is certainly out of his head! or has been among the quakers. Now come be candid, William, and tell me, have you not been hearing Tom Loe?

Yes, father, I have, said William, very firmly; and I hope I have not learned from him to think less reverently of truth.

Nor of duty to your father neither, I hope, sir, rejoined the admiral tartly. And as proof that you have not, I expect you will go back to-morrow, and by proper concessions, recover your high standing in the University, and by instantly quitting your silly quakerism, worship God according to the good old forms of the established church of the nation.

William in the most respectful manner replied, tha he should be exceedingly happy to obey his honoured father in all things lawful, and especially in this late matter, the attack on the students about their dress, which he was already ashamed of as a mere spirit of "*zeal without knowledge*," and entirely contrary to the spirit of Christ who forbids his disciples to strive or to propagate the truth by violence. But that as to abandoning the Christians called Quakers, and confining himself to the established church, he hoped, he said, his father would not insist on that.

Why not, sir? replied the admiral angrily.

Why, because, father, I hope you will never think of abridging my liberty of conscience by compelling me to be a churchman when I wish to be a quaker.

But why do you give that silly preference of quakerism to the established church?

Why, father, peoples' tastes are different. And if I preferred a particular dish, I should hope you would gratify me in it, especially if it was quite as wholesome as another dish, even though I could not assign the reason of my preference of the first; then much more in this case where the reason is so plain.

Well, sir, I should like to hear your reasons, *so plain*, for preferring quakerism to the established church you were brought up in.

Father, I may not have arguments to satisfy you but they are such as fully satisfy myself.

Then pray let me hear them.

Well, father, when I look into the gospel, I see nothing there but lessons and examples of the most perfect HUMILITY and LOVE. All are "*sinners*," and therefore all should be HUMBLE. And, on repentance, all are received into favour, and therefore all should love. But father, look into the established church, and do you see any thing like humility and love there? Nay, don't you see the most glaring marks of PRIDE and SELFISHNESS? Don't you see both among the priests and their people a constant vieing with each other, who shall have the grandest houses, and the richest furniture; who shall appear in the finest clothes and the most dazzling equipage; and who shall be the greatest TALK of THE TOWN for these things? Now father, is there any humility in this? And as to LOVE, look at their endless challenges and duels, their cuffings and fightings, their law-suings and bickerings. Can this be a church of Christ? Then where's the propriety of driving me into fellowship with such a church as this?

Yes, replied the admiral, I know this is the common slang of the dissenters against the established church, and I doubt not you heard enough of it from Tom Loe, but it amounts to nothing: for there are good and bad in all churches.

Yes, father, but do you know any such character as a drunken quaker, a gambling quaker, a duelling quaker a law-suing quaker.

Well, well, admit there are more disorderly characters among them, it reflects nothing on the *Church*.

I don't know, sir, how you can prove this. There can be no effect without a cause. And we cannot be long at a loss for the cause in this case when we look at the glaring corruptions of the clergy. Christ and his apostles had not where to lay their heads, but our bishops and archbishops live in kings' palaces. Christ and his apostles had neither scrip nor purse; but these ride in gilt coaches, and enjoy, each of them, a revenue sufficient to maintain five hundred poor families. Christ and his apostles wanted only the plainest language to tell sinners their misery and danger: but our clergy must have their Latin and Greek, and a thousand other things equally useless. And they set so high a price on these, and lay themselves out so entirely to get these, that they never get the spirit of Christ's preachers; hence, instead of that burning zeal with tears and vehemence we read of in the prophets and apostles, these gentlemen run over their prayers and sermons, like lazy school-boys impatient of their lessons and anxious to get through them. I hope therefore, my dear father, you will never compel me to a church with whose spirit and manners I can have no fellowship." The admiral listened to this discourse of his son without interrupting him, and with looks still gathering, as William went on, a deeper and a deeper shade of saddest disappointment, till at the close, strongly clasping together his uplifted hands, with a kind of sardonic grin he thus exclaimed,—"Well! my pigs are all brought to a fine market! And here's a pretty ending of all the bright castles that I have for years been building in the air for this boy! A lad of genius—getting a complete college education—the only child of a British admiral—great friends at court—the high road to preferment all ahoy before him—and yet determined to turn his back on all, and live and die a poor despised quaker! Why, God's mercy on my sou boy! can you submit to all this? you who might have been among the first in the realm in any walk you had chosen to turn yourself too. If to the army, a general—if to the navy, an admiral—if to the law, a chief justice—to medicine, a court physician—to divinity, a bishop or lord primate! And now with all these grand prizes completely under your guns, will you haul down your colours, and in a three-buttoned drab, and broad beaver, go sneaking about the world, or sitting half asleep and twirling your thumbs at a silent meeting with Tom Loe; a superstitious blockhead, no more to be compared to one of our learned divines, than a Duch cock-boat, to a British line of battle-ship."

William, but little affected by this glittering landscape which his father had so eloquently run over, was about to reply, but the admiral, with anger flashing from his eyes, interrupted him, saying, "Harkee young man! I know you have a clear head and a fluent tongue. till this most unfortunate hour they were my delight; but in such a cause as this, I never wish to hear them. All that I have to say to you is, that you will let me know, to-morrow morning, whether you will go back to the University and do as I have desired you, or not. And take notice, sirrah, that if you do not, you are no longer a son of mine, and never again shall you darken my door. Retire with your mother to her chamber. I know she has always been a greater favourite with you than myself. Perhaps she may do something with you."

Having long been accustomed to command his headstrong thousands, among whom disobedience is instant death, he had learned, when angry, to curl his whiskers and clothe his looks in such terrors, that the gentle Mrs. Penn durst make no reply. So taking her son by the arm she slowly retired, in tears, to her chamber, leaving the admiral in a state of feeling which my readers can better conceive than I describe.

CHAPTER IX.

On retiring to her chamber, Mrs. Penn threw her arms around William's neck, and sitting down with him, still locked in her embraces, she shed many a pearly drop into his bosom. Melted by this dear parent's kindness, he tenderly asked,—"Mother, do you blame me for doing what I thought my duty?"

In tones soft as the whispers of love from a mother's lips, she replied—"No, my son, I do not. But still it grieves me that you should ever have done any thing to offend a father who so dotes on you. Besides, why can't you be religious and yet attain all the HONOURS and CONSEQUENCE in life that are before you?" William, with a look inclined to smile, for which he was, through life, most remarkable in the gloomiest scenes, said, "Why, mother, you are the main cause of all this." Astonished, she asked him what he meant. "Why, my dear mother, it was your dialogues, your blessed dialogues in the nursery, that first brought me to God, and will you now be so cruel as to pull me back again?"

"No! no! not for ten thousand worlds," replied she earnestly; "but can't you walk with God, and yet be rich and great in this world? We read in the scriptures of Joseph, and Daniel, and others who were great saints, even in the courts of idolatrous kings."

"Aye, mother," said William, shaking his head, "all this is possible, but it is dangerous. Christ, you know, says, 'not many rich, not many great' are among his *humble and loving family*. Many, indeed, are called, and for a time make a goodly show; but the smiles of the world, and the deceitfulness of riches, prove too strong for them; so that though '*many are called*, but *few are chosen*.' A sweet flower is sometimes seen on the highways and among the rocks, but it is rare. A fit soil, mother, is not more necessary for flowers than a fit society for saints; and had they but enjoyed such, there would have been more Daniels and Josephs than one in Egypt, and Chaldea. And besides, mother, what is all this pomp and grandeur of the world, which my father so anxiously covets for me? These CHIEF JUSTICES and LORD MAYORS, these GENERALS and ADMIRALS, these BISHOPS and ARCHBISHOPS, are great names; yet, after all, what are they but *splendid paupers;* and many of them, in the midst of their fancied greatness, as mean-spirited, and griping, and furious, and miserable as the beggar who knows not to-day where he is to get his brown crust to-morrow."

His mother here giving him a brightened look, as if to say, "Yes, indeed, all this is but too true, my son," he thus went on.—"Yes, mother; and look here at my dear father: he is all that he wishes *me* to be, that is, a great and prosperous man—he is high admiral of the British navy—a great favourite at court—has his town houses and country houses, his clocks and carpets, his rich plate and gilt coaches, and, in short, every thing that his heart can wish; and yet, mother, what is he the better for it all? O where's his HAPPINESS, that '*one thing needful*,' which certainly every reasonable being should propose to himself as the only *true* end of all his riches and grandeur? Where his meekness and sweetness of spirit? and where's that majesty and charm of goodness which expresses true LOVE? O if he loved God truly, would he not rather a thousand times see me, like Moses, ready *to suffer persecution with the people of God, than enjoy even in a palace, the pleasures of sin, which are but for a season!* And if he loved me truly, would he not a thousand times rather see me pass my moment of earthly being in the sweet and safe vallies of humility and innocence, than on the dangerous mountains of pride and worldly mindedness?"

Such truths from the lips of an only son whom she

so delighted in, contributed greatly to comfort Mrs. Penn in this affliction. So, after some pause of sweet and grateful thought, she said, "Well, William, what will you answer to your father to-morrow concerning the requirement he made of you just now?"

"Why, mother," answered William very firmly, "I will never forsake God. I owe HIM every thing: yes, my dear mother, as you so often told me, when I was a child at your knee, I owe God every thing; and feel that I ought to give myself back to him. And besides, he alone is worthy of my affections, and he alone can to all eternity give me that mighty happiness I was created for. I am determined, therefore, never to 'eave him, nor to form any connexion that may jeopardize my devotion to him."

As Mrs. Penn was too well acquainted with her husband's temper to cherish the most distant hope that he would ever relax one iota of his threats, she began to study how William should be disposed of, when turned out of doors by his father, which she foresaw was inevitable. Several expedients were proposed; but that finally adopted by them both, was, that he should go into Buckinghamshire, and live with her mother, until his father's anger should be turned away from him.

The expulsion of a child, an only child, and that a son so faultless and beloved, is an idea so unnatural, that most mothers would sicken and turn from it with horror. Fortunately for Mrs. Penn, her soul was greatened by religion. She had ever wished above all things that her son should be a lover of God. But still she had fondly hoped that, together with this greatest of all honours, he might enjoy the honours of this world too. And though it was a sad disappointment that this could not be; and that he must give up the one or the other, it still afforded her inexpressible satisfaction, that her dear boy, young as he was, yet possessed faith sufficient to trample the world unde-

his feet, when it came in competition with his duty to God. Such were the thoughts which accompanied this amiable mother to her pillow, there sweetly to revolve that security and peace which she had such good reason to hope would attend her son through life. "William may not be *great*; but, which is far better, he will, I trust, be *good*; and though *fools may account his life to be madness, and his end without honour, yet I hope he'll be numbered among the sons of God, and his lot among the saints.*" Nor did William pass that night in such sleepless trouble as might have been expected. 'Tis true, that as he pulled off his clothes to go to bed, he felt a strange shock at the thought that this night might be the last night he should ever pass in that dear chamber. And when he looked around him on his venerable forefathers, whose pictures were hanging on the wall, the idea that he was about to be exiled from their family, and by his own father, too, occasioned a sudden sinking at heart. But, favoured youth! his eye was singly fixed on God, and on the glory of doing his will; and thenceforth sprung up that "*peace which passeth all understanding.*" In this frame of mind he sought his bed, where, amidst thoughts soft as the summer moon-beams that silvered the bosom of night, he composed himself to sleep, happy as the youthful sailor-boy who, amidst his descending slumbers, hears, without alarm, the crash of surrounding billows, because he remembers that his ship is of the strong-ribbed oak and iron, and that his father, a skilful pilot, presides at the all-directing helm.

CHAPTER X.

The next day, immediately after breakfast, which was passed in perfect silence, the looks of the admiral and Mrs. Penn expressing most eloquently their respective characters—his the angry sternness of parental authority disputed, and hers all the solicitudes of conjugal respect and maternal tenderness combined. Soon as breakfast was over, the admiral, taking his lady and William into his study, with a constrained kindness thus addressed the latter:—"William, you are my child, my only child, the child of all my affections and of all my hopes. I feel, therefore, that I must be most unhappy if I part from you, and especially by your own undutifulness. I hope you have thought seriously of these things. Now will you go back to the University, and, by proper concessions, recover your honourable standing, and also renouncing Tom Loe and his silly quakers, return to the bosom of the ESTABLISHED CHURCH?"

With all the meekness yet firmness of an honest quaker, William replied, that he had "*turned his thoughts to the light within;* and that while he felt, with exceeding affection, how much he owed to his earthly father, he owed still more to his heavenly, and therefore could never offend him, by sinning against the light, and endangering his own soul."

"Well, then, you will not go back to the ESTABLISHED CHURCH!" replied the admiral, angrily.

"While my present convictions remain, father, I can never leave the quakers."

"Well then, sir," rejoined the admiral, quite dark with rage, "you must leave me:" and ordered him instantly to quit the house.

Deeming it fruitless to reply or remonstrate, William took up his hat and went out of the room, leaving his father in a frame of mind not to be envied. His eyes on fire—his motions furious and convulsive—and his face alternately deformed with deadly red and pale, a true index of the stormy passions within. He has turned out of doors his only child—has turned him out in helpless inexperienced youth—not for any crime that he has done, nor for the shadow of a crime, but only for wishing to be more devout—he sees the eyes of his son, glistening on him through tears, as he goes away—he hears the clap of the door behind him, and the sound of his departing feet, as it dies away along the descent of steps. All is silent, save the cries of his mother in her distant chamber, for her "*poor banished boy.*" He rolls his eyes around him on his spacious halls and splendid furniture. "*Sideboards!* and *clocks!* and *pictures! what are you all to a wounded spirit!*"

To be wretched in poverty and obscurity were nothing. There would be no sting of disappointment to evenom the smart. But to be wretched in spite of titles—in spite of court favours—in spite of all his branching honours and golden treasures! this is hell unmixed. Alas! poor man! He is miserable but knows not the cause. He knows not that it proceeds, as his own child had told him, from lack of HUMILITY and LOVE.

But leaving the admiral and his grand castle and gaudy carpets, to confirm the words of eternal truth, that "a man's life consisteth not in the abundance of the things he possesseth," let us see what has become of William. Like the first ancestor, Adam, turned out of Paradise, so fared it with the youthful Penn, expelled from his father's house, "*some natural tears he shed, but wiped them soon.*" His conscience was clear; his heart was cheered; so, deep inhaling the luxom air, and breathing his pious ejaculations to heaven, he sprung forward to his journey, fully trusting in the promise that "all things shall work together for good to them that love God." His course, according to the aforesaid concert with his mother, was towards "*the traveller's rest*," in Buckinghamshire, the elegant and hospitable mansion of his grandmother, who received him with exceeding joy. This great lady was pious in an uncommon degree; and having, just as William arrived, got a letter from her daughter, stating at large the history of this extraordinary transaction, she was so charmed with him on account of his early piety, that her eyes sparkled on him with pleasure. "*What, my dear, dear child*," said she, pressing him to her bosom, —"sweet image of your mother!—*turn you out of doors because you could not content yourself with being a poor dead formalist and hypocrite! Oh my Lord what will this world come to! parents turn their children out of doors only because they wish* TO BE GOD'S CHILDREN! And worse still, can bear to see *their children bloated with pride, pale with envy, burning with rage; and yet think them good enough if they have but been baptized, go regularly to church, say their prayers after the priest, and take the sacrament! Oh! what signify all these proud titles, and grand castles, and court-smiles, when their owners can be so blind and miserable!*" I have not been able to ascertain how much time William passed in the society of his excellent grandmother; but it is more than probable that the days of his exile were not many. The heart of his father yearned towards his ruddy-cheeked boy; and this tender attraction, added to the eloquence of his lady's importunities, soon prevailed. William was, of course, recalled home, to the infinite joy of the whole family; not excepting the servants, who doted on him; for from his childhood, he was remarkable for his affectionate spirit to that despised class of people; always speaking to them with great tenderness, and often making them little presents—his excellent mother purposely furnishing him the means.

Finding that his *seriousness* still stuck to him, his father proposed to him a trip to Paris, begging he would make himself *master of the French language*, *which he said was always to his ear like music.* But the admiral's principal motive was to divert his mind from what he called his *fanaticism;* with the hope, too, that from the mixture of William's *extreme gravity*, as he thought, with the *excessive gaiety of the French*, there would arise a *tertium quid*, a happy mediocrity of manners, that would render him the delight of the nation. To give this pill a richer gilding, and to render it more imposing on William's palate, the admiral took advantage of a party of young noblemen going over to the French capital; so dressing him up in the richest apparel, yet, as William begged, of a *plain fashion*, and filling his pockets with money and letters of introduction to great men, he packed him off for France.

CHAPTER XI.

The admiral was not altogether disappointed in his calculations on the result of William's trip to France. The balmy softness of the climate—the rich variety and beauty of its scenes—its silver flood smoothly gliding along the verdant meadows, or boldly rushing through romantic hills adorned with clustering vines and snow-white castles, contributed much to dissipate the gloom occasioned by his late persecution. But far more exhilarating still were the manners of its inhabitants. William's natural bias was benevolence. The hand that made him had so kindly attuned his nerves to the harmonies of moral beauty, that every look and note of love awakened his soul to joy. Then among what people on earth could he have fallen with such chance of fascination as among the French? That extraordinary people, who study no science but to *please*—who forget themselves, to make others happy—

and who with all they do, mingle so much of suavity and endearment, that whether they frown or smile, whether they grant or refuse, they almost equally oblige: for they frown with such delicacy, and refuse with such grace, that all must fall in love with them. William Penn fell in love with them. And as love naturally assimilates itself to the beloved, he quickly, as the apostle enjoins, in things indifferent, "*became all things to them*,"—he learned their language with the facility of a mocking-bird—he caught their manners by instinct—his limbs forgot their proud British stiffness—and his muscles their cold unlovely rigidity—and whether he stood or moved; whether he bowed or smiled; in standing, moving, bowing and smiling, shone forth the elegant and all accomplished Frenchman.

It was in this style that William, after twelve months' absence, presented himself before his father at Pennwood. The admiral was quite delighted with this "*charming change*," as he observed to Mrs. Penn, "that had *taken place in William's appearance*." He introduced him at court—he carried him about as in triumph among all his illustrious friends—and for fear he should relapse into his old *gloomy ways*, as he termed them, he resolved to send him over at once to Ireland, to take the management of an estate that had lately fallen to him in the neighbourhood of Dublin, the metropolis. And to insure him a full round of dissipation, his pockets were filled with letters from the admiral's court friends, introducing him in the most flattering terms, to the lord lieutenant and his numerous friends, the great ones of Dublin. The calculation from all this was, that if William, now put into such a hopeful way, by the polite and sweetly mannered French, could but be associated for a season with the gay and warm-hearted Irish, he would be confirmed an *elegant* man of the world beyond the power of superstition to shake him.

The packet-boat soon wafted young William over

to Ireland, where he commenced the career prescribed by his father, with great spirit. He applied himself very diligently to the settlement of his estate; visiting and spending his intervals of leisure in the society of the lord lieutenant and his friends, who paid uncommon attention to him as an amiable young man, and the only son and heir of sir William Penn, high admiral of the British navy. It is no where said that William ever followed this fashionable "*multitude to do evil*:" but it is well known that many who began well in the spirit, and once stood fair for heaven, have miserably ended in the flesh, and become cast-away. And this might have been the deplorable end of young William Penn, had not God in great goodness sent one of his shepherds after him. I ascribe it to the divine goodness, for I cannot otherwise account for an event that manifests too much *design* to be called *accidental*. Sitting one evening in the lord lieutenant's palace, and casting his eye on a Dublin paper, his attention was caught by a NOTICE, that "ONE OF THE PEOPLE CALLED QUAKERS WAS TO PREACH IN THE MARKET-HOUSE THE NEXT DAY." Though William had, for some time past, conformed rather too much to the world, yet he had never lost his partiality for the quakers; and therefore immediately resolved to go to meeting. On the rising of the preacher to speak, whom should his eyes behold, but the smooth and placid countenance of his old friend Thomas Loe? nor was friend Loe less surprised, as looking round him like a father about to address his children, his mildly-beaming glances met the florid cheeks of his young friend William Penn. From the professions which William, with tears, had made him two years before; and also from the severe persecutions which, by report, he had suffered both at the University and in his father's own house, friend Loe had counted on him as a dear child in the gospel; but William's *fashionable* dress excited his alarms. Whereupon with a countenance strongly marked with melancholy and a deep sigh, looking at William, he began with these remarkable words, "*There is a faith which overcometh the world; and there is a faith overcome by the world.*" William was startled. From the *particular stress*, as he thought, laid on the text, he felt as though the preacher had taken it *entirely for him.* But if so alarmed at the bare words, how much more when friend Loe, with the looks and voice of a tender father towards a truant child, went on to expose the folly, the cowardice, and hypocrisy of those who, when they hear the great truths of the gospel, will show the most fixed attention; will change colour; will heave the deep sigh and shed the copious tear, thus springing joy in the heart of the preacher that a *soul is born to God;*" and yet after all these goodly signs of faith, can suffer themselves to be overcome by the world and its vanities! To place such guilty conduct in a stronger light, he went on to show the wide difference between these two kinds of faith. He compared the one, which he called HEAD-FAITH, and which is *overcome by the world*, he compared to a light; but only such a light as that of the *moon, a cold barren light*, which, though it please the eye with its silver lustre, yet it imparts no heat to the soil; hence no vegetation appears, and the beholder wonders that the fields, though bright, are naked and sad. But the other faith, which *overcomes the world*, and which he called HEART-FAITH, he compared to the sun; a warm fertilizing light, which, soon as it falls on the earth, sets the grass to grow and covers the fair face of nature with fruits and flowers. Even so this HEART-FAITH, soon as it fires the soul, vivifies every precious seed of virtue, and calls forth all the sweets and charms of heavenly affections. He then showed too that as head-faith like the moon, is cold and barren, so like that orb which belongs only to this low planet, it is often obscured in clouds and storms; but that, HEART-FAITH, like the pure sun-beam, comes from the place of God, and like its source, enjoys perpetual serenity and shine. And though its possessor, as a dweller on this turbid planet may sometimes feel the shadow; yet it is but transient. For as the heart of the wise can well bear the gloom of winter because he sees the bloom of opening spring at hand; so the man of true faith regards not "the short afflictions of this life which are but for a moment," because his eye is fixed upon "that exceedingly great and eternal weight of glory that glitters before him." Animated by this he looks undismayed on the Jordan of death, and even in the last agony smiles as for victory, and whispers, through tears of transport, "*I wait for thy salvation, O God.*"

Here the cheeks of William began to redden over from his labouring heart, and his sighs to thicken, while pearly drops, such as angels love to see in mortal eyes, came trickling down. But still the lips of friend Loe continued to pour their honied streams of holy eloquence, as burning in his zeal he went on to show the widely different effects of these two kinds of faith, even in the life that now is—that while the one is held in derision even of the wicked world, by whom it is overcome, the other is honoured even by the wicked world whom it tramples under foot—that while the one suffers the mortification of shameful defeat, the other enjoys the triumph of the most glorious victory—that while the one dies amidst the horrors of despair, the other expires in extasies of hope—and that while the one shall come forth to shame and everlasting contempt, the other shall awake to all the transports of eternal life.

As the fearful difference between vice and virtue were hardly ever painted in more pathetic colours than by this pious quaker, so, rarely has such painting produced a deeper effect on the pupil of wisdom than in the case now before us; for soon as the sermon was ended, young William, with the sweet dejection of conscious guilt reclaimed, drew near the man of God, and taking him by the hand, acknowledged that, though he had not been entirely overcome by the world, yet he feared, he said, he had conformed too much to its vanities; but now, hoped, through the help of that good spirit which bringeth salvation, he should be established for ever. Thomas Loe, looking on him with a countenance kind as when an angel looks on the tender babe, and with tones of equal sweetness, said,—*I hope my young* friend thee will keep in mind the words of the Lord Jesus, how he said, "the servant is not greater than his Lord"—"If the world hated him," who was the perfection of goodness, "they will hate thee if thou become his follower." But remember, friend William, never canst thou love thyself as God loves thee; never canst thou desire thine own happiness as God desires it. O then meditate on SUCH LOVE, and far above all things in heaven or earth, strive to get thy whole soul inflamed with it. Then shall God himself enter into the palace of thy heart, and "*sup with thee, and thou shalt sup with him.*"

In uttering these words he pressed William to his bosom with all the fervent tenderness of a father; adding at the same time, while the tear hung glistening in his eyes, "God be gracious to thee my son, and give thee wisdom like Jacob to wrestle with God, and also to prevail."

This was to William a day of the sweetest emotions he had ever known.

Joy sprung up afresh in his heart, the joy of glorious hope, far beyond what the young seaman feels when becalmed on his voyage to some golden coast, suddenly a sweet breeze of the ocean springs up, and borne along upon the curling billows he beholds the happy shores of the long promised land, all brightening before him. O how rare is that preacher, whose eyes, whose voice, whose every gesture preaches to the *souls* of his hearers! William, young as he was, could not but mark this preaching in Thomas Loe. He could not but mark the wonderful difference which religion makes between a stranger who possesses it, and one's own father who is destitute. "*Yes*," thought he to himself, "*when struck by this good man's preaching I first felt my unhappy state by nature, and wished to seek to God for comfort, my own dear father instead of congratulating smiles, gave me nothing but angry frowns; and even thrust me from his door! But here this good quaker, though an absolute stranger, seeing my infant wishes to return to God, is moved even to tears of joy on my account, and presses me with a mother's tenderness to his heart. O then how God-like a thing must religion be! How certainly must that fit for the society of angels hereafter, which makes men so much like angels here.*" Such were William's thoughts on his way from the meeting. I hardly need tell the reader that William was now in no frame of mind to go back, as he had been pressed, to the lord lieutenant's, and to the *giddy* and *gay ones*, at his palace. From the religious impressions early made on him by his mother in the nursery, and afterwards deepened at college by friend Loe, William may be said to have always had a turn for those dignified pleasures which naturally beget a disrelish for trifles. To see young gentlemen reddening into indecent passion about the "MINISTER and his MEASURES," or about STAGE BOXES and FENCING MASTERS! or to see young ladies tossing their snowy arms, and rolling their diamond eyes in extasies of *wonderful* OPERA DANCERS; or stage players.—These, though the two ordinary themes of conversation in high life, had *always* seemed to him very uninteresting. But in this present holy and heavenly frame of mind, the very idea of them was so disgusting, that he declined going back, as we have seen, to the lord lieutenant's; and indeed studiously avoided many of the great families in Dublin, because they took no delight in talking of God and those great subjects which he most of all delighted in.—This seclusion of his was soon noticed by the hospitable lord lieutenant and the gay circles of the metropolis, who presently began with much impatience to ask, "*where is young Mr. Penn?*" In a little time the fatal secret came out, that—*he was turned quaker.* The report spread a general gloom among his Irish friends. And no wonder. William was now about eighteen: the very season when youth, rising into manhood, enjoys the double charm of tenderness mixed with dignity, rendering the character peculiarly interesting: this, added to a masculine mind sharpened by a fine education—polished by Gallic manners—and above all finished by a quaker sweetness, had rendered him very dear to the lord lieutenant and his wealthy friends; independent of his rank and fortune as the only child and heir of Sir William Penn, high admiral of the British navy. The loss of such a young man to their society could not but have excited a deep regret on their *own* accounts, mingled too with some contempt of *him* for joining a people who, in those days, were so much despised. It was not long before the admiral learned this most unwelcome piece of news. It came, in the way of letters, to his friends in London, all speaking in the most flattering terms of William, and expressing their sincere sorrow that a youth so amiable, and of such high promise, should have *thrown himself away* after this most unaccountable rate. The admiral came home quite in a fever about it. Mrs. Penn seeing his agitation, eagerly asked him what was the matter?

Matter! replied he abruptly, *matter enough to run a parent mad! that silly boy of ours will be the death of me, that's a clear case.*

"Why, what has he done now?" said Mrs. Penn, much startled.

Done! returned the admiral, why he has fallen in with Tom Loe, who has made a fool of him again

Well, I hope William has not neglected the business you sent him to Ireland upon.

Why no, he has not suffered Tom Loe to make him such a fool as that. On the contrary, I learn from a variety of quarters that he is a prodigy of industry.

O, well then, said Mrs. Penn cheerfully, while his religion keeps him innocent and industrious, we need not much trouble ourselves about him.

No, indeed! replied the admiral hastily; now that's the very reason I choose to trouble myself about him. A youth of his genius and education, with the advantages of such rank and friends and industry, my God what might he not do! How easily might he become one of the greatest men of his age. And such he shall be, I'm determined on it. I'll write for him to come home immediately. And if he doesn't *'bout ship and go upon another tack*, I'll disinherit him, that's the long and short of it. I'll not keep in this hot water any longer. If he choose to despise me and run after Tom Loe, he must do it, but he shall never see my face again.

CHAPTER XII.

If his infant son were suddenly lost in some wild wood, where dark pit-falls gaped, and ravenous beasts lay in wait to devour, what father but would instantly rush forth, with throbbing heart, in search of him? And if happily his listening ear but caught the feeble moanings of his child; or he beheld him at a distance with bleeding feet winding his tortured way through piercing thorns, would he not fly to the dear rescued boy, and, clasping him with transport to his bosom, kiss away the pearly drops from his bloated eyes? Yes, such would be the joy of this world towards a child saved from the deaths that threaten the body. But, alas! to save him from that which would destroy the soul; to save him from ENVY, HATE, and all the haggard passions which inflict wounds and deaths beyond the rage and venom of serpents and tigers, no such solicitude is felt. And this often causes the hearts of good men to bleed within them, that when a young person in the wilderness of this world is brought to a sense of his danger, and wishes to fly to his God, instead of being met by his friends with tears of joy congratulating his happy escape, he is often frowned upon and driven back to sin and hell. Such was the treatment shown to young William Penn by his father, and at a time too when he stood most in need of every encouragement. He was at a great distance from home, and from a pious mother whom he doted on. He was spending his days in diligent attention to his father's business, and his nights in reading and devotion by himself; for he had no kind friend to commune with, no kindred soul to comfort and strengthen him. In the midst of this, he receives a letter from home. But that letter, instead of breathing the joy of a happy father, congratulating his dear boy for being so early in the family of God, begins with reproaching him for his *fanaticism*, and ends with ordering him instantly to come home.

William's spirits were at first, as might have been expected, a good deal depressed by this letter; but the depression was only momentary. Religion soon administered her cordial. An ever present God; a glorious life in his service now, and an eternal Heaven hereafter; how could he long be sad? so, packing up his clothes and books, and taking leave of a few friends, he set out for London; not neglecting to strengthen himself on the road, by frequent reflection on the truth and importance of the hopes before him; for he foresaw that they were to be brought to a severe trial. His calculations were abundantly correct; for while his mother received him as usual with transports of joy, his father's countenance was hard and angry; then scarcely allowing time for the customary salutations, he said—"and so Tom Loe has taken you in tow, and made a fool of you again!" William's face, that had been rosy red with joy at sight of his parents, now all at once turned pale on hearing these cutting words; but, soon recovered by conscious integrity, he replied, "Yes, father I have been with Thomas Loe, but I hope that instead of making a fool, he will, under God, make a wise man of me.

Yes, to be sure, and there's a pretty sample of it, returned the admiral sarcastically, pointing at William's simple quaker habit. Tom Loe will no doubt make a wonderful wise man of you. In place of your handsome dresses brought from Paris, see that ugly drab! and that monstrous beaver, broad brimm'd and darkening over your brow like an umbrella! These are precious tokens of wisdom! And is it possible that for such stuff as this you can reject such honours as are courting you from all quarters?

I don't know, father, said William, of any honours that are courting me from all quarters.

No, indeed! well then,, let me ask you, was there ever a young Englishman so talked of at Paris as you were all the time you spent there? And was that no honour? And on your return here to London, was not the whole town running after you?—was that no honour? And when you went to Dublin, did a single mail ever come over but brought letters from the lord lieutenant and the great ones there, all extolling you to the skies—was that no honour? And now what nobleman is there in all the land but would glory in your friendship?—what place is there so high but you might easily obtain it? what heiress so wealthy, but you might marry her as easily as kiss your hand? Are these no honours?

Well, father, said William, these I know are called honours: and let them pass for such. But after all, what would they signify to me, unless they made me happy?

God's mercy on the boy, cried the admiral, getting angry, what would you want more than all this to make you happy!

Why, as to that, father, you know that to be happy we must have what suits our taste, and that the *right* taste too. But I am morally certain, that while I keep my present taste, I shall never be happy, if I have nothing better than great worldly riches and rank. I feel, father, that I am born for better things than these.

Well, but what's the reason you can't take these things and those better ones too?

That's impossible, sir. There's no going to heaven in "golden slippers."

But why, in the name of God, can't you be good and happy as a GREAT man, as well as a *mean* one: and by dressing like a gentleman as well as like a monk? Can Tom Loe have made such a blockhead of you, as to make you believe it a sin to wear a suit of clothes in the fashion?

Father, the quakers don't stand upon the fashions.

And pray why don't they; can they be such fools as to think that religion has any thing to do with the colour and cut of people's clothes?'

The quakers think, father, that religion has to do with every thing that tends to God's pleasure or displeasure, in the happiness or misery of man.

Well, and what has this to do with the fashion?

Why, certainly, father, to set the heart upon the fashion, as if it were the chief end of being—to make it a great theme of our conversation—to resolve to keep up with it no matter what it *cost*—to honour the basest wretch if he have on a fashionable dress—but despise the most godlike, because of his mean apparel—does not this betray a shameful devotion to trifles? yea, worse still—a horrible *insensibilty* to the charms of goodness, wherein consists our main happiness?

The admiral here remaining silent, as if at a loss what to reply, William thus went on,—Yes, father, many people I know, think that dress, no matter how vain, has nothing to do with religion. But these, sir are looked upon by the quakers, as persons utterly unacquainted with the religion of Christ, which, treating the soul as the only divine part of man, is continually striving to turn his attention to the care of the soul; that by enlightening his understanding with the true wisdom, and exalting his affections to the true good, it may give him a relish for that happiness which is godlike and eternal. Hence it is, sir, that the quakers will have nothing to do with the dresses and fashions of the world, which only serve to make people childish and vain in their minds, and averse from the true happiness, and likewise so to impoverish their circumstances as to put it out of their power to *be honest;* yea, and oft times to practise those dark and base frauds and villanies which ruin them for ever.

This being a style of sermonizing rather too stubborn for the admiral to gainsay, William was permitted to go on, which he did at this rate: "Yes, sir, the religion of Christ, and consequently the quakers, (its expositors in the simplest sense,) will encourage no idolatry of the flesh; being fully persuaded, that in proportion as this rises the soul sinks. And what but this is the meaning of those awful passages which run throughout the religion of Christ—"The flesh lusteth against the spirit"—"If ye live after the flesh ye shall die"—"They that live in fleshly pleasures are dead while they live."

The admiral said it was droll how a man could be *dead* while he *lived.*

It is, nevertheless, awfully true, sir, replied William. For a creature born with capacities to *love God*, and thereby put on the immortal beauties of his likeness, to neglect such ineffable glories as these, and meanly pride himself because of fine clothes and gaudy equip age for this poor mortal body, is not such a creature dead, while he liveth? yea, utterly dead to the true end of living, that is, HAPPINESS; which consisteth not in such unworthy gratifications, but in that perfect love which feels the presence of God, banishing all grief and kindling a perpetual heaven. Such were William's arguments; but all his arguments, cogent and conclusive as they were, availed nothing with his father. Indeed they appear to have wrought a very contrary effect in him, as, looking on William's person, and listening to his speech, he was the more grieved to think, that his only child, a youth of such a figure, such a mind, such eloquence, and born for the highest honours, should become the dupe and castaway, as he called it, of the most *pitiful and grovelling quakerism*. In hope yet to avert so great a calamity as he thought it, from his family, he resolved to make one more effort; and to try, since argument had failed, what might be done by menaces. So, fixing on William a stern and angry eye, he said, "Well, sir, I have heard you out: and now let me tell you, that with all your ingenuity and eloquence you have not started me one inch *from my moorings*; no, sir, there is no reasoning like facts. To say that a man can't be great and yet wise and good, is all nonsense. It contradicts daily observation, sir. Look at our nobility, sir, our HONOURABLES, and RIGHT HONOURABLES—look at our clergy, our REVEREND and RIGHT REVEREND, the bishops and archbishops! these are the GREAT ONES, sir, of the realm; these are the first talents and titles, the first riches and learning of the nation. And will you say that none of these are good?"

William, with a modest firmness, replied, that he did not take upon him to judge of others, but that he well knew this, that Christ every where speaks of the pleasures of FILIAL FRIENDSHIP WITH GOD, as being of a nature so entirely different from those that flow from the pride, and ambition, and lusts of this poor polluted world, that they can no more exist together than light and darkness. And also, that for his own part he could truly say, from oft and sad experience, that it was not possible for him to enjoy blissful communion with God, and at the same time conform to the spirit of the world.

Here the admiral, with looks more angry still, replied, "I perceive, sir, that you are determined for ever to misunderstand me. I don't mean that you should *conform to the world* in any thing *base and villanous.* No, sirrah, I despise that as heartily as you and your friend Tom Loe. But I mean that you should conform to the world as our bishops and archbishops do —that is, that you should be rich, and great too. And such you shall be, I'm determined on it. And therefore let me tell you, sir, that if you do not instantly forsake that quaker fool, that Tom Loe and his principles, you must no longer look on yourself as a son of mine.

William appeared much shocked. But after some pause, observed, that his father must, to be sure, do as he thought proper; but at the same time, he could not help humbly craving his father's reasons for his dislike of Thomas Loe. Is he not acknowledged, sir, said William, to be a HOLY MAN, against whom not even his bitterest enemies can say any harm? And as to his principles, are they not the simple expressions of the humble and benevolent spirit the gospel? And after all, sir, continued William, what harm has Thomas Loe ever done me? on the contrary, indeed, have we not great cause to be thankful on his account?

Thankful on Tom Loe's account! retorted the admiral quite in a rage. A plague on him! what has he brought on us but trouble and vexation ever since his vile name was heard by the family.

I think, sir, replied William, modestly, that, under God, I owe Thomas Loe much for what he contributed towards the comparative innocency of my life, at college.

You pay no great compliment to myself or your mother, in saying that, sir. Did you not go to college as innocent a youth as any in the realm? and do you thank Tom Loe for that?

But, sir, replied William, was not the preservation of my innocence a great blessing? And that I have been less disgraced by vice than many other young men, as well at the University as in the large and dissipated cities wherein I was so early exposed, I feel myself, chiefly indebted to the affectionate and powerful eloquence of Thomas Loe. For considering my weakness of youth and inexperience, and separated too as I was from you and my mother, had it not been for the strong hold which his discourses took on my heart, I do not see how I should have withstood that torrent of bad example which swept away so many of those once amiable young men who came to college as innocent as myself. So I think, sir, that if you love me and prize my honour and happiness, you ought to love Thomas Loe, who was to me, of God, the good guardian angel that in your absence saved me from much disgrace.

I am sure, retorted the admiral, you have no great cause to brag of his saving you from disgrace at the University; for it was all owing to him, that you came by the disgrace of being *expelled.*

Yes, sir, replied William, blushing, I own I was expelled from the University, and that too through Thomas Loe: but still it was not for any *vice*, that I should either hate him or abhor myself. It was for an act of zeal, *intemperate* indeed, but still well meant and flowing from a love for the young men whose vain ornaments I assisted to tear off. I confess it was *error*, but thank God not *shameful vice*, such as many others have been expelled for. And therefore I shall always thank God for the poor quaker Thomas Loe, that while many other young men have been expelled for drunkenness, I have drank nothing but water—that while others have been expelled for gambling, I never touched a card—that while others have been expelled for commerce with lewd women, I have been unspotted from the world—that while others, though great sticklers for the high church, have run their fathers to large expense for horses, and dogs, and gaudy dresses, and balls, and masquerades, I have never brought any cost upon you for these things—and that while many others, because their fathers were rich, have thought themselves privileged to be lazy, I have, thank God, in my studies at college, and in acquiring the French language at Paris, and the law at the Inner Temple, and in settling your business in Ireland—have done all I could to please you. But, continued William, though my earthly father may forget my honest endeavours to please him, yet I have the promise that my heavenly father will enter in his book of life every good act that I perform from a single eye to his glory. And as to my poor quaker friend, Thomas Loe, against whom you have taken up such a dislike, let me once more assure you, father, that he has never weakened but greatly strengthened me in all my duties. And above all, he has taught me that, *to do good for evil is the end of the religion of Christ;* and that I am not to look for the *crown hereafter* if I do not cheerfully bear the *cross here.*

"*Phew!*" returned the admiral with a tremendous whistle, as of a boatswain, calling all hands on deck, "why, Tom Loe has made a preacher of you already! Well, go on, young man, go on with your canting. But let me tell you that all this, and all your cross-bearing to boot, though it might have done in former times, is all mere nonsense now.—Yes, people may be *rich* and *great* in this world, and take their pleasures too, and yet after all go to heaven. Many of our lords, both temporal and spiritual, are daily doing it, to my own certain knowledge, and so may you: yes, and you *shall* do it too, let me tell you that, or be no son of mine. If you are determined to go and play the fool, you must go and do it some where else; you shall not do it in my family. And as I have had no hand in your folly, so I will not be eternally suffering the mortification of it, that I am determined on."

William, of course, was turned out of his father's doors. But though the admiral endeavoured to screen himself from the reproaches of his own conscience, and also from those of the world for this most unnatural act, yet it was abundantly plain, from his looks and motions, that INHUMANITY is a breach of the eternal law, (of love) never to be reconciled to the moral sense.—"HONOUR! HONOUR!" cries the infuriated duellist, as he is about to murder his fellow man; but does the monster ever enjoy sweet peace afterwards? So, no plea that pride can prefer will ever silence that voice of God in the soul of man, which ceaselessly cries against cruelty. The admiral was a proof of all this. Even in the act of driving William from home his every look evinced the torture of a soul engaged in the horrid work of self-murder. Nor did the rolling in his bosom subside with the storm that had excited it. For after the son was gone, the father was seen striding about the apartment dark and angry in his looks; and often stroking down his whiskers, as it is said he was wont, when going into battle. Nor was his anguish diminished by the melancholy looks of the servants as they passed by him in silence, and still less by the cries of his lady, in the adjoining room, bewailing her "*poor exiled son!*" After some time he went into her chamber where she lay a crying on the bed, her face muffled up in the clothes. He sat down by her side to console her; but she turned her face still more away. He repeated his tender efforts; but with no better success. Such treatment from an elegant wife whom he doted on, stung him to the quick. At length after a gloomy silence, he clasped his hands and lifting his eyes of mingled grief and rage, he exclaimed—"My God! what a life is this!"

She making no reply, he still went on—"and here have I been all my miserable days, striving through toils and tempests, through fightings and blood, to raise my poor family to something: and after all have only got to a serious doubt, whether I had not better be dead than alive; whether I had not better at once cut my throat than bear this cursed state any longer."

Alarmed at such expressions, Mrs. Penn half raised herself from the bed, and turning to the admiral with much of wildness in her red, tear-bathed eyes, said, "*why, Mr. Penn*, why will you make use of such dreadful language."

Mortal man, replied he, never had better right to use such language; yes, and ten times worse if I but knew where to find it. I wanted to make my son, my only son, a great man, but he won't hear of it. I wanted to comfort you and you wont allow me to comfort you.

"Comfort!" answered she, with a deep sigh, "don't talk to me of comfort. I was never born to enjoy comfort in this world. I had but one child, and he every thing that my heart and soul could desire, and yet his life and mine too have been made bitter to us both ever since he was born."

"Well, whose fault is it," cried the admiral, furiously, "whose fault is it but his own, a poor, sneaking, mean-spirited blockhead!"

"Don't call him so," said Mrs. Penn, "for I have heard you say, a thousand times, he was a boy of genius."

"A boy of genius! yes, the boy has genius; and a fine genius too; but what signifies his genius? what signifies his education, and all his other rare advantages, if, like a poor fool as he is, he won't improve them, won't let them make a great man of him?"

"A great man of him!" exclaimed she. "Ah my God! there's what I fear will be the downfall of us all. A great man of him indeed!"

"Yes," replied the admiral, "I want to make a great man of your son. And pray what can be more natural? Isn't that the aim of the whole world? An't the poor constantly aiming to become rich? and the rich to become nobles? and the nobles to become kings? and kings to become greater and greater still?"

"Yes, Mr. Penn, and it is the aiming at this sort of greatness that has filled the earth with so many wretched beings."

"What do you mean by that?"

"Why, do not the holy scriptures assure us, that it was by aiming at a greatness of this sort that our first parents lost Paradise, and filled the world with sin and death? Nay, was it not by aiming at this sort of greatness that Satan and his angels lost their high place in heaven and sunk to hell?"

"But how does that apply?"

"Why, Mr. Penn, is not this greatness of riches, and pomps, and places, all from PRIDE, and not for HAPPINESS—which is the only end that rational creatures should propose to themselves in all their actions? And, therefore, did not that dear child, whom you just now turned out of doors, did he not ask you 'what is the true end of greatness but happiness?' And if he thought that the greatness you so press upon him would not make him happy, was he not in the right to despise it?"

"Despise greatness!" exclaimed the admiral.

"Yes, Mr. Penn, such greatness as that. I honour my son for despising it; for what is the greatness that consists merely in possessing great town houses and country houses—in entertaining great lords and ladies—in having our gates constantly thronged with coaches and chariots—wasting the day in idle visitings, and the night in plays and cards—not an hour to call our own, but all swallowed up in one continued round of hurry and dissipation—and all this, too, among the VAIN and WORTHLESS, whose manners are childishly frivolous;

whose conversation is about nothing but fashions and slander; whose looks ever wear the simper of folly or the sadness of discontent and envy; and who court us not from friendship, as we well know, but from vanity and convenience because we are rich; and would desert us on the first reverse of our fortunes."

"You draw a very pretty picture of the great, I think, madam."

"Yes, Mr. Penn, but not one shade too black, nor, indeed, half black enough. For, contemptible as such a life may seem, yet there are thousands who, when enslaved to it, like poor drunkards to their cups, will sacrifice every thing to keep it up; will gamble, and forge, and even rob on the highway! yes, and will beggar and disgrace their wives and children, to preserve only a show of such pitiful greatness. And, because our dear boy was blessed with the rare wisdom and fortitude to discover and abhor such madness, you could turn him out of doors, even in the tender and helpless morning of his days!"

Here the admiral begged his wife to talk no more at that rate, for that he loved William very dearly, though he had turned him out of doors. Nay, that he had treated him in this way altogether out of love, that he might constrain him into his views, and make something of him.

"Make something of him!" cried Mrs. Penn, "O my God! that you should possess one of the richest blessings in all this world, and yet not know it; I mean a PIOUS child. For O! what on all this earth can be matter of such joy and triumph to a fond parent as a PIOUS CHILD?" To me it was every thing. I thought of nothing else. I prayed for nothing else. '*Vain, delusive riches and honours!*' I said, *come not near my son. You are not one ten thousandth part good enough for him. Only let my son love God. Only let him have this, the sweetest spur to every virtue, the strongest curb from every vice, the best cordial under every affliction, and I ask no more!*' Well, God, in his infinite mercy, heard my prayer. He gave me that which I esteem above all worlds—a PIOUS SON. And lo! you turn him out of doors! He has not ambition enough! he won't be RICH enough! nor GREAT enough to please you! O what millions would not many of our rich and great friends here in London give if their sons had but half his virtues!—There's the rich lord Sterling!—His eldest son and heir of all, can't dine abroad, but he must be brought home *drunk!* and his face is now so bloated and fiery, that his friends are ashamed to look at him!—There's the great lady Warwick!—Her only son crippled and shortly to die, mortally wounded in a duel!—There's the earl of Coventry!—His only son sneaking about the house, like a blackguard, for losing at cards in a single week fifty thousand pounds left him by an aunt!—And there's young lord Spencer! though heir to a dukedom, and covered over with stars and garters, yet eaten up in youth, of foul diseases!—In short, what with drunkenness, or duelling, or gambling, or raking, or some other detestable vice, there's hardly one in ten of all our great families but is shrouded in melancholy. Fathers, mothers, and sisters, throughout the town, mourning their disgraced and ruined sons and brothers. And here, amidst all this shame and sorrow, our child, our *only* dear child, not only not disgraced with such vices, but adorned with all the opposite virtues—harmless as an infant! temperate as a saint! devout as an angel! and yet, in place of shouting incessant praises to God on his dear account, you turn him out of doors! O Mr. Penn, Mr. Penn, can you ever forget that look he gave you when taking up his hat to go away, as you ordered him, he said, "*Father, had I been turned out of your doors because of any crimes I had done, I should be wretched indeed. But, thanks to God, I go away with a conscience unstained by an act that should cause you or my dear mo-*

ther, to blush for me." Here she burst into a flood of tears. But it was plain they were not bitter tears, for they flowed from eyes piously rolled towards heaven, and bright with the joy of hope that her dear boy would yet one day come out more than conqueror. And O power resistless of truth! this great British admiral, whom not all the thunders and lightnings of hostile navies could have daunted, was so confounded by the still small voice of sacred truth, that he turned away pale with shame and trouble, and walked the floor silent and humbled as a weaned child.

CHAPTER XII.

BUT leaving the admiral and his amiable consort under the excitement of feelings of a very opposite character, let us turn to William. On the first glance at that dear boy, though but through the eye of fancy, we can scarce refrain from crying out—O, come here young men! come here! and mark the difference, the wide, wide difference between the child of God and the slave of Satan in the persecutions they suffer for vice, or virtue's sake! The young sinner, who, for debauching his neighbour's daughter, or murdering his son in a duel, is kicked out of his father's doors, flies from home like a ravening wolf from his wintry den. And while the curses of the injured are beating upon him from behind, conscious guilt, like a deadly frost, has blasted every flower of hope in front, and left him nothing but dreariness and despair. Then seizing the accursed halter he chokes himself over some convenient gate-post, and dies, as he deserves, the death of a mad dog. Such are, ofttimes, the effects of persecution for wickedness' sake. But the persecution for righteousness' sake, O what is it like, or whereunto shall we compare it? It is like unto a whirlwind in a garden of cinnamon, which, though it create a transient tempest, yet serves to reveal the richer glories of the place; for by shaking the beds of spices it fills the air with sweetest odours and spreads abroad a ravishment unknown before. Such was the effect of his father's persecution of young William. It excited, indeed, an agitation that alternately bleached or reddened his cheeks, and called forth his tears. But still as it was for HIM "who will be no man's debtor," he quickly found in it, that "peace which passeth all understanding!" 'Tis true his mother's eyes, following him to the door, melted him for a moment; but scarcely had he passed the gate and entered on the fair clover-covered lawns of Pennwood, and eyed the spacious skies, before his heart was revived by a flood of joys of the noblest kind. The painful state of halting between two opinions is now over, and, as he hopes, for ever. He has at last bravely seized the cross. In thought he ascends the mount of God, with his anchor of HOPE fast moored in heaven, and his eyes of FAITH, bright as the everlasting hills, on which they are placed. And while a voice within seems to whisper—"well done good and faithful servant!" thou art now free—thou art now for God—"thou art now living to the great end of thy creation,"—he felt what he had often read, but never felt before—"the joy unspeakable and full of glory."

In this happy frame he repaired without loss of time to London, in hopes of meeting his revered friend Thomas Loe. But learning that he was not yet returned from Ireland, William inquired where he might find any of the "PEOPLE CALLED QUAKERS!"

Such an inquiry from the son of admiral Penn, and in the meek looks too of one of that people excited much surprise, but he was presently directed to the house of one George Whitehead, an eminent minister among the quakers. As God would have it, there was a meeting that day, at Whitehead's house, which gave great joy to William, who went in and took his seat among the friends. He had not sat long before he found himself very happy with his company. The modesty of their dress—the sweet spirit on their countenances, shining at once with reverence and affection in a noiseless but fervent devotion, filled his heart with all the delights of a most heavenly fellowship. He felt himself as he thought, among "*the excellent ones of the earth*,"—with them worshipping the best of all beings—seeking the greatest of all goods—and by means well suited to the end they aimed at, even by a simple culture of the heart in those divine loves which alone can *take of the things of God and give them to the soul*. Soon as meeting was over, and the younger people and the women gone out, Whitehead, with several of the friends, approached William Penn, where he still sat, to salute him. William rose and giving his hand told them his name. They appeared greatly pleased, and said they were glad to see him, for that two years ago, they had heard friend Loe speak often and much concerning him. Here William blushed. They then asked him wether he was not very lately from Ireland? for that they had just received letters from friend Loe speaking of having seen admiral Penn's son at meeting there, and giving a very favourable report of him. Thinking this a good opening, William told him his whole exercises in Ireland with friend Loe, also his persecutions and banishment from Pennwood. Moreover he told them with a sigh, that for some time past he had been "halting between two opinions," but that now his mind was made up; that being fully convinced that to love the world is the veriest madness and misery of man, and to love God his highest wisdom and happiness, he was resolved to forsake the world and cleave to God for ever.

As William made this confession, the countenances

of the FRIENDS were brightened with joy. And when he was done they assured him how happy they were that one so *young* and of such *high standing* in the world, should think of making an offering of himself to God. William then told them, that he was indeed thankful, and could never be sufficiently so, that God had called him while so young, to the glory of his service. And, as to his *wealth* and *high standing* in the world, he felt there too that the more he had, the more he owed to God, and the stronger his obligations to a pious life: and that now he was come on purpose to cast in his lot among them.

They all smiled, and asked him if he was in good earnest. William looked surprised.—They said they had asked him this question because they were afraid he had not *counted the cost.*

O yes, replied he, I trust I have.

They all shook their heads; when Whitehead, with great meekness, said, I fear, friend William, thee art almost too young for calculations of this sort. Thee ought to remember that we are a "*little flock*," and withal much despised, and that "not many rich, not many wise, not many great of this world," have sought fellowship with us.

William said he had pondered all these things.

Well then, said Whitehead, thee has done well in so doing; but still, friend William, there is something against us much worse than all this yet.

William wanted to know what that was.

Why, friend William, said Whitehead, thee must know that our religion is the *hardest* in the whole world. Here, William seeming to look as if he did not entirely comprehend this, Whitehead repeated "yes, friend William, ours is the hardest religion in the world." Other religions go chiefly on NOTIONS, ours on LOVE. And thou wilt learn, by and bye, that it is easier to harangue about a *thousand new fangled notions*, than to mortifiy one *old lust.* If thou soughtest fellowship with many other societies, thou mightest easily gain thy point by subscribing to their articles; contending for their creeds; confessing their notions, as about the trinity, and baptisms; &c. and by assenting that all ought to be burnt who differ from them in these things. But friend William, we have not so learned Jesus. If his religion stood in these things, it were easy to be a Christian. Corrupt nature has always had a strong leaning to religion of this sort. The heathens gloried in their showy temples and gaudy sacrifices. The Jews vaunted in their tythings of mint, anise and cummin. Many CHRISTIANS also make a great to do about *creeds* and *catechisms*, about *sacraments* and *notions;* because all the zeal they display on these points, though it may bring them much fame and wealth, need not cost them one dear lust or passion! But the quakers, friend William, put no confidence in these things. We feel ourselves constrained to a deeper work, even that hard lesson of Christ, "*the perfect love out of a pure heart.*" And now since thou art come to join our society; and, as is common when persons apply for membership with us, we would ask thee a question or two, but not concerning thy NOTIONS, but concerning thy *affections.* Hast thou then a perfect hatred of sin, and dost thou sincerely desire to be holy? Hast thou the "faith that worketh by love?" and does this vital principle in thy heart manifest itself in every thought and act of thy life? Is it the staid purpose of thy soul never to shed thy brother's blood in war or private strife? Wilt thou never provoke him to hate by suing him at the law? Wilt thou never indulge thyself in gaudy attire, or furniture, or equipage, to the depriving thy *poor brother* of the comforts of thy charity, and thyself of the pleasure of extending it to him? Wilt thou not only not put thy bottle to him, but wilt thou drive from thy house all GIN and ardent spirits that might prove a stumbling block to him? Wilt thou never thyself rob him of his liberty, and wilt thou set thy face against those who would? Wilt thou in thy furniture and equipage, also in thy cookery and manners of living, maintain whatever is plain and cheap, lest by a contrary example thou shouldst tempt him to live above his means, and thus involve him in debt and suffering?

These things, friend William, will serve to show thee the genius of our religion; what we would be ourselves, and what we expect of all who enter into communion with us. Now as thou art young and of a great family in the world, thou mayest not relish doctrines so mortifying to pride and carnal sense, and which require that simplicity and perfect love so distasteful to corrupt nature. We would therefore advise thee to take time and revolve these things in thy mind, lest thou shouldst fall into the condemnation of those who are very ready to follow the Lord in the days of "*the loaves and fishes*," but soon as he begins to preach his heavenly morality that would pull down the brute and set up the angel in man, strait they are "*offended and will walk no more with him.*"

William's eyes sparkled, as friend Whitehead spoke in this way; then with a smile he replied, that he had no need to take time to revolve these things. He was already persuaded, that every pulse of the heart towards the world and the flesh was but fostering a fever fatal to true peace of mind; that it was the desire of his soul to be crucified to the world and the flesh, as the *only wisdom for a happy life.* And as to the SIMPLICITY and SELF-DENYING doctrines of the people called quakers, and also, the contempt they put on all NOTIONAL religion, in comparison of that "PERFECT LOVE" which so strongly inclines to do, in all cases, to others, as we would they should do to us, he was always *charmed* with them. He would not he said, so highly prize the religion of Christ, if it were not for this sweet spirit that runs through and animates the whole. He had within himself, added he, the witness of the divinity of this religion of Christ—its tendency to heal all the ills, and brighten all the goods of life. Repeated experience had taught him, that in proportion as his heart was warmed and sweetened with this divine charity, he had a disposition to feel for his brother as for himself; to pity him; to forgive him; to mourn his vices and misfortunes, and to rejoice in his virtues and prosperities; and therefore instead of being offended thereat, he thought it the very best employment God could set himself upon in this life to crucify inordinate self with all its pride, and envy, and hate, and to perfect himself in that pure love which, by giving him a tender interest in the welfare of others, would make him a partaker in all their good."

Upon this, they all gave him the right hand of fellowship, and he was formally received as a FRIEND, not more to the surprise and comfort of that benevolent and despised people, than to the astonishment and displeasure of the proud ones and great of the dominant church, who from that day marked him as the butt of their spite.

CHAPTER XIII.

It was about the twenty-fourth year of his life that William Penn became a preacher among the quakers; whence it appears, that, being only eighteen when he joined them, he must have been *six* years preparing himself for his "*high calling*," the ministry. What we are to learn from that singular fact in the life of Christ, that he was nine years after he came of age, as we say, before he began to preach, I know not. But of William Penn we may safely say this in the hearing of young candidates for *holy orders*, that when they remember that his talents were certainly of the first class, and his life equally spotless; and when they remember too that his convictions of the transcendent charm and worth of religious affections, were very early and deep, and yet he delayed coming forth to the public until his twenty-fourth year, they ought, we think, to be very cautious, lest, "running before they are sent, they fall into the snare of the devil, and by bringing much reproach on their holy profession, pierce themselves through with many sorrows."

What particular books and bodies of divinity Willim Penn studied during those six years of seclusion, I have never been able to learn; but on reading the numerous tracts, which, like polished shafts of the quiver, flew from his pen against the adversaries of the *humble* and *loving gospel*, (as set forth in the lives of the quakers,) we are at a loss whether most to admire the extent of his reading, or the powers of his memory and judgment.

As a skilful chemist, from a waggon load of plants, will extract an essence which though compressible into an ounce vial, shall yet contain the choice odour and virtues of the whole heap, leaving the residue a mere caput mortuum fit only for the dunghill—so, in passing through the alembic of William Penn's brain, the grossest bodies of divinity appeared all at once decomposed; the bonds whereby sophistry had coupled truth and error, are instantly dissolved; and the vile and the precious are shown in such characteristic colours, that a child can easily mark the difference. The result of all this was a plainness and purity in his principles and practice which can hardly be enough admired and imitated.

We read of the wise king of Israel, that after all his sprightly songs, and pregnant proverbs, and grave discourses, he winds up with a single text—"fear God and keep his commandments; for that is the whole duty of man." Even so, William Penn, after all his deep reading and reflection on that great subject, throws the whole of religion into two words, HUMILITY and LOVE. Those who are in the habit of despising a religion that is not bundled up and bloated with CREEDS and CATECHISMS, SACRAMENTS and CEREMONIES, will no doubt think as meanly of Penn's simple religion of HUMILITY and LOVE, as Naaman did of Elisha's simple prescription for the leprosy, "*go and wash.*" But it is enough for us to know that this religion, simple as it may seem, is from God. And it is also enough for us to know that the foolishness of God is wiser than man. Man must always have a tedious "*round about*" way to come at his object. God goes point blank to it at once. Man must have a thousand springs to move one effect; God touches but one spring, and lo millions of effects leap into motion! Since then his power is so great why may not God, if it please him, give command, and a single pair of *parent* virtues shall instantly give birth to innumerable beauties in the moral world? He does so in the natural world. Look at wintry nature clad in her dreary shroud of ice and snow—her lovely vegetable family all enhearsed!—her nobler animal offspring drooping in silent despair! "*Alas! shall these dead bones live.*" Yes, let the sun but come forth in his strength—let the soaking showers smoke along the ground—and straightway the little plants peep forth, laughing, from their clods—the lambs gambol on their hills—and the birds fill the spicy groves with songs! —and all this wondrous change effected by the sole agency of the sun and the shower! And what is that sun; and what is that shower in the natural world, but *humility* and *love* in the moral? For as the warm sun and shower unbind the ice of winter, and fill the lap of nature with precious fruits and flowers, so by the tear of humility and the glow of love, the ice of human nature is dissolved—the long dead seeds of virtue begin to sprout—the man is revived—his face blooms benevolence—his thoughts breathe kindness—and his lips utter a language sweeter than the song of birds, and more refreshing than the odour of precious spices.

Thus NATURE, by her still small voice of analogy, proclaims to man that humility and love are the true religion and life of the moral world. But for further proof let us go up from nature to nature's God; from his works to his *word.* And here, passing by the prophets who all assure us that Jehovah asks not our "*thousands of rams nor tens of thousands of rivers of oil,*" but only that we "do justice; love *mercy;* and walk *humbly* with God." Passing by the apostles also, who with one voice declare that HUMILITY and LOVE are the very "*end of the law*"—and that without these all our zeal, though hot as the martyr's flame, and all our faith though stronger than mountains, will avail us nothing. Passing, I say, by the prophets and apostles, let us come to a greater than all prophets and apostles, I mean God himself "*manifested in the flesh,*" and in him we shall see cause for ever to exclaim, "was ever love, was ever humanity like his?"

His mother—an obscure virgin!

His supposed father—a poor carpenter!

His birth-place—a stable!

His cradle—a manger!

His heralds—shepherds!

His disciples—fishermen!

His family example—washing his disciples' feet!

His miracle—giving eyes to the blind, &c.!

His new commandment—love one another!

His favourites here—they that resemble little children!

His courtiers hereafter—they that feed the hungry, &c. &c.!

His coming into the world—to seek those that were lost!

His LIFE—doing good!

His death—on the cross to save sinners!

Now what does all this point to, but to humility and

love—to a love stronger than death, and to a humility lower than the grave!

And for those who hold no authority equal to reason, what says reason? Why the only religion in the universe must be humility and love—because, BY HUMILITY WE ADORE GOD FOR ALL THAT HE GIVES TO OURSELVES; AND BY LOVE WE PARTICIPATE WITH OTHERS IN ALL THAT HE GIVES TO THEM.

But still a blind world will not be reconciled to HUMILITY and LOVE. They are too heavenly for earthly natures—too much against the grain of flesh and blood, to be submitted to. "What!" says Pride, "be the servant of all! take the lowest seat! wash the disciples' feet!"—"What!" says Hate, "bear to be called a liar! love my enemies! do them good for all their evil to me! no, never."

This is poor human nature all over. Whether Jew or Gentile, Turk or Christian, they can't stomach humility and love. If God will but excuse them from these, they will do any thing for him. Let them but have their PRIDE and REVENGE, their COVETOUSNESS and LUST, and they will give him thousands of will-worship. The heathens will sacrifice their hecatombs of fat bullocks and lambs; yea and their own children too, on a pinch. The Jews will give him prayers in the streets by the hour, with loads of mint and anise into the bargain. The Mahometans will shear their whiskers, and make scores of pilgrimages to the prophet's tomb—and the Christians, with all their better light, will get baptized in every mode, whether of sprinkling or dipping; and will take forty sacraments, if there be as many. And yet, after all, what good was ever done to the world by these alone? Have they ever yet made mankind one jot the better or happier? Alas! can we be ignorant that with the most pompous display of these, the world has all along been "dead in trespasses and sins?" The heathens universally, idolaters, gladiators, cannibals. The Jews, extortioners, and devourers of widows' houses. The Mahometans, polygamists, s ave holders, robbers. And the Christians—(O shame! shame! shame!) the Christians—drunkards, gamblers, swindlers; duellists in private life; and in public, butchers of one another in endless and bloody wars.

But to come nearer to our own case as individuals, let us suppose a man disordered with the leprosy of sin. And for argument's sake, let us suppose, reader, that you are that man; from the sole of your foot to the crown of your head all distempered, all grievously afflicted. Let us suppose that you are tormented with ENVY, so that like Cain, the prosperity of even your own brother stirs a hell within you—or bloated with PRIDE, so that, like Haman, not all the smiles of a monarch and his court can appease your vengeance for the neglect of a beggar. Now under such cruel distempers as these, will you look for a cure in the externals of religion? Alas! have you not discovered, that all your *bodily exercises* "*profit nothing?*" Have you not found, that after all your shiftings from one religion to another; after all your humble kneelings and solemn sacraments; all your china bowl baptisms, or your deeper plungings,—your heart has continued just as hard, and your life as much embittered with malignant passions and the dread of death as ever? But say, O happy reader, when at some subsequent period the God of Elijah had descended into your heart, in streams of humility and flames of love, have you not experienced a change beyond all that you could have conceived? Have you not found the haughty proudling converted into the weaned child—through tears smiling on injuries which formerly would have been insupportable—delighting in works of love which you would once have utterly loathed—with brotherly tenderness washing the feet of the meanest disciple—with angel sympathy cleansing the ulcers of the poorest Lazarus—and, more wondrous still, with godlike generosity taking the bitterest enemy to your arms, and even rejoicing in the divine work of doing him *good for evil!*

Of the wonderful difference between this religion of Christ and that of the world—between the showy religion of ceremonies and the simple religion of humility and love, few men perhaps ever had a livelier sense than William Penn; and few ever took truer pains to impart that sense to others. This was the end of all his life's extraordinary labours—to caution men against what he called WILL-WORSHIP. "Don't think," he would say, "that preachings and prayings, singings and sacraments, can make you Christians. Baptism by water *washes away only the filth of the flesh;* 'tis baptism *by fire and the Holy Ghost* that is to burn up our lusts, and restore union and *oneness* with God. 'Tis in vain you eat the flesh, and drink the blood of Christ, unless they nourish in you his spirit, which is humility and love. Without which there is no salvation, because there is no qualification for it. For without humility how can there be gratitude? and without gratitude, how can there be enjoyment? And without a child-like love of him, how can we *walk with God* in the blessedness of sweet obedience in this life, or in the joys of beatific vision in the life to come? Thus humility and love are required, not as arbitrary terms for God's pleasure, but as loving prescriptions for man's happiness, to which indeed they are so absolutely essential, that without them God himself could not make us truly happy: for, without them, we could no more enjoy the ravishing glories of his presence than we now can enjoy beautiful pictures without eyes, or savoury dishes without health.

CHAPTER XIV.

Now one would have supposed that all men would have been well pleased with William Penn, for thus eloquently persuading people to exchange their *barren notions* for *divine loves*, which alone can restore the "golden age" of pleasure, to man and beast. One would have supposed that every child, laughing with plenteousness of bread; and that every animal gamboling with fat, would, by thus manifesting the blessed effects of his doctrine, have caused all good men to rejoice in it. At any rate, one would have supposed, that though KINGS and their MINIONS, rioting on the nation's substance, might hate such levelling doctrines, yet assuredly their "*thread bare subjects*," and above all, the *oppressed dissenters*, would have supported him in a doctrine so well calculated to lighten their burdens, and better their own condition. But alas, poor human nature! let a man wear a coat never so black, or a face never so grum, yet, without LOVE, (the soul of all MAGNANIMITY,) he will soon manifest himself the slave of some pitiful passion. And as slaves on a West-India plantation, the worse they are treated by their masters, the more cruel they become to one another; so in a country where religion is not left free to make men the children of God in humility and love, but is enslaved to make them the "hewers of wood and drawers of water" to a despot, the worse they are afflicted and chafed in their minds by him, the more apt are they to hate their fellow sufferers.

Another reason may be assigned for the very unexpected persecution of William Penn by the dissenting preachers. Man is seldom placed in a situation that entirely extinguishes his strong natural wish to be *somebody*. Hence the dissenters in England, though shamefully kept under hatches by the national church, yet never shed their liquorish tooth for power. And although they could not get what St. Paul calls "a good thing," *i. e.* a *bishopric;* yet they affected to come as near to it as possible. They must, (as our Saviour charged their fathers,) be called "Rabbi! Rabbi!" They must be seated in the "*uppermost places at the feast*—be the *chief men in the synagogues*, and receive *praises of men.*" Well, those among them who possessed talents and education, often attained these objects of their ambition—they gathered hearers—made proselytes—built meeting houses—drew up their catechisms and confessions of faith—published their hymn books and discipline—and thus *mimicked* most bravely a church of Christ. But though apparently, "*so nigh unto the kingdom of God, yet one thing they lacked. They did not this for God,—but for filthy lucre sake*—and *for glory from men.*" Yes, they must be great doctors of divinity and heads of churches. Some of them, as before observed, succeeded. Success often tempts even the pulpit to pride; and pulpit pride, like all the rest, kindles at opposition and sickens at talents superior to its own. The shepherd who loses his lamb to the wolf, loses nothing but his lamb; the fleece and flesh, that's all. His own character, in the mean time, as a man, and therefore lord of the wolf, stands undisputed. But the proud priest who loses his disciple, loses not only his fleece and flesh, his taxable and tytheable, who feeds his vanity and fattens his purse, but he loses his reputation too! The world will say of him that though he was great, another was greater. "Saul slew his thousands, but David his tens of thousands." This were a stab incurable; he could never get over it. And as such an idea must never go abroad, he must pull down his rival, that's a clear case.

Such was the wretched spirit manifested against William Penn, by *some* of the dissenting preachers of his time. I mean not such "*great and shining lights*," as the Watts's and Baxters and Doddridges and Wesleys, and Gills, of latter times, whom God, in mercy to the world, has all along raised up to check the corruption and decay of the gospel by wickedly mixing it with this world, as popes and politicians have done. But I am speaking of such, and such there are in the purest churches, who preaching for fame and for the fleece, would not thank St. Paul himself to take away one of their hearers. It was a dissenting preacher of this stamp who rose up so furiously against William Penn. The case was thus— The divine sweetness of his countenance when he stood up to speak, and the truths which fell from his lips with such demonstration of light and love, produced the effect that might have been counted on. Numbers were convinced and joined themselves to the gospel. Among these were some persons belonging to the meeting of a popular dissenting preacher of the name of Irvine. This gentleman had, for some time, been much displeased with William Penn for reflecting on his favourite doctrine, "*justification by faith alone*,"— "*imputed righteousness*," and other such notions which some are fond of putting in place of the harder precepts of *humility and faith working by love*." As yet he had kept his displeasure to himself. But soon as he heard that William Penn had drawn away some of his flock, he could contain no longer, but broke forth against him into the most indecent passion, calling him a JESUIT; a FALSE PROPHET, and a preacher of DAMNABLE DOCTRINES.

Happily for William Penn his labours in religion had been chiefly in quest of that treasure which is *better than the merchandize of gold*, i. e. love. By virtue of this he had learned to look on his fellow man, when tormented with sin, as no object of hate but of pity. He therefore made no reply at first to such abuse, but by his sighs. At length fearing that silence might, by weak persons, be considered as a tacit acknowledgment of a bad cause, he permitted a public notice, that "*he and his friend William Mead, would meet James Irvine at any time and place he should think proper to appoint, and in the spirit of meekness endeavour to answer the very uncharitable charges which he had made against them.*"

If a rumored fight between the elephant and rhinoceros has always excited curiosity sufficient to fill the largest amphitheatre, then how much more when Christian divines, of highest reputation in their respective churches, are coming forward to public dispute on the all-important subjects of religion and eternal life. The crowd of hearers was immense. William Penn, and his friend Mead being handed up to seats prepared for them on a platform, Mr. Irvine in his pulpit commenced with very formally charging William Penn, as an utter enemy to the glorious doctrine of the trinity.

William Penn denied the charge.

Mr. Irvine set himself with great pomp to prove his assertion in a lengthy series of subtile scholastic arguments.

William Penn with his usual simplicity and brevity, showed that both his reasoning and language, being utterly unscriptural, ought not to be relied on.

Finding that William Penn and his friend Mead had a great deal more to say in favour of their opinions than he had imagined, and that the controversy was like to take a very different turn from what he had expected, Mr. Irvine lost his temper and became quite abusive. His disciples kept pace with him in his rage, which they now indulged, not only without restraint, but even with *complacency*, as thinking they were doing God service by abusing "*false teachers*," and "*vile jesuits*." In short, after an altercation continued till late at night, Mr. Irvine, filled with holy wrath, could refrain no longer, but leaping down from his pulpit and snatching his hat, darted out of the meeting-house with a soul as dark and stormy as the night he rushed into. This served as a signal to his party to maltreat our poor quakers at pleasure, which they accordingly did in the most indecent manner. They shuffled their feet—they hissed—they put out their candles—and at length pulling them down from the platform, thrust them out of doors.

Seeing no chance of getting any thing like justice from such blind persons, William Penn determined to bring his defence before the public. Accordingly he fell to writing and presently came out with a pamphlet entitled "*the sandy foundation shaken.*" Now though in this famous piece he only said what his divine master had said a thousand times before him, viz. that all manner of dependence on Christ save that which worketh HUMILITY and LOVE, will only turn out like the *house built on the sand*, yet he soon discovered that, in writing it, he had brought himself into the predicament of that notable peasant, who, in running away from the wolf, stumbled upon the lion. In place of the skin-deep scratches of a few feeble dissenters, he was all at once in the strong clutches of the bishop of London and his formidable clergy. These reverend and right reverend gentlemen, with scarlet ribbons at their knees and long swords by their sides, had for some time past been frowning on William Penn, and for the same goodly reasons for which certain worthies in his day had so grinned at St. Paul, i. e. because he wished "*to be their friend.*"

Every body knows that William Penn did not dread the prince of darkness half as much as he did a NOISY, SHOWY RELIGION. Knowing, as he did, that the heart of man is "*deceitful above all things and desperately wicked,*"—and knowing also, that most men are such extravagant lovers of themselves, that like certain saints we read of in the gospel, if they only make a *bow at the altar*, think themselves full holy enough to "*despise father and mother!*" or if, like the pharisees, they do but offer to God a sprig of mint, they set themselves down at once for *Abraham's children!*—Or if, like Christ's *own disciples*, who only for leaving their beggarly trades and walking about a short season with their divine master, who, by the bye, was every day working miracles to fill their *hungry bellies* and pay their *taxes*, yet they could boldly lay claim to the "*first seats in his kingdom!*"—Knowing, I say, as William Penn did, all this incalculable pride and naughtiness of the human heart, had he not abundant cause to tremble for the bishop of London and his clergy, when he saw the mighty noise and show which they were making "*for God's sake*,"—darkening the skies with their tall cathedrals and spires—distracting the air with their bells and organs—dazzling all eyes with their rich pulpit-cloths and altar-pieces—keeping the people on the stare at their constant change of gowns, and cassocks, and the church in a holy bustle of kneelings and risings, with loud responses and amens? Had not he good cause, as St. Paul speaks of certain *ostentatious saints* of his day, "*to stand in fear of them*," lest, after such wonderful exploits in religion, they would, in the old way, begin to "thank God that they were not like other men?" And because he thus feared for them, and often out of pure christian love expressed his fears, the bishop of London, in place of taking it in good part, kindled into wrath, and by way of revenge, had him attainted of heresy, on account of his book, and thrown into prison!!

The clergy, many of whom had already raised the old war-whoop, "Great is Diana of the Ephesians," now felt themselves perfectly at liberty to fall upon William Penn, which they did in the most virulent manner. One of them went so far as to say, "*he did not see how it was possible for God, consistently with the Bible, to save a quaker!*" Another reverend gentleman, going still further, published a book against William Penn, wherein he asserted roundly, that "Parliament would not be doing half as much harm to the nation by *tolerating* gamblers, *horse-thieves*, *duellists and all that pack of vermin, as by tolerating the quakers.*"

Had a whale or a grampus, during a heavy blow at sea, put into the mouth of the Thames, no historian of those days would on any account have missed relating the wonderful and portentous event. And yet this reverend whale of spiritual ignorance and bigotry, who made his appearance in the city of London so late as the year 1669, is no where noticed by Hume, Smollett, or any other British writer that I have seen. So much apter are men to notice monsters in the natural than in the moral world! thus dipping, like wanton swallows, at mere feathers on the surface to amuse a vain fancy, when they ought to be diving like men to the bottom of moral truths, for the precious pearls of true wisdom.

After lying for some time in durance vile, William Penn was let into the grand secret of his confinement there, viz. *for denying the divinity of the Saviour!* He was also given to understand from the good bishop, that unless he recanted that *damnable error*, he *should die and rot in prison!!* Soon as possible he procured pen and ink, and presently came out with another pamphlet, entiled "TRUTH WITH HER OPEN FACE" In this work, so far from making the Saviour less, as his enemies slandered, he makes him much greater than they do. Instead of making him the *second* person in the *trinity*, he makes him the *first*—yea, he makes him as the scriptures make him, "*The mighty God*"—"*The everlasting Father*"—"*The* ONLY WISE GOD OUR SAVIOUR," even "God himself manifested in the flesh"—who was "with God from the begin ning, and who was God." The bishop, a sturdy ATHANASIAN, did not altogether like this exposition of the trinity; but it gave great comfort to some, even to those whose pious souls had often been grieved to hear the blessed God misrepresented as having *less love* for them than Christ has. To them it gave unspeakable joy to find, as they did in this publication of William Penn's, that God was still *their* God, their infinite friend and father, who so loved them even in their death of sin, that he came into the world for their redemption; yea, that it was "God himself who in the person of Christ redeemed the world." William Penn is, however, in prison, where we mean to visit him, next chapter.

CHAPTER XV.

William Penn in prison; his mother visits him.

A THOUSAND great things and glorious have been said of RELIGION and her family of pleasures. But if ten thousand times ten thousand more were added, still would the happy Christian have cause to exclaim, as did the queen of the East, when with rapture-sparkling eyes she beheld the riches and glories of Solomon's royal state, "verily the half was not told me." O, who, in praising can ever do half justice to that blessed frame of mind which in every thing sees and feels the presence of the Deity, with that holy joy which antidotes all the ills of life, and makes men content in every state—content in poverty—content in sickness—yea, content in bonds and imprisonment where duty calls and the pleasure of pleasing God, is felt. This blessed influence of religion was fully experienced by William Penn in a very important event of his life about this time.

Because he could not think of the TRINITY exactly as St. Athanasius thought, he was, as we have just seen, locked up in prison by the bishop of London. Under circumstances of this sort, the *falsely* GREAT have been known to exhibit symptoms of extreme dejection and impatience; bitterly lamenting their own misfortunes, and as keenly reflecting on the authors of them. But far different was the state of William Penn in prison. Iron bars and bolts could shut him in, but they could not shut out his God. As to please him by pulling down falsehood, and setting up truth, appeared to Penn the highest glory of man, so it inspired the tenderest pity of those who were blind to its importance, and who did not greaten life by pursuing it. Hence, all the malice of the bishop and his clergy, in place of harm, wrought him much good, by exercising and strengthening in him that divine charity which draws the sting of injuries, and spontaneously breathes that sublimest of prayers, "Father forgive them for they know not what they do."

With so much of heaven in his bosom, what wonder that his confinement should have entirely changed its nature, and instead of seeming dark and dreary as a dungeon, should have reflected the gay and lightsome air of a palace.

How long he had laid in prison before the news thereof reached that affectionate parent, I know not. And as little do I know by whom it was conveyed. Certainly, it was not by him, for she was the last person on earth to whose tender bosom he would have imparted such a pang; especially knowing, as he did, that all her sighs and tears could avail him nothing. The news, however, was brought to her that he was in prison. The reader, especially if a parent, will ask no poet's pen to describe the feelings of this tenderest of mothers on hearing that an only son, and one so beloved, *was in jail!* And her sufferings must have been more than ordinarily severe, as, from the silence of the historian concerning him, it is more than probable that her husband, the admiral, was from home at this distressing juncture. Her coach was instantly ordered to the door, and, with all the trembling eagerness of maternal affection, she threw herself into it and set out for the prison, mournfully revolving no doubt as she went, the dark cloud now obscuring those bright prospects which she had so often formed for her son. Her reveries were soon broken off by the appearance of the prison. But if her tender spirits were chilled with horror at sight of the gloomy walls and iron gratings around that house of woe, what must she have felt, as passing along those crowded chambers of sin and suffering, her gentle senses were assailed with the filth and rags and pallid looks of the wretches that, on all sides, stared at her as she walked. Following the steps of the sullen turnkey, she arrived at William's chamber, whose iron door, reluctantly opening with discordant jar, gave her eager eyes the dear object they sought for. Absorbed in his studies, and sitting at an opposite window, William Penn had not marked the entrance of his mother, who, soon as she beheld him, could not repress her feelings, but involuntarily uttered a scream, calling on his beloved *name*. Starting from his chair, William Penn wheeled him around to that well known voice, presenting to his mother a face as like an angel as innocence and filial love, in rosy youth could look. O never was the charm of virtue more sensibly felt than now; and never was that charm more needed. Mrs. Penn had come to weep over her imprisoned son, and to bathe him with her tears. But far from her were all such thoughts when she beheld him, as leaping from his chair, and with all heaven in his countenance, he flew to embrace her.

My Mother!

O my son! was all that nature, near swooning with ineffable tenderness, could utter. After a moment of delicious tears shed on his bosom, the happy mother raised herself to feast her eager eyes on his beloved face. It was a feast indeed. "*O the difference! the difference!* her joy sparkling eyes seemed to say as they darted over his looks—"*O the difference between this my son and the ghastly wretches I but now beheld! They, the dismal forms of guilt, disease, and death; but* HE, *all that fancy can conceive of the lovely reverse! Health in his cheeks, heaven in his eyes, and in every feature innocence and bliss.*" These honours of her son were too bright and precious to escape her keen searching inspection. She caught and enjoyed them all to ecstasy. Then pressing him once more in transport to her bosom, and looking at him with great tenderness, she said, "O William, my son, my son, what a medley of sweetest pains and pleasures has my life been made to me; and all through you!"

Sweetest pains, my mother, and all through me!

"Yes, William, sweetest pains indeed, and all through you. God be praised, you never gave me the pang of a single vice. O no, your life has all been brightened over with virtues. But still, William, through some rare dispensation of heaven, even your virtues have caused me pains; but, as I said, they have been sweet pains. Your early seriousness and devotedness to God, were certainly the greatest of all virtues: but then your father's violent persecutions of you for it, and especially for your joining the quakers, was cause of great pain to me, though it was, I confess, accompanied with much pleasure because of the pure principles and firm, yet amiable spirit, you displayed under it all. And now your confinement in this prison has cost me many tears, but still, blessed be God, they are comparatively sweet tears, because not shed for grief of any crime that you have committed, but rather for joy of your angel innocence and honest adherence to what you think your duty." But, my dear son, although your looks, shining with heavenly innocence and peace, do cause me to feel myself the happiest of mothers, yet I must confess, William, that my joy would be still more complete if you were not in this place."

Yes, mother, and could I obtain it on terms consistent

with duty, I also would prefer freedom to these bonds. But with my present views of things how can I ever expect it?

Why not, my son? replied Mrs. Penn, eagerly.

Why, mother, I am in this prison not for any moral law of God that I have violated; not for any harm that I have ever done to any, or even for suspicion of such thing, but merely because I will not conform with the national church. But how can I conform to that church while there is so much of antichrist in their worship?

Of antichrist, William!

Yes, mother, of antichrist: for what is antichrist, but to invent substitutes, no matter how costly or how apparently holy, in place of the simple worship which God has declared will please him? Now God every where tells us that he "IS A SPIRIT"—a spirit of "HOLINESS AND LOVE"—that, this being his OWN NATURE, "HE SEEKS FOR WORSHIPERS"—"*none but those who thus worship him in spirit and truth.*" He also every where assures us that there is nothing which his soul so abhors as all attempts, in place of these, to invent *outward substitutes*, such as *grand temples—rich offerings—thousands of rams—tens of thousands of rivers of oil—bowings of the head like bullrushes—observings of new moons and sabbaths—tythings of mint and anise—disfiguring of faces—long prayers—frequent fastings—giving alms in the streets*, &c. "WHILE THE HEART IS FAR FROM HIM," and of course the life filled up with crimes, such as "devouring widows' houses"—and not providing proper food and raiment even for "*their own household.*" Now, my dear mother, look at our national church, my non-conformity with which has caused the bishops to throw me (*uncharged with a crime*) into this prison; I say look at our national church and see how awfully it has fallen into these abominations—see how, leaving the *simple, inward, spiritual* worship of Christ, that naturally leads to imitate him in all moral virtues, they have substituted an outward, showy, gaudy worship, like the Heathens, which is consistent with all their old sins of pride, indulgence of self, and frauds and cruelties to others. Look at their grand churches and cathedrals which they have built for Christ! do these show any thing like his HUMILITY in *life*, *doctrine* and *example*, which "*he has left that we might follow his steps.*" Do these show any thing of his LOVE, who "made himself poor that we might be rich"—who requires "*mercy and not sacrifice*"—and who said "let nothing be lost," no, not a scrap of broken meat, because there is always some poor starving Lazarus who wants it.

"And look at the ornamentings and furniture of these grand churches and cathedrals, which they say they have built for Christ; their costly carvings and paintings; their rich altar-pieces and pulpit-cloths, flaming with crimson and gold; their piles of massy plate; and, above all, their tall and towering steeples and spires, reaching to the clouds! Do these things suit the genius of his simple humble worship; or do they match with his precepts of "perfect charity," which are as angels sent to earth, with their eyes bright through tears, eagerly looking around for the poor and miserable, that they may relieve them; and not throwing away their precious means on such blinding, deceiving, and fatal vanities. For "*who hath required these things at your hands, saith the Lord God. Behold the heaven of heavens cannot contain me: and will you build me houses of brick and mortar, which perish before the moth? Is not this the sacrifice that I have chosen, even to deal thy bread to the hungry? and that thou bring the poor that are cast out of thy house? when thou seest the naked, that thou cover him; and that thou hide not thyself from thine own flesh?*" And then for the *worship*, both by the priests and the people, which is offered unto Christ in these their grand churches, what precedents have they for it in his gospel? When the multitude was come together to hear the words of eternal life from his lips, did he amuse them with changes of garments, surplices, and gowns, and cassocks? or did he keep the impatient crowds in suspense, wearying and fatiguing them with repetitions of long prayers, which, though excellent in themselves, and apt to be very savoury and profitable to the *devout*, ought not to be forced upon the multiude? And as to his worshippers, did he, whose chief delight is in the '*humble and contrite ones*,' ever look to be served by giddy crowds driving up to his house in proud carriages, alas! too often bought with monies taken from their creditors; or, worse still, taken from the '*poor* to whom he had appointed them his own *stewards?*' or did he expect that persons profaning his house with pomps and vanities of attire so opposite to the charitable spirit of his religion, would set themselves down as his disciples, because they had gone a formal round of outward devotions, while in their tempers and manners they betrayed the most deplorable ignorance of the Saviour whom they had been so pompously worshipping—living in their old scandalous neglects of those moral duties which even heathens honour, to the great disgrace of the religion of Christ, and to the filling the world with infidel philosophers, thus taught to *laugh* at all revelation!"

As William Penn uttered this, which he did like one who strongly felt what he was speaking, his mother, who had been eagerly imbibing every syllable, thus passionately replied:—"Oh William, my son, what a horrible picture have you given of the degeneracy of the church in these wretched days! and the more horrible because it is so true."

"Yes, mother," replied he; "and yet, because I cannot conform to such horrible corruptions of Christ's gospel; because I cannot bring my feelings to go to such churches and to partake of all that outward, noisy, showy, unspiritual worship, my name is cast out as evil; my property is confiscated and sold; and I am here, you see, mother, locked up in prison, cut off from the common blessings of air and liberty, when all the time no man dare come forward and say I ever did him harm; and all this under the eyes of the bishops of the church, whose tythings, and revenues, and palaces, and pomps, and pleasures are, in part, maintained out of the substance thus torn from the poor quakers; and their children beggared and ruined by such inhuman robberies.

"Well, William," replied Mrs. Penn, embracing him, and her looks shining with heavenly joys, "you have given me more of divine comfort to-day than I ever experienced in one day in all my life. Such bright lights on your duty, and such fortitude to adhere to it, in spite of all discouragements, O what glory has it not shed over your person in my eyes; and what ceaseless gratitude to God that he has given to my dear son the honour to be such a champion and martyr for his glorious truth, which yet shall triumph."

"Yes, mother," replied William, catching up that word, "yes, Christ's truth shall yet triumph over Satan's lies—and his heavenly love over hellish hate. The fruits of his righteousness shall yet fill the earth, and then all those who have honestly laboured for that great change, 'shall shine like the firmament, and as the stars for ever and ever.'"

"Well, William," returned Mrs. Penn, getting up as to go away, "I came here to comfort you, but thank God for ever, you have much more comforted me. Yes, I am going home very different from what I came; not with eyes flowing with bitter tears, but with a heart overflowing with sweetest joys. But now I must be going. I forgot to tell you that I expected your dear father yesterday. He will, I think, certainly come to-day. He is coming home sick. I long to pour of my joys into his bosom And besides, my dear son, this shameless imprisonment of you may bring about great good. You know what a high spirited man he is; and that, after all his life's dangers and hard fightings for his king and country; after all his large loans of money for the glory of the British nation, you, his child, his only child, should be thus rudely thrown into prison, it cannot but rouse his indignation. At any rate, it must set him to thinking; and he may thence make such discoveries of the scandalous corruptions in the national church, as shall produce an entire change in his respect for it, and even make him honour you for quitting it." Mrs. Penn then took a tender leave of her son, not without promising to come and see him the next day, and, perhaps, to bring his father with her.

CHAPTER XVI.

On her return Mrs. Penn found the admiral had just got home and very uneasy about her, as none of the servants could tell him where she was gone. His surprise in hearing from her that she had been to the prison, was changed into the deepest horror on hearing the cause—that she had been there to see William! The effect on his spirits was such as she had predicted, that after all his hard fighting, and liberal spendings for his country, his only son and child, though innocent of crime as a lamb, should thus be thrust into prison like a common felon, and that too by an English bishop, for the slightest insult of whose sacred lawn he would have fought to the knees in blood; oh it was like the stab of a dagger. But he felt not as he once would have done. His health, which for a considerable time past, had been on the decline, had experienced such rapid decay during the last four months' cruise that his impoverished heart could scarely furnish blood enough for his cheeks and eyes to express their resentments. Mrs. Penn did not fail to aid his returning reason and conscience by all the arguments she honestly could. She gave him an account of the interview with their son in prison. She told him that instead of finding William dejected and unhappy, she found him an angel of innocence and serenity; cheerfully pursuing his studies, and in his looks showing a heroic spirit, nobly triumphant over all his enemies. She then related their son's vivid description of the horrible corruptions of the gospel by worldly minded bishops, substituting outward forms for the inward *power of godliness;* and the still more horrible corruptions of the bishops themselves as too evident in their pride and ambition, living like princes in their palaces, while thousands of widows and orphans were pining for bread; and likewise their shutting up in prisons and robbing of their substance, thousands of the most humble and harmless souls, merely because they chose to worship God in a way of greater simplicity and purity.

The admiral showed signs of deep contrition at this, and with tears in his eyes, told his wife that he was afraid he had treated that amiable boy, his son, too harshly. He added that ever since his disputes with William, his own eyes had been, he believed, opening; and that he had for a good while past, been thinking that there was a wide difference between the precepts and example of Christ, and those of the great hierarchs who call themselves his bishops—that he began now to be satisfied that they were, most of them, a pack of *worldly-minded*, SELF-SEEKING hypocrites and impostors, whom he would never more go to hear preach as long as he lived. "But, my dear," added he, let us waste no more time in talking thus while our son is in prison. I long to see William; I long for an entire reconciliation with him; and to encourage him to persevere in his good walk, though I am afraid, poor boy, the times are so bad he will meet with much persecution." The next morning while they were at breakfast, they were all at once surprised and delighted with the fine, open, sweetly shining face of William, who had received his discharge from prison early that morning, through a friend to whom the admiral had privately sent money for the purpose. Mrs. Penn as usual, flew to embrace her son. But his father, suddenly struck with the recollection of his former harsh treatment of William, manifested a momentary embarrassment; but quickly recovering himself he rose, and with a slight suffusion on his cheeks, stepped forward reaching out an eager hand, and calling, "come, William, my dear son, welcome to your father's embraces. You saw me a little embarrassed, but no matter for that; if I was angry with you, I meant it for your good as I thought; but, thank God, I have lived to see my error; and also to congratulate you, my dear child, that you were so early a favourite of your God." Such a speech from so great an officer as admiral Penn, ought never to be forgotten by the young, whom it should instruct that the bravest men have always been the first to *acknowledge* error, and to seek the heartfelt satisfaction of making friends with the injured. From a father, ever so highly honoured, this speech greatly affected William Penn, especially when he saw in the looks of that honoured *father* such evident symptoms of a constitutional decay and speedy dissolution. The admiral understood the meaning of the tender melancholy that so suddenly settled on William's countenance; with his frequent sighs, which served but to attach him the more to his beloved child. "I am going, my son," said he to William, "I am going; and very fast toc; and I am thankful above measure that you are with me, and that things have worked about into such a good trim at last, as I have been so long wishing. And now my dear boy you must stay with me and see the last of me."

William Penn had his hands full at this time, many assailants having risen up rudely attacking himself as well as the religious opinions of the people he patronised. In addition to this he had just commenced his career as a preacher of the gospel, to which his heart was entirely devoted. But when he saw the low and languishing state of his father; and in his pale and emaciated looks recognized the dear author, under God, of his own existence, with all his advantages of education and high standing in life, he was so affected that he resolved to stay at home and aid his mother in the pious work of cheering his declining hours and smoothing his rapid descent to the grave. Then was seen the *blessed*, BLESSED power of religion to open the understanding to a sense of parental obligation, and to warm the heart with such filial gratitude, as to cause a young man cheerfully to give up every thing else and find no place so dear to him as the bedside of a sick parent. Then also was seen the wide difference between gold and love to qualify for the tender offices of nursing and waiting in the house of mourning. The coarsest hireling can bring to the sick man his food, and can administer his physic. But it belongs solely to love to perform these offices in such an endearing way as to give them their proper refreshing effect. And here it was that William Penn shone in full lustre. He was not the ESAU, the *rough man* whose duties coldly and reluctantly performed, only served to show ingratitude and to grieve a father's heart; but he was the fond and affectionate JACOB whose love made him all eye, all ear, all attention to anticipate his wishes and make him fly to supply them even before they were breathed. And whatever he did, whether it was to raise his father in bed, or to smooth his pillow, or to wipe the cold sweat from his brow, or the phlegm from his lips, all was done with such alacrity and tenderness as to cause the good old admiral daily to lift the eye of gratitude to God for such a child. And indeed few parents ever had more cause to be thankful for such a child. For William Penn's ardent love and unwearied attention to his father was but a small part of his recommendations. His extraordinary talents, his studious habits, his rare acquirements, together with his gravity, his dignity of deportment, his unsullied morals and sublime principles of religion, all, all conspired to furnish this happy parent with an overwhelming flow of joy and thankfulness on his dear account. And to see such a son as this, taking all these his rare advantages and attainments, and with the sweetest humility and affection, laying them at the feet of his aged father, as if he had received all from him, and found no pleasure equal to that of returning all to him again. O how gratifying must this have been to the soul of admiral Penn, especially when he recollected that he had, twice, turned this same child out of doors. How fully now must he have been convinced that this his son "*had learned*, as he ought, *the truth as it is in Jesus!*" It appears that he became completely a convert to the same blessed faith as it is preached and exemplified in the simple child-like spirit and manners of the FRIENDS. Then it was that the pride, and ambition, and worldly mindedness of the bishops and clergy began to lay heavy upon his heart; and he often said in his latter moments, that he was "*awfully afraid that the corrupt examples of the national church, with those of the dissolute nobility would overwhelm the country with ruin.*" Feeling his end approaching, and seeing the dark cloud of persecution hanging over his son's head, because of his religion, he sent a friend to the Duke of York, (afterwards King James II. under whom he had fought that great battle against the Dutch fleet) desiring it of him as a death-bed request that he would protect his son in case of persecution; and to ask the king (Charles the 2d) to do the same. They both returned a comfortable answer—"*that they would assuredly be William's friends.*" The day before his death, he said, "son William, I am weary of the world! I would not live over my days again if I could command them with a wish, for the snares of life are greater than the fears of death. Three things I commend to you. *First and above all,* let nothing ever tempt you to *wound your conscience! O be tender of your conscience!* so you will have peace at home and a rich feast in a day of trouble. *Secondly,* whatever you design to do, lay it *justly* and time it seasonably; for that gives security and despatch.—*Thirdly,* be not troubled at losses and disappointments; for if they may be recovered, well; if not, *trouble is vain.* If you could not have helped it, be content, and trust in Providence, whose afflictions are for our good. And if you could have helped it, *let not your trouble exceed instruction for another time!*"

His dissolution which had been rapidly advancing, began now sensibly to appear upon him: he felt its cold and icy approach without the least alarm. His last words contained the highest eulogy ever pronounced on the TRUTH. "*Son William,*" said he, looking at him with the most composed countenance, "*if you and your friends keep to your plain way of preaching, and keep to your plain way of living, you will make an end of the* PROUD PRIESTS *to the end of the world.—Bury me by my mother—live all in love—shun all manner of evil; and I pray God to bless you all! and he will bless you all.*" He then bowed him in his bed and gave up the ghost.

By the death of his father, William Penn became owner of a very handsome estate, supposed to be worth at that time 1500*l.* sterling per annum, equal to 15,000 dollars now; besides an immense sum of money due to him from the CROWN, for loans made by his father, and which he had been kept out of for a long time, as we shall see in the next chapter.

CHAPTER XVII.

"*WHO can tell what is good for man in this life?*" was a question which staggered Solomon himself, with all his wisdom; and which, indeed, he proposes not with any idea of ever solving it, but rather of throwing out to us a comfortable hint that there is ONE who knows what is good for man in this life, and that we should bow with reverential joys to that adorable will which can easily convert what we think the heaviest misfortune into the greatest blessing.

To be kept out of their money, especially if a large sum, is felt by the most of men as a serious misfortune. It was so felt by admiral Penn, William's father. This patriotic officer, for the glory of the British navy, was continually making it loans out of his own private purse, and with such a sailor-like neglect of calculation, that when he came to cast up the account, he found, to his utter astonishment, that the government owed him the affrightening sum of sixteen thousand pounds sterling, equal, as money now goes, to two hundred thousand dollars! After a world of fruitless applications to the crown, the good admiral sickened and died, leaving this vast debt to his son to collect. William's applications to government were equally unavailing; but, happily, his mind was so greatened by the mighty objects of religion, that he suffered but little from this disappointment. After a lapse of many years, and his prospects of payment from the crown continuing as gloomy as ever, he proposed to the king, Charles the Second, an exchange of his claim for a grant of lands in North America. William Penn had his reasons for this.

In the first place, he saw no chance of ever getting his money out of the hands of the king. And, in the second place, he saw no end to the persecutions of himself and his poor friends, the quakers. Even at this time, 1680, so lamentably ignorant of the spirit of the gospel were the bishops of the established church that they not only tolerated, but even encouraged the mad multitude in the most cruel abuses of the quakers. Headed by the sheriffs and magistrates, the populace would snatch off their hats and bonnets in the open streets, even of Liverpool, Bristol, and London, and dash them in their faces, or tread them under foot. They would burst into their meeting-houses, even while assembled in the worship of ALMIGHTY GOD! and utterly regardless of the divine presence, drive them out like dogs; break the windows; split up the benches; tear down the galleries; and then nail up the buildings as forfeited to "HIS SACRED MAJESTY, CHARLES THE SECOND, BY THE GRACE OF GOD DEFENDER OF THE FAITH!!" and yet, instead of being ashamed of themselves for such brutal acts, or being disarmed of their fury by the meekness and patience of such gentle sufferers, they became more brutal against them still, keeping a closer watch over their proceedings—dogging them from place to place—attacking them at their meetings, even in *private houses*—and, after shutting them up too, as "CONVENTICLES *forfeited to the king*," they would then drive them, like convicts, to the jails, and, without any regard to the weather, or to age or sex, turn them into dark and dirty rooms, often in such crowds as to endanger their lives, for want of fresh air; the women, even the most delicate, forced to sleep on the hard planks, and the men in hammocks stretched above them, while such as were supposed to have property, were fined at the most inhuman rates, even, in some instances, at twenty pounds sterling a month, for *no attending the established church!* and when the money could not be raised by these poor people, as was often the case, the sheriffs would distrain their property, such as cows, calves, horses, beds, household furniture, and utensils, and sell them off, frequently at half price; thus actually reducing many an innocent and hard-working family, with their unoffending children to beggary. And all these public robberies committed under the eye of king Charles and his CLERGY!—the former, great part of his time, revelling with his harlots and jesters! and the latter, in all the solemn pageantry of sanctified looks and lawn sleeves, devoutly lifted to heaven, returning "THANKS to Almighty God. that they were ever born in a *Christian country;*" and making long prayers "*for the poor Jews and heathens!*"

William Penn, I say, seeing no end to these cruel persecutions of himself and innocent followers, very naturally turned his thoughts to North America, whither the ROMAN-CATHOLIC Christians, and the PRESBYTERIAN Christians, had just before been flying, by thousands, from the fury of the CHURCH of ENGLAND Christians! (O glory to God that there is yet *one government left on earth* where the demagogues of one church are not permitted to persecute and plunder the rest.)

But the generous wish to place his friends beyond the reach of persecution was not the sole motive with William Penn for looking towards North America. He had a nobler motive still. His mind had long been ravished with the beautiful ideas of a state of society formed on the humble and loving spirit of the gospel. That blessed state, where religion, stript of all her harlot-like trumpery of *barren forms*, and adorned in her matron robes of divine simplicity, fruitful of love and good works, should so illumine the wilderness, that the Heathens, enamoured of her divine charms, should press to become her converts and children. Eager to plant such a colony of brothers in America, William Penn applied to king Charles for a grant of land in that country, "*which, as was expressed in the petition, he was willing to receive in exchange for the sixteen thousand pounds so long due to his family.*"

It would appear that that hand, which is so visible in the growth of the lily and in the preservation of the sparrow, was with William Penn in this great matter. It was this hand, it is presumed, that had, so early as 1661, turned his thoughts to North America, as to an asylum for his oppressed brethren. And it was this hand, it is still believed, that had led him, in 1675, to be concerned in the settlement of a small colony of FRIENDS in East (now called *New Jersey*) and principally about Mount Holly and Burlington. From these people he often learned that the Indian country on the western side of the great river Delaware was most beautiful to look on--"*the plains,*" said they, "*along the winding flood, are in most places covered with corn and natural meadows and marshes; while all on the back of this, a mighty forest rose, tall and stately, darkening the western sky with its blue shade, and stretching itself north and south with the river far as the astonished eye can travel.*" They stated too, that sundries of their people had, at different times, gone over the great river to trade; and that all of them, on their return, had made the same very favourable reports both of the inhabitants and their country. And first of the INHABITANTS. "*With respect to these,*" said they, "*we were never so agreeably disappointed.* We had expected to find a people fierce and rude as the bears and panthers of their forests: but we met a people the most friendly that we had ever seen. As we approached their towns, they would hasten forth to bid us welcome, shaking hands with us very cordially, and signifying, by the kindest smiles and nods, how glad they were to see us; and with great vehemence and affection, addressing us in words which the interpreters said, were to tell us how welcome we were to our INDIAN BROTHERS. After this they would take us to their towns, and spread down skins for us to sit on; and while the men entertained us with *smoking*, the women would bring us barbecued turkies, and venison, and roasting ears to feast on.

"And as to the COUNTRY, we can truly say of it, that it is a land most rich and desirable to dwell in; a land of fountains and brooks, a land of mighty oaks and elms, and all manner of precious trees for timber, a land whose soil, especially on the water-courses, was a black mould very deep and rich, insomuch that the Indian corn, without the aid of the plough, grew there to an enormous size, with two and sometimes three large shocks on a stalk; and we have counted seven and eight hundred grains on a shock! And then for the GAME in those ancient forests—it was wonderful to look at; far sarpassing in abundance any thing that we had ever thought of. For in walking through the woods, we were ever and anon starting up the deer in droves; and also frequently within sight of large herds of the buffaloe, all perfectly wild, and wallowing in fat, and seeming, in their course, to shake the earth with their weight. And, indeed, no wonder; for the grass, particularly in the low grounds, grew so rank and tall, that the buffaloe and deer, on flying into it, which they were wont to do when frightened, would disappear in a moment.

"The rabbits and partridges too were exceedingly numerous; and as to the wild turkeys, we have often seen them perched in such numbers on the nut-trees, especially the beech, that the branches seemed qûite black with them. Nor had the Creator been less mindful of the waters in that great country; foı they were made to bring forth abundantly of fine fish of various kinds, especially the sturgeon, of which the great river was so full, that at no time could we look on it without seeing numbers of those great fishes leaping from it into the air, not without much fright to the natives, whose canoes they have many a time fallen into and overset. And for water-fowl, such as geese and ducks, they were in such quantities, that he who should tell only one half of the truth, would be counted a romancer; for indeed the whole surface of the mighty river seemed covered over and black with them; and when at any time they were disturbed and rose up, their rising all at once was like the sound of distant thunder, and the day itself was darkened with their numbers. We saw also the wild vine in that country, the spontaneous birth of the woods, growing to an enormous size, and spreading over the trees to an astonishing extent, bending the branches with their dark-blue clusters, most lovely to sight and taste, and capable, no doubt, of yielding a very pleasant wine. Nor were the bees forgotten in that favoured land; for we often saw them at work among the sweet-scented bells and blossoms of the wild wood-flowers. And besides, at the simple feasts spread for us by these friendly heathens, we were frequently regaled with calabashes of snow-white honey-comb."

Now, counting all these advantages of this Indian country, the nobleness of its waters, and the richness of its lands, with that plenteousness of fowl and fish and flesh of all sorts, how can we but say that it is a land which the Lord has blessed; and that it only wanteth a wise people to render it like the ancient Canaan—"*the glory of earth.*"

Such were the accounts which the settlers in New Jersey often reported in their letters to William Penn, concerning the great country on the western side of the Delaware. They produced on him their proper effect. Looking on all this as a finger pointing him to a place of long-desired rest, he immediately presented a petition to king Charles the 2d, "*praying that, in lieu of the monies due to him from the crown, he, the king would be pleased to grant him a sufficient portion of lands on the western side of the Delaware river in North America for a settlement for himself and his persecuted followers the Friends."* The king was well pleased with the petition, himself, and had it laid before the LORDS COMMITTEE OF COLONIES AND COMMERCE.

Soon as the petition was read, and it was known that both the petitioner and his followers were quakers, the board appeared as if struck into a strange sort of dilemma. "*A colony of quakers among the North American Indians!*" The very name and sound of the thing excited a general stare. And it was unanimously agreed that no good could possibly grow out of it, either to the *nation* or the *individuals*. As to the first, "*it was ridiculous*," said sir John Warden, agent of the Duke of York and Lord Baltimore, who having grants of "THE PLANTATIONS OF NEW YORK AND MARYLAND," were opposed to the petition.—"It was ridiculous," said he, "to suppose that the interests of the British nation were to be promoted by sending out a colony of people that would *not fight*." "What! a pack of noddies that will have nothing to do with gin or gunpowder; but will gravely tell you that gin was never invented to make savages drunk, and cheat them out of their lands; but only for physic to cure the cholic withal. And that guns were invented, not to kill men, but hawks and wolves! God's mercy on us, my lords! what are we to expect from such colonists as these! Are they likely to extend our conquests—to spread our commerce—to exalt the glory of the British name —and above all to PROPAGATE our MOST HOLY RELIGION? No, my lords, I hope it will never be so supposed by this NOBLE BOARD.—And as to this crack-brained fellow, this William Penn and his tame, yea forsooth, followers, what can they promise themselves from settling among the fierce and blood-thirsty savages of North America, but to be tomahawked and scalped, every man, woman, and child of them!"

This speech, pronounced with due emphasis, made such an impression on the *board*, that they were on the point of rejecting William Penn's petition at once. And thus that beauteous city of Philadelphia, that loveliest monument of the blessings of God on human virtue, would have been lost for ever. But he whose glorious prerogative it is to make even "*the wickedness of man to praise him*," appointed one of the lords of the BOARD to advocate William Penn's petition; which he did with singular ingenuity. With trembling voice and changeful countenance, as of a man about to utter unwelcome truths, he began with assuring the board that he was *no quaker*, nor any friend to that *silly people*. "No, my lords," continued he, raising his voice, "I am *no quaker*. And I pray you let no gentleman in this noble house, hold me in such *misprison*. But still, my lords, I am in favour of the petition for the quakers to go off to North America. The reason, my lords, to my mind is very plain. The *swinish multitude*, my lords, *profanum vulgus*, my lords, the *swinish multitude* as we properly call them, must have a government; yes, my lords, and *an iron government too*. They have not sense and *virtue enough to govern themselves*. All the boasted REPUBLICS, or governments of the people, have, on trial, turned out no better than BABELS of confusion and destruction to their foolish undertakers. No, my lords, there is no government on earth for the PROFANUM VULGUS, comparable to that of KINGS, PRIESTS, and NOBLES. Now if this be true, and I challenge the board to deny it, then William Penn and his quakers ought gladly to be permitted to leave the COUNTRY. Nay, I even assert, my lords, that William Penn cannot stay in this country consistently with the safety of the government; for if ever he should get the ear of the populace, he would bring such contempt on those glorious privileged orders of KINGS, PRIESTS, and NOBLES, that no man of spirit would have any thing to do with them. *For, my lords*," said he, "*what* nobleman is there, with a drop of English blood in his veins, but would blush for his STARS and GARTERS, when, as he rolls along the streets in only a fashionable coach and four, he hears on all sides, the groans of these quakers upbraiding him for being "*a lover of pleasure more than a lover of God*," and for squandering on *vanities* that precious gold, which if laid out in feeding and clothing the *fatherless and widow*, would yield him a feast of never-failing pleasures! And as to our lords spiritual, our BISHOPS and our ARCHBISHOPS would it not make these our HOLY FATHERS in GOD, ashamed of their SACRED LAWN SLEEVES and MITRES, to be told every day by William Penn and his quakers, that these are '*the marks of the beast*,' the vain trappings of carnal pride seeking glory of men, and that those who use these things are none of Christ's--that his poverty can have no fellowship with their palaces—nor his staff and sandals with their gilt coaches, and horses covered with silver harness, and grooms bedecked with gold lace. But this is not the worst yet; no my lords, let William Penn alone, and his sacred majesty himself will soon have an uneasy seat of it on his throne. How can he otherwise, my lords, having it rung daily in his ears, that '*kings are sent of God merely in his wrath as a punishment of wicked nations*.' And that if they will but repent and become good quakers, following the *light within*, they shall no longer have a king to reign over them; for that God himself will be their king, and will break all other yokes from off their necks. God's mercy, my lords! who would be a king to be rated after this sort? Surely then, my lords, you will agree with me, that it is high time for William Penn and his quakers to be off. Yes, my lords, I repeat it; they *must be off;* or this excellent government of kings, priests, and nobles, is gone for ever, and chaos, and wild uproar is come again."

This speech produced the desired effect. The petition was unanimously recommended to the approbation of his gracious majesty, accompanied with a note, "*humbly praying that his majesty would be graciously pleasedto make unto William Penn a grant of the lands in North America, which he had petitioned for.*"

Charles, who, like Herod of old towards the honest Baptist, had a great liking for William Penn, was well pleased with this award of the board in his favour; and knowing that the news would be very acceptable, immediately despatched a *special messenger to him on that errand.* The king was right in this conjecture. The news was indeed very acceptable to William Penn. His heart had been much in this North American enterprise. The glory of God in the spread of human happiness—the beauty of gospel virtues to charm the savages—to overcome their hatreds—to conciliate their loves—and to unite them, like brothers, with his gentle followers, these were lovely ideas to his mind. Nor less were the fair scenes thence ensuing—the white men bringing to their red brethren all the rich productions of their looms and anvils; on the other hand, the red men smiling with friendship, bringing to their white brothers, their venison and corn, with grants of rich lands for them to dwell together in. Then to see them both rising, like brothers indeed, to the glorious toils that crown life with comfort—erecting pleasant habitations and spreading beautiful farms—while, aided by science and religion, human nature shakes off its brutal character and becomes angelic, presenting a spectacle of all others the most lovely to the eyes of God and good men. Such was the picture which William Penn's benevolent fancy had long been painting in North America—"*the desert blossoming like the rose, and the wilderness like the garden of God.*" Thousands of prayers, had he put up that God would realize such bright visions; and thousands of gold and silver had he expended to settle such a colony in the new world. And now having prayed his sovereign for permission to pass over that Jordan and take possession of the desired land, he was waiting to see whether the Lord would prosper his way or not. It was a moment big with anxiety and hope. No wonder then that the news of such full success should have excited the sweetest emotions. "*Yes, God has heard the voice of his prayer! God has appointed unto him the honours of Joshua—to lead a remnant into the land of rest: the nobles have been made to consent, and even the king himself is stirred up to convey the greatful tidings.*"

Soon as possible he hastened up to court to make his acknowledgments to the king; but not so soon but that the king, in right royal generosity, had gotten in readiness, fairly drawn up and endorsed "A DEED OF A CERTAIN NEW PROVINCE IN NORTH AMERICA, FOR MY BELOVED SUBJECT AND FRIEND WILLIAM PENN." It is not easy to conceive the feelings of this amiable man, when, introduced into the drawing-room of the palace, he was met by his sovereign and presented with the above deed. "Well, friend William," said the king in his frolicksome way, "you'll see in this paper that I have done something handsome for you. Yes, *man*, I have given you there a territory in North America, as large as my own Island of Great Britain. And knowing what a fighting family you are sprung from, I have made you governor and captain general of all its coasts, and seas, and bays, and rivers, and mountains, and forests, and population. And now in return for all this I have but a few conditions to make with you."

William Penn begged the king would please to let him know what they were.

Why, in the first place, replied Charles, you are to give me a fifth of all the gold and silver you may find there. But as you quakers care but little about the precious metals, I don't count on much from that quarter.

In the second place, friend William, you are to be sure not to make war on the nations without my con sent. But in case of a war you are always to remem ber that you are an Englishman, and therefore must never use the *scalping knife.*

In the third place, if any persons of my religion, the *honest Episcopalians*, would wish to come and settle in your quaker province, you shall receive them kindly: and if they should at any time invite a preacher of their own, he shall be permitted to come among you. And moreover, if they should like to build what we call a church, (but you a *steeple-house*,) you will not forbid it."

William Penn smiled and said that FRIEND Charles, for so he often called the king, "should certainly be gratified in all these things: for," added he, "I who have drank so deeply of the bitter waters of persecution myself, will never, I hope, consent to persecute others on the score of religion." On retiring from the royal presence, William Penn hastened to inspect his charter to the new province; when lo! at the very threshold he met an article that set his cheeks all on a glow—he found that his province was named PENN-SYLVANIA! that is, in English, "THE WOODY LAND OF PENN." Blushing at the bare idea of the enormous vanity which this name might argue, he hurried to the recorder and begged he would change the name. The recorder, who happened to be a Welshman, said to him, "*well then, what name would hur like to give to hur province?*"

New Wales, replied William Penn. The Welshman answered that this name being a compliment to his own native country, ought certainly to be very acceptable to him. But, continued he, "*though hur should be well pleased to hear hur province called New Wales, yet hur has no business to alter the present name.*" Upon this Penn drew his purse and offered him twenty *guineas* to alter the name. The Welshman still refusing, Penn repaired to the king to have it done. To this the king, in his jocose way, replied that as he had stood God-father for the new province, he had, as he thought, a fair right to give it a name: that he had accordingly given it a *very good name;* and should *take the blame on himself*."

Having obtained his charter under the great seal of England, Penn lost no time to inform the public of the fair territory which he had purchased in North America, and also the terms on which he meant to dispose of it. This publication excited considerable emotion throughout Great Britain. It was observed,

In the *first place*, That "while lands in England, sold from *twenty* to *sixty pounds sterling per acre*, William Penn offered his lands, *fresh and heavy timbered*, for *forty shillings the hundred acres!* being but little more than *four pence an acre!* with but one shilling per hundred acres as quit rent, to the proprietor for ever!"

"Secondly, That while lands in England rented from one to three pounds sterling, per acre, William Penn offered his for one shilling!"

"Thirdly, That while in England it was a transportation offence to kill a rabbit or partridge! and few, except the nobility, ever tasted venison, in Pennsylvania any boy big enough to draw a trigger might knock down a fat buck in the woods whenever he pleased. And as to rabbits and partridges, they were so abundant that the very children, if they but knew how to set traps and pack-thread snares, might always keep the house full of such savoury game."

If these are talked of by all, as great *natural* recommendations of Pennsylvania, the *moral* recommendations were still far greater; for it was observed,

"Fourthly, That while in England the servants were a people but poorly rewarded for their services; in Pennsylvania all servants, men or women, were to be allowed fifty acres in *fee simple*, to be paid them with a good suit of clothes at the expiration of their servitude! And the more cheerfully if they had acted with fidelity as servants, doing all things cheerfully as with an eye to the glory of God.

"Fifth, That while in England, there was but *one creed*, *one catechism*, *one form of prayer*, *one baptism*, from which no man or woman might dissent without peril of the *whipping post*, or *pillory;* in Pennsylvavania, all who acknowledged "one almighty and eternal God to be the moral governor of the world, and honoured him as such by an *honest and peaceable life*, should be equally protected in their rights, and made capable of promotion to office, whether they were Jews, Gentiles, or Christians."

"Sixth, That while in Virginia, Maryland, and New England, the settlers were charged with cheating the Indians, by putting bad merchandize upon them in exchange for their furs; in Pennsylvania all merchandize offered in trade was to be brought into market and exposed to public inspection, so that the Indians might no longer be imposed on and provoked.

"Seventh, That while in the *other* colonies the Indians were treated very little better than dogs, whom every blackguard might kick and cuff, to the exceeding diversion of the *white Christians;* in Pennsylvania it was enacted that the PERSONS and RIGHTS of the INDIANS should be held SACRED: and that no man, whatever his rank or fortune, should affront or wrong an Indian without incurring the same penalty as if he had committed the trespass against the proprietor himself.

"Eighth, That while in most new countries settled by Christians, if a Christian was injured by a native, he might instantly avenge himself even to the knocking out the brains of the offender; here it was enacted by William Penn, that if "*any Indian should abuse a planter, the said planter should not be his own judge upon the Indian, but apply to the next magistrate who should make complaint thereof to the king of the Indian for reasonable satisfaction for the injury.*

"Ninth, That while other Christian adventurers thought they had a right to treat the inhabitants of the countries they discovered, as mere animals of the brute creation, whom they might abuse at pleasure, William Penn framed his laws with an eye of equal tenderness for the Indians and the quakers, ordering that "*all differences between them should be settled by a jury of twelve men, six chosen from each party, that so they might live friendly together as brethren*"—thus extending with impartial hand the rights of justice and humanity to these poor people, who in proportion to their weakness and ignorance, were the more entitled to his fatherly protection and care.

"Tenth, That while in England the children of the rich were, too generally, brought up in pride and sloth, *good for nothing to themselves or others;* in Pennsylvania all children of the age of twelve were to be brought up to some *useful trade*, that there might be none of the *worthless sort* in the province; so that the poor might get plenty of honest bread by their work, and the rich, if brought low, might not be tempted to despair and steal.

"Eleventh, That while in England, from the millions given to the KINGS, LORDS, and CLERGY, the number and wretchedness of the poor were so increased, that every year hundreds of them were hung for stealing a little food for themselves and children; in Pennsylvania there were but two crimes deemed worthy of death, *i. e.* deliberate murder, and treason against the state. As for offences requiring confinement, it was ordered by William Penn, that in the punishment of these an eye was to be constantly kept on the reformation of the offender. And hence all prisons were to be considered as workshops, where the criminals might be industriously, soberly, and morally employed."

The perusal of this manifesto of William Penn's, diffused a most lively joy through the hearts of all honest Englishmen; then what must have been its effects on the spirits of those benevolent people the FRIENDS? To them it would have been welcome as a ray from the dawning millennium, no matter by what hand, God had been pleased to send it. But that one of their own long afflicted tribe should be thus raised up of God to set such an example to the whole world, and revive the hearts of the humble and contrite ones, was peculiarly dear.

The change produced by it among that long oppressed people was wonderful. Till now their appearance in the streets was but rare; and even then they made no stop, but hastened along to their business, serious and shy, like persons who know that the public favoured them not. But now they are frequently seen stopping each other and standing in the streets in large groups, shaking hands with glad faces, as men are wont who have heard good tidings. And amidst their mutual congratulations on the bright prospects dawning on themselves and a darkened world, the pleasant name of William Penn was often heard. It was heard in tones of pious joy triumphant, as when the patriarch beheld a ray of hope from the distant Shiloh, descending on the head of his beloved Joseph; even on the head of him who was separate from his brethren. "William, thou art a lovely vine; even a lovely vine by a well, whose branches run over the wall."

The archers have sorely grieved him, and shot at him, and hated him.

But his bow abode in strength; and the arms of his hands were made strong by the hands of the mighty God of Jacob--from thence is the SHEPHERD--the stone of Israel."

It now remains to be mentioned that this publication of William Penn was followed by consequences far beyond what he himself had ever counted on, even in his most sanguine moments. It reminds us of that other wonder of the world, *Solomon's temple.* We read of this heaven-ordered edifice, that when the noble materials, the stones and timbers were all hewn and fitted for the purpose, and the golden trumpet sounded to the work, straightway the workmen, whether Jews, Tyrians, or Sidonians, all rose up as one man, and the sacred building was put together with such perfect harmony, that no discordant sound of a hammer was even once heard to disturb that sacred silence. Such throughout Great Britain was the effect of William Penn's publication. The general confidence inspired by it is without a parallel in the annals of a private man. Trading companies immediately bought their thousands and tens of thousands of acres: while crowds of individuals from all parts of the empire were seen leaving their homes and the bones of their ancestors, that they might go to "THE LAND OF WILLIAM PENN," and there, safe from the red scourge of persecution, lead *a peaceable and quiet life in all manner of godliness.*

Nor were they the quakers alone who followed his fortunes to the western world. Numbers of the poor and pious of other churches, won by the unusual benignity of his looks, which they had seen as he travelled and preached through the realm, and confiding in that good name which all seemed to delight in giving him, offered themselves to partake of the good or ill fortune that awaited him beyond the seas. Having sent off *three* ships laden with poor adventurers, and a fourth, in which he meant to embark himself, being ready for sea, he hastened up to London, to take leave of the king (Charles the Second) who, though by no means the man after his own heart, had yet shown great good will towards him, and even a particular friendship.—"Well, friend William," said the king in his jocular way, "I have sold you a noble province in North America, but still I suppose you have no thoughts of going thither yourself."

"Yes, I have," replied William Penn, "and I am just come to bid thee farewell."

"What! venture yourself among the savages of North America! Why, man, what security have you that you'll not be in their war-kettle in two hours after setting foot on their shores?"

"The best security in the world," replied William Penn, calmly.

"I doubt that, friend William: I have no idea of any security against those cannibals but in a regiment of good soldiers, with their muskets and bayonets. And mind, I tell you beforehand, that, with all my good will for you and your family, to whom I am under obligations, I'll not send a single soldier with you."

"I want none of thy soldiers," answered William Penn, pleasantly. "I depend upon something better than thy soldiers."

The king wanted to know *what that was.*

"Why, I depend on themselves," replied William Penn, "on their own *moral sense;* even on that '*grace of God which bringeth salvation, and which hath appeared unto all men.*'"

"I fear, friend William, that that grace has never appeared to the Indians of North America."

"Why not to them as well as to all others!"

"If it had appeared to them, they would hardly have treated my subjects so barbarously as they have done."

"That's no proof to the contrary, friend Charles. Thy subjects were the aggressors. When thy subjects first went to North America, they found these poor people the fondest and kindest creatures in the world. Every day they would watch for them to come ashore, and hasten to meet them, and feast them on their best fish, and venison, and corn, which was all that they had. In return for this hospitality of the SAVAGES, as we call them, thy subjects, termed *Christians*, seized on their country and rich hunting grounds for farms for themselves! Now is it to be wondered at, that these much injured people should have been driven to desperation by such injustice; and that, burning with revenge, they should have committed some excesses?"

"Well, then, I hope, friend William, you'll not complain when they come to treat you in the same manner."

"I am not afraid of it."

"Aye! how will you avoid it? you mean to get their hunting grounds too, I suppose."

"Yes, but not by driving these poor people away from them."

"No, indeed! how then will you get their lands?"

"I mean to buy their lands of them," replied William Penn, firmly.

"Buy their lands of them! why, man, you have already bought them of me."

"Yes, I know I have; and at a dear rate too: but I did it only to get thy *good will*, not that I thought thou hadst any *right* to their lands."

"Zounds, man! no right to their lands!"

"No, friend Charles, no right at all. What right hast thou to their lands?"

"Why, the right of discovery—the right which the Pope and all Christian kings have agreed to give one another."

"The right of *discovery!*" replied William Penn, half smiling, "a strange kind of right indeed! Now suppose, friend Charles, some canoe loads of these Indians, crossing the sea, and *discovering* thy island of Great Britain, were to claim it as their own, and set it up for sale over thy head, what wouldst thou think of it?"

"Why—why—why," replied Charles, blushing, "I must confess I should think it a piece of great impudence in them."

"Well, then, how canst thou, a CHRISTIAN, and a CHRISTIAN PRINCE too, do that which thou so utterly condemnest in these people whom thou callest SAVAGES?"

The king being rather too much staggered to make a reply, William Penn thus went on:—"Yes, friend Charles, and suppose, again, that these Indians, on thy refusal to give up thy island of Great Britain, were to make war on thee, and having weapons more destructive than thine, were to destroy many of thy subjects, and to drive the rest away, wouldst thou not think it horribly cruel?"

The king, with strong marks of conviction, agreeing to this, William Penn thus added:—"Well then, friend Charles, how can I, who call myself a *Christian*, do what I should abhor, even in heathens. No, I will not do it. I will not use the right to their land, though I have bought it of thee at a dear rate. But I will buy the right of the proper owners, even of the Indians themselves. By doing this I shall imitate God himself in his justice and mercy, and thereby ensure his blessing on my colony, if I should ever live to plant one in North America."

Tradition does not report the reply which king Charles made to this modest yet cutting reproof; but it is hoped that the AMERICAN YOUTH will take notice how very small indeed, a wicked king appears when placed by the side of an honest man.

"A king may make a belted knight,
A marquis, duke, and a'* that:
But an honest man's above his might,
Good troth he dare not paw that."

BURNS.

Having performed this duty of respect to the king, he went down to his country-seat at Worminghurst, where he spent one sweetly mournful day with his

* A', in Scots, means *all*.

wife and children, whom he was so soon to leave, and perhaps never to see again. The day was passed in a very interesting manner, sometimes in the consolatory exercises of devotion, or of valuable conversation, seasoned with a heavenly love, and sometimes in writing the following letter, which as it is said by good judges to be one of the richest pieces of tender, heart-touching, family eloquence any where to be met with, I do the more cheerfully give it, word for word, to the reader.

"Worminghurst, 4th of the 6th month (June.)

"My dear wife and children,

"My love, which neither sea, nor land, nor death itself can extinguish or lessen toward you, most endearedly visits you with eternal embraces, and will abide with you for ever, and may the God of my life watch over you, and do you good in this world and for ever! —Some things are upon my spirit to leave with you in your respective capacities, as I am to one a husband, and to the rest a father, if I should never see you more in this world.

"My dear wife! — remember thou wast the love of my youth, and much the joy of my life; the most beloved, as well as most worthy of all my earthly comforts; and the reason of that love was more thy inward than thy outward excellencies, which yet were many. God knows, and thou knowest it, I can say it was a match of Providence's making; and God's image in us both was the first thing, and the most amiable and engaging ornament in our eyes. Now I am to leave thee, and that without knowing whether I shall ever see thee more in this world, take my counsel into thy bosom, and let it dwell with thee in my stead while thou livest.

"First: — Let the fear of the Lord, and a zeal and love to his glory dwell richly in thy heart; and thou wilt watch for good over thyself and thy dear children and family, that no rude, light, or bad thing be committed else God will be offended, and he will repent himself of the good he intends thee and thine.

"Secondly:—Be diligent in meetings for worship and business; stir up thyself and others herein; it is thy duty and place; and let meetings be kept once a day in the family, to wait upon the Lord, who has given us much time for ourselves: and, my dearest, to make thy family matters easy to thee, divide thy time, and be regular; it is easy and sweet. Thy retirement will afford thee to do it; as in the morning to view the business of the house, and fix it as thou desirest, seeing all be in order; that by thy counsel all may move, and to thee render an account every evening. The time for work, for walking, for meals, may be certain, at least as near as may be: and grieve not thyself with careless servants; they will disorder thee: rather *pay* them, and *let them go*, if they will not be better by admonitions. This is best to avoid many words, which I know wound the soul, and offend the Lord.

"Thirdly:—Cast up thy income, and see what i daily amounts to; by which thou mayest be sure to have it in thy sight and power to keep within compass: and I beseech thee to live low and sparingly, till my debts are paid, and then enlarge as thou seest it convenient. Remember thy mother's example, when thy father's public-spiritedness had worsted his estate (which is my case.)

"I know thou lovest plain things, and art averse to the pomps of the world; a nobility natural to thee. I write not as doubtful, but to quicken thee, for my sake, to be more vigilant herein: knowing that God will bless thy care, and thy poor children and thee for it. My mind is wrapt up in a saying of thy father's, "I desire not riches, but to owe nothing;" and truly that is wealth: and more than enough to live is a snare attended with many sorrows. I need not bid thee be humble, for thou art so; nor meek and patient, for it is much of thy natural disposition; but I pray thee be oft in retirement with the Lord, and guard against encroaching friendships. Keep them at *arm's length*, for it is giving away our power, aye and self too, into the possession of another; and that which might seem engaging in the beginning may prove a yoke and burden too hard and heavy in the end. Wherefore keep dominion over thyself, and let thy children, good meetings, and friends, be the pleasure of thy life.

"Fourthly:—And now, my dearest, let me recommend to thy care my dear children; abundantly beloved of me, as the Lord's blessings, and the sweet pledges of our mutual and endeared affections. Above all things endeavour to breed them up in the love of virtue, and that *holy plain* way of it which we have lived in, that the world in no part of it get into my family. I had rather they were homely than finely bred as to outward behaviour, yet I love sweetness mixed with gravity, and cheerfulness tempered with sobriety. Religion in the heart leads into this true civility, teaching men and women to be mild and courteous in their behaviour, an accomplishment worthy indeed of praise.

"Fifthly:—Next breed them up in a love one of another: tell them it is the charge I left behind me; and that it is the way to have the love and blessing of God upon them; also what his portion is, who hates, or calls his brother fool. Sometimes separate them, but not long; and allow them to send and give each other small things to endear one another with. Once more, I say, tell them it was my counsel they should be tender and affectionate one to another. For their learning be liberal. Spare no cost; for by such parsimony all is lost that is saved: but let it be useful knowledge, such as is consistent with truth and godliness, not cherishing a vain conversation or idle mind: for ingenuity mixed with industry is good for the body and mind too. I recommend the useful parts of mathematics, as building houses or ships, measuring, surveying, dialling, navigation; but agriculture is especially in my eye. Let my children be husbandmen and housewives. It is industrious, healthy, honest, and of good example, like Abraham and the holy ancients, who pleased God, and obtained a good report. This leads to consider the works of God and nature, of things that are good, and diverts the mind from being taken up with the vain arts and inventions of a luxurious world. It is commendable in the princes of Germany, and the nobles of that empire, that they have all their children instructed in some useful occupation. Rather keep an ingenious person in the house to teach them, than send them to schools, too many evil impressions being commonly received there.

"Be sure to observe their genius, and do not cross it as to learning: let them not dwell too long on one thing; but let their change be agreeable, and all their diversions have some little bodily labour in them. When grown big, have most care for them: for then there are more snares both within and without. When marriageable, see that they have worthy persons in their eye, of good life, and good fame for piety and understanding. I need no wealth, but sufficiency; and be sure their love be dear, fervent, and mutual, that it may be happy for them.

"I choose not they should be married to earthly, covetous kindred; and of cities and towns of concourse beware; the world is apt to stick close to those who have lived and got wealth there: a *country life and estate I like best for my children.* I prefer a decent mansion, of a hundred pounds per annum, *i. e.* a neat house and fifty or sixty acres in the country, before ten thousand pounds in London, or such like place, in a way of trade. In fine, my dear, endeavour to breed them dutiful to the Lord, and his blessed light, truth, and grace in their hearts, who is their Creator, and his fear will grow up with them. 'Teach a child,' says the wise man, 'the way thou wilt have him tc walk, and when he is old he will not forget it.' Next, obedience to thee, their dear mother; and that not for wrath, but for conscience sake; liberal to the poor, pitiful to the miserable, humble and kind to all; and may my God make thee a blessing, and give thee comfort in our dear children, and in age gather thee to the joy and blessedness of the just (where no death shall separate us) for ever.

"And now, my dear children, that are the gifts and mercies of the God of your tender father, hear my counsel, and lay it up in your hearts; love it more than treasure, and follow it, and you shall be blessed here, and happy hereafter.

"In the first place, remember your Creator in the days of your youth. O how did God bless Josiah because he feared him in his youth! and so he did Jacob, and Joseph, and Moses.

"O my dear children, remember, and fear, and serve him who made you, and gave you to me and your dear mother; that you may live to him, and glorify him in your generations! To do this in your youthful days, seek after the Lord, that you may find him; remembering his great love in creating you; that you are not beasts, plants, or stones, but that he has kept you, and given you his grace within, and substance without, and provided plentifully for you. This remember in your youth, that you may be kept from the evil of the world: for in age it will be harder to overcome the temptations of it.

"Wherefore, my dear children, eschew the appearance of evil, and love and cleave to that in your hearts which shows you evil from good, and tells you when you do amiss, and reproves you for it. It is the light of Christ that he has given you for your salvation. If you do this, and follow my counsel, God will bless you in this world, and give you an inheritance in that which will never have an end. For the light of Jesus is of a purifying nature. It seasons those who love it and take heed to it, and never leaves such, till it has brought them to '*the city of God, that has foundations.*' O that you may be seasoned with the gracious nature of it! hide it in your hearts, and flee, my dear children, from all youthful lusts; the vain sports, pastimes, and pleasures of the world; redeeming the time, because the days are evil!—You are now beginning to live. What would some give for your time? Oh! I could have lived better, were I, as you, in the flower of youth!—Therefore love and fear the Lord; keep close to meetings; and delight to wait on the Lord God of your father and mother, among his despised people, as we have done; and count it your honour to be members of that society, and heirs of that living fellowship which is enjoyed among them, for the experience of which your father's soul blesseth the Lord for ever.

"Next:—Be obedient to your dear mother, a woman whose virtues and good name is an honour to you; for she hath been exceeded by none in her time for her plainness, integrity, industry, humanity, virtue, and good understanding; qualities not usual among women of her worldly condition and quality. Therefore honour and obey her, my dear children, as your mother, and your father's love and delight; nay, love her too, for she loved your father with a deep and upright love, choosing him before all her many suitors; and though she be of a delicate constitution and noble spirit, yet she descended to the utmost tenderness and care for you, performing the painful acts of service to you in your infancy, as a mother and a nurse too. I charge you before the Lord, honour and obey, love and cherish your dear mother.

"Next:—Betake yourself to some honest, industrious course of life, and that not of sordid covetousness, but for example, and to avoid idleness.—And if you change your condition and marry, choose with the knowledge and consent of your mother if living, or of guardians, or those that have the charge of you. Mind neither beauty nor riches, but the fear of the Lord, and a sweet and amiable disposition, such as you can love above all the world, and that may make your habitations pleasant and desirable to you.

"And being married, be tender, affectionate, patient and meek. Live in the fear of the Lord, and he will bless you and your offspring. Be sure to live within compass; borrow not, neither be beholden to any. Ruin not yourself by kindness to others, for that exceeds the due bounds of friendship; neither will a true friend expect it. Small matters I heed not.

"Let your industry and parsimony go no further than for a sufficiency for life, and to make provision for your children, and that in moderation, if the Lord gives you any. I charge you to help the poor and needy; let the Lord have a voluntary share of your income for the good of the poor, both in your society and others; for we are all his creatures; remembering that he that giveth to the poor lendeth to the Lord.

"Know well your in-comings, and your out-goings may be better regulated.

"Love not money, nor the world: use them only, and they will serve you; but if you love them you serve them, which will debase your spirits as well as offend the Lord.

"Pity the distressed and hold out a hand of help to them; it may be your case; and as you mete to others God will mete to you again.

"Be humble, and gentle in your conversation; of few words I charge you; but always pertinent; hearing out before you attempt to answer, and then speaking as if you would *persuade* not *impose.*

"Affront none, neither revenge the affronts that are done to you; but forgive and you shall be forgiven of your heavenly father.

"In making friends consider well first; and when

you are fixed be true; not wavering by reports, nor deserting in affliction, for that becomes not the good and virtuous.

"Watch against anger, and neither speak nor act in it; for, like drunkenness, it makes a man a beast, and throws people into desperate inconveniences.

"Avoid flatterers, for they are thieves in disguise; their praise is costly, designing to get by those they bespeak. They are the worst of creatures; they lie to flatter, and flatter to cheat; and, which is worse, if you believe them you cheat yourselves most dangerously. But the virtuous, though poor, love, cherish, and prefer. Remember David, who asking the Lord "who shall abide in thy tabernacle? who shall dwell upon thy holy hill?" answers, "he that walketh uprightly, and speaketh the truth in his heart; in whose eyes the vile person is contemned, but honoureth them who fear the Lord."

"Next, my children, be temperate in all things; in your diet, for that is physic by prevention; it keeps, nay, it makes people healthy, and their generation sound. This is exclusive of the spiritual advantage it brings. Be also plain in your apparel; keep out that lust which reigns too much over some; let your virtues be your ornaments, remembering life is more than food, and the body than raiment. Let your furniture be simple and cheap. Avoid pride, avarice, and luxury. Read my "No Cross, No Crown." There is instruction. Make your conversation with the most eminent for wisdom and piety, and shun all wicked men, as you hope for the blessing of God and the comfort of your father's living and dying prayers. Be sure you speak no evil of any, no, not of the meanest; much less of your superiors, as magistrates, guardians, tutors, teachers, and elders in Christ.

"Be no busy-bodies; meddle not with other folks' matters, but when in conscience and duty pressed; for it procures trouble, and is ill manners, and very unseemly to wise men.

"In your family, remember Abraham, Moses, and Joshua, their integrity to the Lord, and do as you have them for your examples.

"Let the fear and service of the living God be encouraged in your houses, and that plainness, sobriety, and moderation in all things, as becometh God's chosen people; and as I advise you, my beloved children, do you counsel yours, if God should give you any. Yea, I counsel and command them as my posterity, that they love and serve the Lord God with an upright heart, that he may bless you and yours from generation to generation.

"And as for you, who are likely to be concerned in the government of Pennsylvania, and my parts of East Jersey, especially the first, I do charge you before the Lord God and his holy angels, that you be lowly, diligent, and tender, fearing God, loving the people, and hating covetousness. Let justice have its impartial course, and the law free passage. Though to your loss protect no man against it, for you are not above the law, but the law above you. Live therefore the lives yourselves you would have the people to live, and then you have right and boldness to punish the transgressor. Keep upon the square, for God sees you: therefore do your duty, and be sure you see with your own eyes, and hear with your own ears. Entertain no luxuries; cherish no informers for gain or revenge; use no tricks; fly to no devices to cover or support injustice; but let your hearts be upright before the Lord, trusting in him above the contrivances of men, and none shall be able to hurt or supplant you.

"Oh! the Lord is a strong God, and he can do whatsoever he pleases; and though men consider it not, it is the Lord that rules and over-rules in the kingdom of men, and he builds up and pulls down. I, your father, am a man that can say, he that trusts in the Lord shall not be confounded. But God, in due time, will make his enemies be at peace with him.

"If you thus behave yourselves, and so become a terror to evil doers, and a praise to them that do well, God, my God, will be with you in wisdom and a sound mind, and make you blessed instruments in his hands for the settlement of some of those desolate parts of the world, which my soul desires above all worldly honours and riches, both for you that go, and you that stay; you that govern and you that are governed; that in the end you may be gathered with me to the rest of God.

"Finally, my children, love one another with a true endeared love, and your dear relations on both sides, and take care to preserve tender affection in your children to each other, often marrying within themselves, so as it be without the bounds forbidden in God's law, that so they may not, like the forgetting unnatural world, grow out of kindred and as cold as strangers, but, as becomes a truly natural and christian stock, you and yours after you, may live in the pure and fervent love of God towards one another, as becometh brethren in the spiritual and natural relation.

"So my God, that has blessed me with his abundant mercies, both of this and the other and better life, be with you all, guide you by his counsel, bless you, and bring you to his eternal glory! that you may shine, my dear children, in the firmament of God's power, with the blessed spirits of the just, that celestial family, praising and admiring him, the God and father of it, for ever. For there is no God like unto him; the God of Isaac, and of Jacob, the God of the Prophets, the Apostles, and Martyrs of Jesus, in whom I live for ever.

"So farewell to my thrice dearly beloved wife and children!

"Yours, as God pleaseth, in that which no waters can qnench, no time forget, nor distance wear away, but remain for ever,

William Penn."

The next day leaving his family in tears, but sweetened with pious hope, and accompanied with several friends, he hastened down to Deal, where the ship Welcome, with about one hundred adventurers for the new country of Pennsylvania, were waiting for him.

So general and strong among mankind is the confidence reposed in those who are remarkable for uprightness of life, that, no doubt, every passenger on board the Welcome, thought himself perfectly safe with William Penn, and counted on nothing but a voyage as charming as fine health and smooth seas and pleasant breezes could render it. But all such should remember, that "God seeth not as man seeth." He the infinite King, hath his plans; and be sure they are such as are worthy of his own eternal wisdom and benevolence. Physical ills, such as sickness, form a part of his plan, and therefore should not be looked on as any evidence of his displeasure.

> "If plagues and earthquakes mar not heaven's design,
> Then, why a Borgia or a Catiline?"

Accordingly, the Welcome had scarcely gotten to sea before the confluent small-pox broke out among the passengers, and raged with a fury that presently swept no fewer than thirty corpses of them into the sea. Here was a fair opportunity for William Penn to display that generous sympathy with the unhappy, for which he was always so remarkable. And it is agreed by all, that his attention to these poor sufferers was worthy of a disciple of him who came to wash the feet, and to administer comfort to the afflicted. Day and night he was with the sick, administering medicines, supplying proper diet, washing, fumigating, and sprinkling with vinegar the floors of their cabins; and, above all, chasing from their minds the gloom of melancholy and despair, and lifting their thoughts to that parent power who *wounds but to heal*, and with divine complacency accepts the tear of repentance, even at the eleventh hour.

After a voyage of six weeks, he reached the capes of Delaware Bay, which he entered, and continued his course up the same, until he found it narrowed into a noble river about two miles wide. To one who had been for six weeks beating the gloomy waves with nothing but the same unvaried and monotonous prospect of boundless sea and sky around him, this last day's voyage must have been highly entertaining. To have been sailing up this great bay, in many places from 10 to 20 miles wide, and gradually narrowing itself into such a majestic river, skirted to the waters' edge with natural meadows or marshes of vast extent and most lustrous verdure; and back of these, on either side, far as the exploring eye could reach, it beheld nought save the startling range of huge forests stretched out into an immeasurable expanse, bounded only by the distant skies—to a mind, like Penn's, ardently devout, such magnificent scenes as these must have yielded indescribable pleasure. In the course of the two days sail up this great bay, and at the place where they found it narrowed, as aforesaid, to about two miles, they beheld with great joy, on a vast plain on the left bank of the river, and about ninety miles from the sea, a little town, since called Newcastle, and which, with some small villages, as Wilmington and Christiana, and some country settlements of a few square miles, belonging to a little colony of Swedes and Dutch, who settled themselves there as early as 1727.

These poor people, on seeing the tall ships of William Penn, were exceedingly alarmed, supposing that they were come, according to custom, too common among nominal Christians, to attack and break them up and their families. But when it was seen, on their nearer approach, that the ships carried no cannon for murderous war, but were altogether vessels of peace; and also that the mariners on coming ashore, exhibited nothing of the fierce looks and fiery regimentals of human man-killers, but, on the contrary, were clad in dove-like garments, with looks of answering meekness, their fears all vanished, and they received William Penn and his quakers with exceeding joy and hospitality.—The next day he requested a meeting of the magistrates and people, who all very promptly assembled themselves in the court-house at Newcastle, to hear what he had to say. He told them that he supposed they all knew that the country belonged to the English; but he begged that they would not suffer this to give them any uneasiness, for that having purchased it from his own government, he could very honestly assure them that he was not come to diminish, but greatly to increase, if possible, their enjoyments. He said he placed it among the highest happinesses of his life, that God had called him to the knowledge of the heavenly truth as it is in Christ Jesus, whose divine doctrines are all summed up in that blessed faith which even the poorest and most illiterate may always carry with them, that is, "*perfect love out of a pure heart.*" He declared that, under the guidance of this sweet and *holy light and love within*, which God offers to all, he wanted nothing of them but to make them one people, and equally happy with himself and his followers. That his own sorrowful sufferings from the cruel persecutions of his own countrymen, had taught him most deeply to abhor all persecution for religion's sake. That whatever therefore their country or their religion, they were entirely secure from persecution from him: that even if he should find, on better acquaintance with them, that their religious opinions and practices were not so good as his, he hoped that so far from hating and persecuting them on that account, he should feel a livelier tenderness, and show them greater kindness, as being the only *gospel* way, and therefore the only *right* way to bring them to what he most of all wished —the TRUTH. He concluded with saying, that, for the present, all he expected of them was to "*yield him the legal possession of the country.*"

This was cheerfully assented to by these poor people; and with such an air of honest simplicity as affected him exceedingly. Hereupon he begged they would not reflect on this act with any kind of alarm; for that he felt a comfortable hope that neither himself nor those who came after him, would ever abuse it. As a proof of his friendship for them, he renewed the magistrates' commissions; intreated they would strictly do their duty to discountenance all vicious and disorderly persons; and to encourage and protect the peaceable and honest. He then very pathetically begged them to remember that they were but as "*exiles in a strange land, and as a handful of little children in a wide wilderness;*" that the eyes of God were upon them, marking their conduct whether it was towards his glory by their cheerful and honest industry to make the "wilderness blossom like the garden of God," or by their idle and vicious courses to cover it with the weeds of poverty, and thefts, and murders, and wretchedness. He begged them often to think of the precious "PARABLE OF THE TALENTS," and of the GREAT DUTIES now devolved upon them, as—

1st. How much they owed to GOD who had called them to the honours of so high a trust.

2d. How much they owed to a YOUNG COUNTRY in which they were the *first settlers.*

3d. How much they owed to the natives, the poor HEATHENS, whom, by a blessed example of JUSTICE and MERCY, they might draw to Christ.

4th. How much they owed to their own poor children, even the comforts of a FAIR ESTATE; the bless-

:ngs of a PIOUS EDUCATION; the sweets of a GOOD NAME, and, in short, all that could render time and eternity happy.

These truths, unspeakably interesting in themselves, were rendered much more so by the very earnest and affectionate manner with which he delivered them. In short, they made such an impression on the minds of these poor honest-hearted people, that they could not rest until they had selected one of their nation, a Lacy Cocke, to wait on him with their thanks, and to assure him how heartily they esteemed him, and that they should for ever look on this as "*one of the best days they had ever seen.*"

Having, next morning, taken leave of these poor simple people, who, in a body, followed him as a father to the shore; he went on board and gave command to weigh anchor and proceed to finish the great object of his voyage. As he sailed along up the mighty flood, which he did, that day, about forty miles, his eyes were constantly gazing on the western banks, the destined seat of his Province, and which for beauty and grandeur of appearance, fully answered all the fair accounts which had been told him of it by his friends of East Jersey. But although his eyes, straining with curiosity, were deeply rivetted on those lovely shores, yet his thoughts were not there: they were busily travelling over the future and the past, with all the keenest emotions of alternate joy and sorrow. "*Ye venerable forests, whose sacred silence was never disturbed by the sound of the axe, nor your dark brown shades pierced by the enlivening sunbeam, O who can relate your history! How long has my poor brother man, in joyless hordes, roamed your gloomy wilds, contending for food with beasts of prey, or mingling with each other in murderous fight?*"

But soon the vermilion of joy with its radiant smiles would revisit his cheek, as he remembered the glorious change at hand, when the Gospel of Christ, now about to be set before these poor people, not in barren faiths, but *Heavenly loves*, should seize their hearts with its ravishing excellences, and mould them into one people with his own followers, adopting their gentle spirit and endearing manners; and when quitting their savage usages of hunting and war, and setting themselves to build houses, to plough the fields, and to plant orchards and vineyards, they should fill the land with corn, wine, and oil, and thus attain all the elegant pleasures of civilized man. To a heart humble and benevolent, like his, ever ready to adore God for every notice taken of *himself*, and for every opportunity afforded of doing good to others, what a day of enjoyment must this have been! O William Penn! how far superior thy pleasures of this single day, to all that Cæsar or Napoleon, with their restless pride and tormenting ambition, ever tasted!

> "One self-approving hour whole years outweighs,
> Of stupid starers and of loud huzzas." POPE.

After sailing this day, as aforesaid, about forty miles before the mid-summer's smoky breeze, they opened, on the larboard, a beautiful little river, whose silver waves serpentining from the north-west, joined the parent Delaware through a mouth almost hid amidst the luxuriant grass, hence by the Dutch called Schuylkill; the Indian name was MANAJUNG. Having passed this, and also a long grassy point, he beheld the great river gently winding to the left, and then as gradually turning out to the right again, thus, in the shape of a magnificent half moon rolling along its mighty flood, with a beautiful little island lying out to the right; and on the left an extended level of handsome elevation, and shaded with massy oaks—and a little further up, two Indian villages near the water. A site combining so much natural grandeur and convenience, could hardly escape the discerning eye of William Penn, who was, at once, so struck with it, that he ordered the anchors to be cast, which was instantly done, nearly opposite to the Indian towns: and this he did the more readily, as it was now in the afternoon, and the flood-tide almost spent. Of these two little Indian towns, the first was named COAQUANOC, standing on the upper part of what is now Philadelphia: and the other stood a little higher up, about Kensington; this last was called SHACKAMAXON by the Indians. They both stood near the water: the Indian name of the Delaware was POWTAXAT. Soon as the ship was anchored, the boat with an interpreter was sent on shore to inform the Indians that the sachem or chief of the Whites wished to have a "*grand talk with his Red brothers the next day, when the sun was at the half-way house in the sky.*" Soon as the natives saw the boat put off from the ship, they came down from both villages, men, women, and children, to meet them: and although from a total ignorance of each others' language, there was no conversation between them except a little by signs, and a word or two through the interpreter, yet the interview was highly interesting, each party marking the colour, features, and dress of the other with all the pleasures of surprise.

On the return of the boat, the interpreter reported to William Penn, that the Indian chiefs on hearing that he wished to have a grand talk with them, replied in their language, "*well, very well.*" They added, also, that they had been told by their friends "the Raritons," (an Indian tribe then living below Burlington and Mount Holly,) that *this* sachem of the Whites was a *good man*, and that his white children which he had sent into their country in the *big canoes*, had never done them any harm." The interpreter also informed William Penn that the Indian chiefs had said that they would send their *young men* to their towns and let all their friends know, so that there might be a *good many at the talk.*

As to William Penn, he did not set foot on shore that night, but rather spent it in fervent prayer that God would, in his great mercy, now realize all those bright visions of love and happiness between the Red and White people, which he had so often and with such pleasure dwelt upon. Indeed it was a most serious night to William Penn. He felt how much was at stake. On the one hand, he himself had always most confidently maintained that, " the grace of God which bringeth salvation, appears to all men," i. e. that the moral sense is universal, and of sufficient efficacy to conciliate the affections even of heathens to strangers visiting them, provided those strangers in all their dealings, would be most scrupulously *honest* and *kind* to them: on the other hand the British king and ministry had equally ridiculed these opinions of his as utterly visionary, and had left him with a handful of his despised followers to make the rash and ruinous experiment. The awful hour for that experiment is at hand, and in a short time it is to be decided whether men are creatures capable of moral and religious control or not; or in other words, whether when Christians have a mind to settle new discovered lands, they must, as heretofore, use all manner of villanous frauds and violence, killing the inhabitants by fire-arms and gin; or whether, by going among them, not with dumb bibles and crucifixes in *their hands*, but its blessed spirit of love in their hearts, and smiles in their looks, and justice and kindness in their actions, they may not change these poor heathens into dearest friends, and in this short and most honourable way to attain all the blessings of the safest and sweetest society in rich and new countries.

CHAPTER XVIII.

Speech of William Penn to the Indians.

The Indians having been informed, as aforesaid, that the great Sachem, (or Chief) of the white men, wanted to have a talk with their nation, assembled themselves together to hear him. Their numbers must have been considerable; for to the quakers, on shipboard, it appeared as though the woods were all alive with the Red men. And marching to and fro, as they did, in their military dresses, armed with bows and arrows, and waving their warlike plumes of many a barbarous hue, they formed a fearful sight; insomuch that some of the meek lamb-like followers of William Penn, thought he was doing wrong to venture himself among those wild people. But the middle of the day, which was the time fixed on to meet them, being come, he got into the boat and went on shore with a countenance serene and pleasant as if he had been going to dine with his friends; thus proving by his own fair example, what has often been observed even by heathen writers, that "a man of innocent life is afraid of nothing. The place where the red and white men met together, was on the western banks of the great river Delawere, on a fine green near the pleasant villages of Shakamaxon and Coaquanoc, where Kensington now stands. As if purposely formed to be the theatre of that memorable event, an elm-tree, of extraordinary size lifted high its towering top, and from its giant arms threw far and wide a refreshing shade over many a grassy acre. Seeing the Indians, men, women and children, assembled under this tree, William Penn, attended by only a few of his quakers, advanced towards them with no other mark of rank but a sash of blue silk, which is still seen in the Penn families in England. The Indians were struck at his presence.

A stranger advancing towards them, with no guards around his person, no weapons of war in his hands, and no armour of defence but the majestic sweetness of his own looks, was a spectacle that impressed them all with veneration. With such sentiments in his favour, they readily obeyed his signal to sit down, which they did in the form of a half moon, the men, women and children of each tribe sitting round their own chiefs. Then, while all eyes were rivetted on him eagerly awaiting his speech, he stretched forth his hand, and with the engaging air and voice of a brother, thus addressed them through an interpreter.

"Brothers, listen! Brothers we are come to bring good words to your ear! We call you brothers, and so you are; and we are your brothers too. Yes, the red men on this side the big water, and the white men on the other side, are all children of the GREAT SPIRIT, and so must love one another, and never *fall out*. The GREAT SPIRIT says so. HE says we have no need to fall out; for he has made this world big—big enough for all, red and white brothers too. And he has made fish, and deer, and turkeys, and corn, and every thing plenty for all. And if at any time the red or white brothers want any thing that the others have, they must not fight to take it away. Oh no; that will make the Great Spirit angry. Now your own eyes see our canoes yonder, (here he pointed to his ships) that they are bigger than your canoes; and our bows and arrows too that they are stronger than your bows and arrows. They send out thunder and lightning; nothing can stand before them. We could easily kill you with our bows and arrows of fire, and take your land; but the Great Spirit shakes his head and says no, you must not hurt your red brothers. You must not touch their land. Didn't I give this land to them and their children to hunt on? And also the buffaloes, and deer, and turkeys, and corn, and beans, and squashes? And havn't I given you good things too—great many good things ? Well, then, give some to your red brothers, and they will give you land ; and so live together like brothers. Now, brothers, lift up your eyes! and see here the good things which the Great Spirit has given us to bring to you."

Here the English sailors, with their usual alacrity, opened out their ready bales of cloths, their *true blues*, and fiery *crimsons*, and *flaming reds*, stretching them along in all their dazzling colours on the grass. And then as by magic, they unpacked their boxes of finely painted guns, with shining tomahawks, and axes, and hoes, and knives, and other articles of choice British goods, which they also spread out to the best advantage, William Penn in the mean time explaining their uses to the Indians, who now no longer able to keep their seats on the ground were risen up, crowded around him with uncontrolled curiosity to look and wonder. But who can paint the pleasure-sparkling eyes and looks of these children of the forest, when with timid step they approached, and gazed, and touched those beautiful things before them, and heard their admirable uses-- the guns of thunder and lightning, so much stronger than their bows and arrows, to conquer the bears and panthers! the keen steel-edged axes so much better than their flint tomahawks to hew down the trees of the forest! the fine woollen cloths so much softer and warmer than the rugged skins of the bear—and then all these good things brought to them by a mildly looking stranger who called them BROTHERS, and said he had brought these good things from beyond the big water to give to them for some of their land. Then was seen the power which JUSTICE has to charm the souls of all men. Those savage faces, but now so cold and hard with hostile passions, were seen to glisten with admiration and friendship: while with broadest smiles, such as Indians are wont towards whom they love, they approached William Penn, and shaking his hands called him BROTHER! *good brother!* They told him too that if he saw they had looked angry at first, it was because they had heard from their friends the Chesapeakes, and Mussawomacs, and Susquehanocks, that the white men beyond them had killed the red men and had taken their land and deer. And also that their neighbours the Passaicks and Manhattans had told them how the white men with bows and arrows of FIRE, had killed many Indians there too. "*Bad white men!*" said they, shaking their heads—"*bad white men to kill their red brothers! But you no bad white man! Oh no; you good white man! You all same as red man! You one brother! you bring red men good things! We love you much! We give you land, and deer, and turkeys plenty! You live with us, all brothers together, long as the sun and moon give light.*"

Great was the joy of William Penn when he heard these words. They served to confirm his belief of that precious scripture truth, "The grace of God which bringeth salvation hath appeared unto all men." Or, as the quakers are fond of terming it—"there is a light within," which teaches all men the difference between right and wrong; and which, while it condemns and troubles them for the one, fills them with joy for following the other. William Penn now saw with his own eyes, this truth most gloriously illustrated in those North American Indians. Judging from the unartificial vehemence of their tones, and their glowing looks and sparkling eyes, it were questionable whether any, the most civilized people on earth, could have expressed a higher admiration of justice than did these uneducated heathens.

After a considerable pause, chiefly to indulge a melancholy pleasure in looking at this branch of the great family of Adam, and remarking their peculiarities, such as their bright copper complexions, their broad faces, their high cheek bones, their long lank hair, black as the ravens' breast, and coarse as the mane of horses—and also their curiosity, which especially in the women, appeared to be as eager and unsatisfied as that of the veriest children; William Penn proposed a *going to business.* This he did by desiring the interpreters to call up the sachems to him. The sachems all instantly gathered around him, and, on learning that he wanted to have a *talk* with them about *buying land,* they replied with great vehemence, "*Yes, brothers!—yes!—good!—very good!*"

One of the sachems then gave a kind of whoop, as a signal to order, after which he told them, in a very short speech, that their good brother, the great sachem of the white men, wanted to *buy land.* Soon as this string was touched on, the Indians, though very fond of the trade, began to look grave and assume an air of business; and one of the sachems, with much of a natural majesty about him, bound something like a chaplet or cushion on his head, with a small horn projecting from it. This, as we read in the Holy Scriptures, was used among the great eastern nations as an emblem of kingly power. And however curious it may seem, was so used among these Indians of North America; for, soon as it was put on by the chief sachem, the rest all threw down their bows and arrows in token of respect, as also of perfect friendship, and seated themselves on the ground, in the form of a half-moon, each tribe around its own sachems. The great sachem then announced to William Penn, that the nations were ready to hear him; whereupon, with his usual look and voice, all serene and loving, he thus addressed them.

"BROTHERS, listen! BROTHERS! the red men and the white men, all children of the Great Spirit, are going to exchange land and good things with one another. BROTHERS, this makes the Great Spirit smile. He sees that this is doing as his good children ought to do. He sees that this will help to make them love one another *very much,* if they do it in true and good hearts. BROTHERS! the Great Spirit sees our hearts whether they be good, like his children, or bad, like foxes and snakes. BROTHERS, since nothing that we get will ever do us any good, if the Great Spirit is angry with us, let us bring something to your ear about the Great Spirit. BROTHERS! The Great Spirit is GOOD—MIGHTY GOOD.—Nobody can tell one half how good he is. The red men know that he is good; but the white men know it better still. BROTHERS, don't be angry Don't you see that the Great Spirit has taught us, your white brothers, to make canoes (meaning his ships) much better than your canoes; and bows and arrows (meaning his guns) much better than your bows and arrows? Well, then, the Great Spirit has given us better *talks* too. BROTHERS, listen! BROTHERS! the GREAT SPIRIT has had *much talk* with your white brothers. He has told them in many talks, that it was he who made the sun, and the moon, and the stars—that it was he who made the skies, and the great waters, and the land, with all the trees and grass, and all the fishes, and birds, and beasts; and made the red men and the white men, and gave *all* to them as his own children, that they might live together as brothers, and do good to one another, as he does good to them. He says, too, that we must not be straitened and narrow in our doing good to one another, for that he is great enough and rich enough for all. And that, if we will but let his words sink deep in our hearts, he will speak to the ground, and to the clouds, and to the skies, and they shall pour down good things on good things upon us, till there be no more room to hold them. He says, "*can you count the sands on the shores;* can you count the leaves on the trees, and the stars in the skies? then you may count how many are the good things which he will give to us. But he says, too, that, if we throw his words behind our backs, and tell lies, and cheat, and fight one another, he will turn all his good things into bad things against us, and so fill up our lives with trouble.—The spring may come;

but no flower shall shine on the ground, no bird sing in the trees; for the sky shall be cold and black like winter. The ground under our feet shall be like stone; and the clouds shall hold back their rain, so that the beans shall be few on their vines, and the ears of corn shrivelled on their stalks. The grass, too, shall wither in the vallies, and the acorns shall fail; so that though we hunt all day, we shall catch no game, and few fish shall come to our hook. And as we delighted to kill others, so the Great Spirit will suffer others, to kill us, yea, after that they have killed our sons in our presence, and tomahawked our little ones before our eyes. Now, BROTHERS, listen! These are the good talks which the Great Spirit gave to our fathers on t'other side of the big water. We bring these good talks to you. We love these good talks ourselves. We are not like those white men who came with the big canoes and bows and arrows *of fire*, and killed the Chesapeakes and Mussamomecs, and Susquehanocks; nor are we of the white men who killed the Passaicks and Manhattans; but we are of the white men who love the good talks of the Great Spirit to our fathers. And we have made a covenant with the Great Spirit, that we will never lie, nor cheat, nor fight, nor kill any of his children, whether red men or white men: but will love them all as our brothers, and will do them good out of the good things which he has given us for them. Now, that you may know that the words which we bring to your ear are true words, look and see that we have brought no canoes of the big bows and arrows of thunders and lightnings to kill you; but have brought nothing but our good things which the Great Spirit gave us to bring and give to you for land. And now, BROTHERS, if it seem good to you to give us land that we may live with you as brothers, tell us; and if not, tell us, that we may turn to the right hand or to the left."

William Penn then sat down, still deeply gazed on by the Indians, whose eagerly projecting eyes and shin ing looks strongly showed how deeply they felt and approved all that he said. And no wonder; for justice is that godlike charm which no eye of man can look on without being enamoured thereof. This was the enchantment practised by William Penn. He was no stupid missionary, telling by rote his dull tale of the apple; nor was he the bigoted priest holding up his idol crucifix and threatening DAMNATION to the uninstructed savages if they fell not down and worshipped it. But he was the true Christian missionary indeed, who set out, like St. Paul, with first preaching up "*righteousness*," and preaching it up too in that "*spirit which giveth life*," even the spirit of love made visible in its precious fruits of justice to these poor heathens, with whom he began by acknowledging them to be the rightful owners of the soil, and to whom he applied for a portion of it, bringing them at the same time in his hands, the best necessaries of life in exchange. For on William Penn's sitting down, after this famous speech to the Indians, the sachem, with the crown and horn on his head, got up, and with the looks of one strongly excited, thus replied—"BROTHER! your words are fire. We feel them burning in our hearts. BROTHER! we believe that the Great Spirit is good. Our mothers always told us so. And we see it with our own eyes. This big water, which runs along by this Shackamaxon and Coaquanoc, with all the fish, speaks that the Great Spirit is good. This ground which grows so much corn and beans and tobacco for us, speaks that the Great Spirit is good. These woods that shelter so many deer and turkeys for us, speak that the Great Spirit is good. The Great Spirit would not have done all this for us if he had not been good, and loved us very much. BROTHER, we ought to be like the Great Spirit. We ought to love one another as he loves us. But BROTHER! the red men here have not done so. The red men do very bad. They sometimes fight and kill one another. The Great Spirit has been very angry with us for it, and has taken away our corn and deer; and then we have become poor and weak, and have fallen sick and died, so that our wigwams (cabins,) are empty. But now we are very sorry and ashamed and will do so no more. And now, BROTHERS, we are ready to sell you land that you may live with us like good brothers, never to fight us as we *red men* have done, but always to love and do good to one another. And then the Great Spirit will make his face to shine upon us as his good children, and will always give us plenty of deer, and corn, and beans, so that we may eat and grow strong again!"

Soon as this speech was ended, the Sachems all gathered around William Penn, and the few FRIENDS he had with him, cordially shaking hands all around, saying to them at the same time, "BROTHERS, the Great Spirit sees our hearts, that they are not like FOXES and SNAKES, but like *brothers; good brothers.*" After this they gave the *calumet* or pipe of lighted tobacco, which was smoked out of by all; the great Sachem first taking a whiff, then William Penn, and then the Sachems and warriors and squaws of every tribe. This is used among the Indians as a most sacred pledge of friendship which, according to their strong language, *should endure long as the sun and moon gave light.* They then proceeded to their great business of dealing for land and goods. How much time was spent in making this famous bargain, I have never been able to ascertain, but the result was as follows—

1st. The Indians agreed to give the great Sachem of the white men (William Penn,) all the land, binding on the great river from the mouth of Duck creek to what is now called Bristol, and from the river towards the setting sun, as far as a man could ride in two days on a hoise.

2nd. William Penn agreed, in return, to give the Indians as follows:

	(*The probable prices now.*)
20 Guns,	$140 00
20 Fathoms match-coat,	20 00
20 Do. stroud-water,	30 00
20 Blankets,	25 00
20 Kettles,	20 00
20 Pounds of powder,	10 00
100 Bars of lead,	25 00
40 Tomahawks,	30 00
100 Knives,	25 00
40 Pair of stockings,	25 00
1 Barrel of beer,	4 00
20 Pounds of red lead,	5 00
100 Fathoms of wampum	50 00
30 Glass bottles,	2 50
30 Pewter spoons,	2 50
100 Awl blades,	25
300 Tobacco pipes,	1 00
100 Hands of tobacco,	12 00
20 Tobacco tongs,	5 00
20 Steels,	2 50
300 Flints,	2 00
30 Pair of scissors,	6 00
30 Combs,	8 00
60 Looking-glasses,	15 00
200 Needles,	25
1 Skipple of salt,	10 00
30 Pounds of sugar,	3 75
5 Gallons of molasses,	2 00
20 Tobacco boxes,	2 50
100 Jews' harps,	6 25
20 Hoes,	10 00
30 Gimblets,	2 00
30 Wooden screw boxes,	7 50

Amount brought over.	$ 515 00
100 Strings of beads,	50
Total	$515 50

Soon as the bargain was concluded and also ratified, as is the manner of the Indians in great treaties, by a second smoking of the calumet all around, William Penn ordered the stipulated price in British merchandize, as the blankets, hatchets, axes, &c. &c. to be all openly counted out to the Sachems and nicely put up for them, which was accordingly done. But so strong was the pulse of gratitude and esteem in the bosoms of these poor heathens towards William Penn, because of this his act of justice towards them, that it appeared as though they could not leave him until they had again shaken hands with him all round, with marks of an immortal affection, calling him father "ONAS," which in their language signifies *quill*, and being the nearest word to Penn, and at the same time assuring him in their earnest and vehement manner, that they would be "*good friends with him and his white children long as the sun and moon gave light.*" After this they took up their goods and went away. But not until William Penn affectionately shaking hands with the chiefs had bade them "*remember* that although he had bought their lands of them, yet they must still use them as their *own;* and fish and hunt and make corn for their children as before: and also that if they had any of these good things to spare, they must bring them to him and he would pay them for them." In a transaction so honourable to human nature as this, every thing seems important; and it would be highly gratifying at this day, to know the number of Indians that were assembled on that memorable occasion. But although we shall never be able to ascertain this, yet it is a gratification that we know something of the history of the famous elm under which Penn's treaty with the Indians was made. From its unusual size it must have been at least one hundred years at that time, which was in 1682; in the American war, which was about one hundred years later, it was still standing, and so justly venerable on account of the glorious scene it had witnessed, that the British, then in possession of Philadelphia, although near freezing of cold, and the fancy-trees and fruit-trees all abandoned to the axe, they placed a sentinel under this tree so that not a twig of it should be hurt. In the year 1811 it was blown down: but still revered like the oak that sheltered the great William Wallace, it was piously wrought into little boxes and cups by the curious, to be sent as presents to friends, or laid up in their own cabinets to keep alive the memory of what that tree had seen.

Having in his own honest and peaceable way obtained of the poor natives a title to that fine province which had so long dwelt on his mind, he then, with great joy and thankfulness of heart, set about having it surveyed. While the survey of the province was going on, he diligently looked about for a good site for his intended city. He was not long in the search. The elegant country round Shackamaxon and Coaquanoc soon arrested his delighted attention: a grand extended surface, level as a die—full twenty feet elevation above the water—bounded on the east by the mile wide Delaware—on the west by the narrow but deep-flooded Schuylkill—and on the south, six miles below Coaquanoc, by the junction of the two rivers—above the surface, a noble forest of oak, poplar and pine, for building—beneath, an inexhaustible bed of choice brick clay—and in the neighbourhood, millions of stone laid up in ready quarries. If king Solomon had been in quest of a site for a royal city for his peerless bride, the daughter of Pharaoh, where could he have found such a spot, and such abundant materials, as the hand of Heaven had here laid up to forward the good work which his servant William Penn was engaged in?

Without loss of time he then sketched off a plan for his new city, which for beauty and convenience, for regularity of prospect and pure ventilation, is so far superior to any other city that we have ever seen or read of, as to incline us to believe that the hand of the GREAT ARCHITECT was with him here also. His first street was to lay on the Delaware, and his second on the Schuylkill, both to run nearly north and south *one mile*, straight as a mathematical line, and from fronting these two rivers, to be called *Front* streets—each sixty feet wide! His third street, to be called High-street, full *one hundred feet* wide, was exactly to intersect his city by running due east and west from the middle of DELAWARE *Front-street*, two miles over, to the middle of SCHUYLKILL *Front-street*. Then, exactly half way between the two rivers, his fourth street, *one hundred and thirteen* feet wide, to be called BROAD-street, was to run due north and south crossing High-street, as aforesaid, in the centre of the city. In this centre point he laid off ten acres for a grand park or square to be handsomely railed in, smoothly sodded with grass, and planted with trees of finest shade, that the citizens, often as they pleased, might here meet and mingle with one another, and although in the midst of the crowded city, enjoy an air and verdure and shade equal to the country. For the same pleasant and beneficial uses, he ordered a park or square of eight acres to be laid off in the centre of each quarter of his city. To complete the streets of his city, which, as we have seen, was to be *two* miles in length, from *river to river*, or east and west, and in width, from north to south one mile, making a surface of upwards of twelve hundred acres, he ordered eight streets to be run parallel with High or Market-street, i. e. east and west; and twenty streets parallel with Broad-street. i. e. north and south; each of these streets was to be *fifty* feet wide, except Mulberry, which is sixty-six feet wide. The streets running north and south were to be named according to their numerical order, as *first*, *second*, *third* street, &c. and those running from east to west after the woods of the country, as *Vine-street*, *Sassafras-street*, *Cedar-street*, and so on. The city having been thus planned, was called PHILADELPHIA, which, in Greek, signifies the CITY OF BROTHERLY LOVE, that being, as he said, " *the spirit in which he had come to these parts; the spirit which he had sworn to Dutch, Swedes, Indians, all alike; and the spirit which he earnestly prayed God would for ever rule in his province.*"

No sooner was the city surveyed and laid off according to this plan, which gave universal joy to the little colony, than the sound of innumerable axes was heard in the woods, with the frequent crash of the falling trees. And so ardent was the passion for building, that, late as the season was, (September,) many families had comfortable houses erected before winter. In addition to these, several who came out in the fall ships, being fuller handed, brought with them houses in frame, all marked and ready for putting together; with furniture of all sorts, and clothes, and provisions: these, of course, went on swimmingly. But a great many coming in late, and being poor withal, had to work day and night to cover in their huts, and provide a good stock of wood for fires, before the deep snows should fall: while others, still worse off, were fain to go down to the shores of the Delaware, and there in the sides of the steep banks, dig large grottoes or caves with chimnies at the tops for the smoke. These places for a long time afterwards went by the name of the CAVES; and homely as they may appear, yet many families, whose posterity have since made much noise in Pennsylvania, passed the winter of 1682, in *those caves*, and in a very snug and healthy style too. Indeed, whether it be that in those times of virtuous necessity, there is generally the presence of him who " *tempers the air to the shorn lamb*," or whether that, having created man to imitate himself in *active*, *useful* life, Heaven a ways gives better appetite, sleep, and health to the steadily laborious; but certain it is, that no adventurers, perhaps, in such numbers, ever enjoyed better health and spirits than did the followers of William Penn, that season. For while of the little colony, only one hundred and twenty in number, who settled, or rather invaded Virginia, in May, 1607, full one half of them were in their graves before Christmas: of William Penn's colony, though exceedingly more numerous, there is no record, that I have seen, of one single case of mortality that season. But after all, the health of this colony, though remarkable, is not so much to be wondered at. "Cheerfulness," says Solomon, "*does good like a medicine;*" and who ever had greater reason for cheerfulness than the followers of William Penn? The cause for which, like faithful Abraham of old, they had left father, mother, and country, i. e. *for God and religion's sake*, was not that enough to make them cheerful? The loving spirit in which they had treated the poor natives, was not that enough to make them cheerful? The attainment, without blood and murder, of the object of their perilous journeyings through the watery wilderness, viz. an earthly Canaan of their own, flowing with the milk and honey of peace and quiet, was not that enough to make them cheerful? The hand of Heaven, so visible in all this, was surely enough to make them cheerful And, to perpetuate their cheerfulness, the same blessed hand was still visibly present with them; for, like quails upon the camps of Israel, so did delicious flesh seem to rain down from Heaven upon them in their time of need. Wafted on by the winds of autumn, the wild pigeons from the Indian lakes, came down upon them in such darkening clouds as overwhelmed them with astonishment: those who had powder and small shot could kill thousands a day; while, as if for the sake of the *poor* who had not such advantages, these savoury birds flew so low, or fed on their berry bushes so utterly careless of man, that they might be knocked down in any quantities that were wanted, insomuch, that besides feeding on them fresh, they salted barrels of them up for future use. As to deer, buffaloe, bear, raccoons, opossums, squirrels, rabbits, turkeys, pheasants, partridges, &c. the lands which William Penn bought of the Indians so abounded with all these varieties of delicious game, that any man who chose to go after them with his gun, might presently return loaded; while such as could not hunt, might have them brought to their doors for a mere trifle—turkeys of twenty pounds weight for one shilling! and fat kidney-covered bucks for two shillings! which was not indeed a fair price for the skin. And all this done for them by those whom the Christians call *Savages*, who appeared to have such a true child-like love for father "ONAS" as they called William Penn, that they could never, as they said, *do enough for his poor children.* And indeed so strong was this generous feeling in their bosoms that if they saw any of "*Onas's children*" so poor that they could not buy at the low rates above, they would, of their own accord, go and hunt for them, and bring them loads of the finest and fattest flesh, and fish, and fowl, for nothing. And, as if there was to be no end to the bounties of God, and to the thankfulness and joy of William Penn and his people, the waters in this new country were no less abundantly stored with dainty food than the air and the land: swans, geese, brant, and ducks of all sorts were here seen in flocks as no European ever had any idea of; while as to the fish, such as sturgeon, shad, rock, perch, &c. the rivers and creeks were so full of them, that with the least industry in the world, a man might feast his family on them every day. And in addition to all this, the Indians had exquisite peaches in surprising abundance; and the woods were, in numberless places, matted as it were with vines, which in the fall season of the year were perfectly black with shining clusters of grapes; not indeed so large as those of Europe, but remarkably plump and sweet tasted, especially after a little touch of the frost. Now with such ample cause of ceaseless gratitude and cheerfulness, who can wonder that William Penn and his humble followers were always so healthy and happy as they appear to have been? William Penn in a letter to one of his friends in England, says, "I thank my good God that I have not missed one *meal's meat*, nor one *night's sleep* since I came into this fair province. *O! how sweet is the quiet of these parts, freed from the anxious and troublesome solicitations, hurries, and perplexities of woeful Europe!*" But leaving the settlers in the new city, driving on might and main as aforesaid, with their buildings, and like sagacious ants laying up the best store they could for the approaching winter, William Penn took his surveyor with him, and went into the country to finish the survey of his grand purchase of the Indians, and also the little district then called the "TERRITORIES," now the STATE OF DELAWARE, which had been ceded to him by the Duke of York; and to divide them into counties. Three counties were created out of each of these districts, those of his province were named as follow: PHILADELPHIA, after his new city: BUCKS, or BUCKINGHAM, after a county in England, dear to him as the long residence of his ancestors:—and CHESTER, which he so named to pleasure his old travelling companion Thomas Pearson, who was born in a county of that name in England. His three counties in the TERRITORIES he named NEWCASTLE, KENT, and SUSSEX: this last out of respect to his wife, whose family for many generations had resided in a county of that name in England. At the sitting of the Assembly, which took place in March ensuing, (1683) he procured a seal to be struck for each of the above counties. That for PHILADELPHIA, was an anchor,—to BUCKS, a tree and vine,—to CHESTER, a plough,—to NEWCASTLE, a cassia,—to KENT, three ears of Indian corn,—and to SUSSEX, a wheat sheaf. Each of these seals, no doubt, had a meaning, and particularly that of Philadelphia, which very fitly denoted his long twenty years' servitude of hope and toil for this blessed land of religious liberty, and CITY OF BROTHERLY LOVE.

Having thus divided his land into counties, as just mentioned, William Penn immediately appointed sheriffs in each county, and issued writs for the election of members both for the Council and general Assembly, as also summons for the formation of Grand Juries! Now that all this was not a mere matter of pride and affectation in him, (which none on earth ever more heartily abhorred) but a course of proceeding to which he was compelled by existing facts, the reader may rest perfectly assured that so entire was the confidence of the people of England in the wisdom and honesty of William Penn, and the probable great advantages which they should derive from settling in his province, that although he did not himself arrive in it till the beginning of September, yet so great was the emigration, and the number of those who had purchased grounds, and settled in the counties by the middle of November, that he found a sufficient population in each of them to require wise laws, and a prompt and just administration of them. Weight of individual character has rarely had such flattering respect paid to it. Nearly three thousand souls, by reasonable computation, to follow a persecuted quaker across a vast ocean to a wilderness, in three months! 'tis wonderful!

Who can tell the joy that reddened over the cheeks of this true FRIEND of man, when on his return from the country, which was in November, he beheld the bright prospects that were opening before him—his new city, of upwards of fifty houses, risen as by magic out of the woods, and thereby promising, what has really happened, the speedy creation of a mighty metropolis—and in addition to this, to see his noble, silver-flooded Delaware already beginning to whiten with the sails of ships; twenty-three of which came in about this time almost in squadron, from different ports in England and Ireland, and even from Wales, making in all upwards of two thousand souls, who had bravely left their country and friends to cross a howling wilderness of waves, and cast in their lot with William Penn for their sweet peace and conscience sake.

And great also was the joy of the colony when they saw that these ships, though tall, carried none of the dread implements of death, nor of those men whose fierce looks, and fiery regimentals proclaim that their trade is human slaughter; but, on the contrary, were filled with men and women whose dove-like clothing bespoke them the children of peace, perhaps, humble and industrious farmers and mechanics, who were come into the wilderness to build up a ZOAR, a city for God, and to aid the great and good cause by their useful labours. The scene that ensued was tender and interesting. Nothing was to be seen or heard on all sides but the noise of the citizens running down to the shore to meet and welcome the stranger *friends*, also with looks and eyes of friendship eagerly searching round if happily they might find some beloved kinsman in this noisy throng. And ofttimes the heart was touched at the sight of dearest relatives rushing to all the transporting embraces of an unexpected meeting; bathing each other's red swollen cheeks of joy with gushing tears, and with sobs and cries rending the air, "*O my brother!*" or, "*O my dear mother*," or "*my dear child!*" These persons had taken leave in England of their relatives; the *first adventurers*, never expecting to see them more.—But finding a void in their bleeding hearts, which nothing else could fill, they had suddenly sold off all and ventured across the seas, that they might, as they said, "*live and die together.*" William Penn was much affected by these things, which served to strengthen him the more, if possible, in his resolutions to leave nothing undone to ensure the welfare of so many poor people who had confided their all to him. And it is highly pleasing to record that what with the very unusual length of the mild and open weather that season, and the most hearty hospitality and great simplicity and industry prevalent throughout this group of *Christian friends*, such good preparation was made, both of huts and provisions, that there was no instance of serious distress and suffering ever heard among them. It is worthy of remark, that nearly the whole of the late arrival of two thousand persons, were QUAKERS, who had followed William Penn, that, as appeared in a London paper of those times, "*they might lead a life quiet and peaceable, free from the vexatious they had experienced; and worshipping the Creator in their own way; and that here, as on a virgin elysian shore, they might shun the odious and infectious examples of European profligacy and wickedness; and lastly, that by manifesting, in all their tempers and actions, a fair example of the humble and loving spirit of the gospel, they might more effectually impress the heathen around them, and thus bring them from darkness to light—even that pure and perfect light which emanated from Jesus Christ.*"

When plain simple Christians can go abroad to win the Heathens to Christ by his sweet charm of "*love and good works*," exemplified in their own divine tempers and actions, we may well expect a good turn out. But when missionaries, calling themselves *Christians*, can travel to the other side of the globe to make *proselytes* to *their own party*, and there, in the sight of the Heathen, wrangle and abuse each other about *baptisms* and *sacraments*, and free grace or election, surely it is time for all good men to pray that God would have mercy upon such "*blind leaders of the blind*," and send fitter "*labourers in into his own vineyards.*"

CHAPTER XIX.

Snug in their huts and *caves*, and well supplied, as we have seen, with food timely laid up, William Penn and his gentle followers passed the winter in much comfort, often amusing themselves with an atmosphere darkened with heavier snows, and the Indian forests howling with far louder tempests than they had ever witnessed in England. In the course of the season, perhaps in January, there occurred an event which, though trivial in itself, served for a while to be talked of in this infant city, I mean the *first birth*, of English parents, in the colony. The child was a boy, of the family of Key, born in one of the *caves*. William Penn took a fancy to record this event by making the child a present of a lot of ground. The neighbours from that day gave young Key the name of *First-born*, which he went by all his life, and that a very long one.

On the 10th of March, 1683, William Penn met his *first Council*, in Philadelphia; two days afterwards he met his *first Assembly*, which sat at the same place.

As a certain very unpromising youngster of Virginia, on reading in a history of the revolution that his grand-father was a favourite officer with general Washington, instantly *took up*, determining to render himself worthy of such a noble ancestor; so I will let the young people of Pennsylvania and Delaware see the names of their great-grandfathers, who had the honour to sit under William Penn in the *first Assembly*, in the year 1683—also on the first grand jury of that venerable period. For the assembly, as follow—Yardley, Darke, Lucas, Waln, Wood, Clowes, Witzwater, Hall, and Boyden, for Bucks; Longhurst, Hart, King, Binkson, Moon, Wynne, Jones, Warner, and Swanson, for Philadelphia; Hoskins, Wade, Wood, Blunston, Rochford, Bracy, Bezer, Harding, and Phipps, for Chester; Biggs, Irons, Hassold, Curtis, Bedwell, Windsmore, Brinkloe, Brown, and Bishop, for Kent; Cann, Darby, Hollingsworth, Herman, Dehoaef, Williams, Guest, and Alrick, for New Castle; Watson, Draper, Flutcher, Bowman, Moleston, Hill, Bracy, Kipshaven, and Verhoof, for Sussex.

For the *first Grand Jury of Pennsylvania*, in 1683. Lloyd, (foreman,) Flower, Wood, Harding, Hill, Luff, Wall, Darke, Parsons, Blunston, Fitzwater, Guest, Curtis, Lucas, Jones, and Pusey.

As to what this famous assembly did—I call it famous, because it was the *first* that ever sat in the glorious colony of William Penn—I say as to what they did, such as what wise laws they passed; who was their chairman; who their great orator, and so forth, they are now all effaced from the memory of man, as though such an assembly had never existed. This most mortifying fact, however overlooked by others, ought certainly to stick awhile on the memory of those ambitious little ones, now-a-days, who vainly dream that if they can but muster enough of whiskey-bought votes to send them to "THE LEGISLATURE," the world is to ring of them a thousand years hence.

But concerning the exploits of the first Grand Jury of Pennsylvania, we are not so completely in the dark. It appears that, early as good William Penn began to draw his net for villains, he did not draw it without catching a miserably bad fish. A very hardened wretch by the name of Pickering, a silver-smith of London, finding what ship-loads of quakers had gone off to Pennsylvania, took it into his head that a capital speculation might be made on these easy unsuspicious people, by palming upon them a barrel or two of counterfeit Spanish milled dollars, and thus handsomely, as he hoped, to strip them of what little property they had saved from the paws of the British monarchy and hierarchy. The better to ensure success, he gets himself a deep drab and broad beaver, and off he sets for

Penn's colony, and there in the guise of a very *pious friend*, begins his villanous trade. His money passes without the least suspicion : for who would think of suspecting FRIEND PICKERING! Success inspires confidence ; confidence makes him forget caution ; his money is questioned, and he is arrested with thousands of it upon him. Now, in England, such a villain as that would, in five minutes, have been in a dungeon pinioned with irons, and soon as possible, have been dangling in a halter *without benefit of clergy.* But what was the award of the first Grand Jury of Pennsylvania in 1683? Why, it ran in these words: "Whereas Thomas Pickering hath been found guilty of coining and stamping silver in the form of Spanish dollars with more alloy of copper than the law allows, *he* the said Thomas Pickering shall, for this high misdemeanor, make full satisfaction in good and current pay, to all persons who shall, within the space of one month, bring in any of his base and counterfeit coin, (which shall be called in to-morrow by proclamation ;) and that he shall pay a fine of *forty pounds* towards the building of a court-house, stand committed till the same is paid, and afterwards find *security for his good behaviour.*"

Having undergone an incessant fatigue of mind for a long time past, and especially during the late session of his Assembly, and Common Council, and Grand Jury, of which he was the prime mover and conductor, William Penn determined, for a necessary relaxation, to make an excursion into the country, and taking a few friends with him, now when the opening spring with all its sweet birds and blossoms were inviting to industry, to indulge the pleasure of a general view of his beloved province. But to a mind like that of William Penn, happily moulded into the spirit of divine love, and, like that, always seeking opportunities of doing good, relaxation only means a change in the great business of being useful. During this grand tour if we may so call it, he made numberless minutes of every thing that he could see or hear that he thought would entertain or benefit, and which may be looked on as a panorama *in miniature*, or *rapid sketch* of the geography, botany, natural history, &c. of the country and its aboriginal inhabitants, or Indians. I should like to give it at length to my readers, were it not for fear that from the lusty growth which our country has made in these sciences during the long lapse of one hundred and fifty active years, it would only excite a smile as at sight of a dwarf by the side of a giant. But there is one thing in this little journal which always affords so much pleasure to myself, that I can, certainly, never withhold it from my readers. i. e. his tender sketches of the poor simple natives of the country. Aye, there William Penn was always at home. This was his first and favourite theme, to be continually looking into the *moral condition* (because all happiness lies there) of his brother man; not indeed so much to scrutinize his *notions* and shiboleths; or to ascertain how far orthodox and strict he was in his sectarian faiths, and catechisms, and creeds, and confirmations, and baptisms, and sacraments, and sprinklings of holy water, and signings with crosses, and other such things; because from *faithful history* of popes, and cardinals, and bishops, and presbyters, William Penn had learned that the utmost formalities in those things are perfectly consistent with the vilest spirit and passions of the world—with the most satanic pride and lust of universal domination—with mortal envies and hatreds of all opponents—with kindlings of bloody wars and crusades among the nations, and most unnatural inquisitions and burnings of their brethren—with multiplying of great titles, and palaces, and revenues of the *established* churches, and imprisonments, and confiscations, and poverty, and starving of the rest!!! William Penn, therefore, in his loving regards to the *moral condition* of his brother man, paid no respect to those things; but much rather to the plain evidences of that "grace which bringeth salvation," and which always manifesteth itself in acts of "*justice*, and *hospitality*, and *kindness*, and *brotherly love*, *without dissembling*."

CHAPTER XX.

William Penn's Narrative of the Aborigines, or native Indians, whom he found in Pennsylvania, touching their persons, language, manners, religion, and government.

"1st. For their *persons*; they are generally tall, straight, well built, and of singular proportion. They tread strong and clever, and mostly walk with a lofty chin. Greasing themselves with bears' fat, and using no defence against the sun, their skins must needs be swarthy. Their eyes are small and black, not unlike a straight-eyed Jew. The thick lips and flat noses of the East Indians and blacks, are not common to them; for I have seen as comely European faces among them as in England; and truly an Italian complexion has not much more of the white, and the noses of many of them have as much of the Roman.

2d. For their *language*, it is lofty yet narrow, but, like the Hebrew, in signification full. Like short-hand in writing, one word serves in place of several, and the rest are supplied by the understanding of the hearer. And I must say that I know not a language in Europe that has words of more sweetness or grandeur.

3d. As to their customs and manners, these in some things, as very curious, especially as regards their children. Soon as these are born they plunge them into cold water, the colder the better, to make them hardy and bold as young otters. Then, having wrapt them up in skins, they brace them out straight on a little board, and thus, when travelling, carry them on their backs, or if at work, set them up nearly erect against the sides of their cabins. Hence the Indians are all remarkably straight. The boys while young, practise a great deal with their bows and arrows, at which they come to be so expert that a sparrow must be lucky that escapes them. At fifteen they take to the woods, eager to figure as men. If they make a brave return of skins, they begin to take airs and talk about wives; otherwise they are very silent. The girls stay with their mothers and help them to plant and hoe the corn, and carry burthens. 'Tis happy that they are timely used to this; for, when wives, they are expected to do all the drudgery. The husband, if he hunts and kills the buck, thinks he has done his share. He comes home, sits down and lights his pipe; leaving it to his wife and daughters to bring in the buck. Their sagacity at finding it seems like a miracle. The husband has but to say a word or two and fling his arm in the direction where it lies, and they go off as straight to it, no matter how thick the swamps and woods, as a buzzard to a carcass.

We Christians call these poor people savages, but indeed, in many of the most Christian virtues, they leave us far behind them. If a white man call at their cabins, they are all joy and gladness to see him. They give him the best place and the first cut. If they come to visit us, and any thing is given them to eat or drink, well, for they will not ask; and be it little or much if it be with *kindness*, they are well pleased; otherwise they go away sullen, but saying nothing.

But in liberality they excel. Nothing is too good for their friend. Give them a fine gun, coat, or other thing, it may pass twenty hands before it sticks: light of heart, strong affections, but soon spent: the most merry creatures that live. They never have much nor want much. Wealth circulates like the blood. All parts partake: and though none shall want what the others have, yet exact observers of property. Some of their kings have sold, others presented me with parcels of land. The pay or presents I made them were not hoarded by the particular owners, but the neighbouring kings and their clans being present when the goods were brought out, the parties chiefly concerned consulted what and to whom they should give them. To every king then, by the hands of a person for that work appointed, is a proportion sent, so sorted, and folded, and with that gravity which is admirable. Then the king subdivideth it in like manner among his dependants, hardly leaving himself an equal share with one of his subjects: and be it on such occasions as festivals, or at their common meals, the kings distribute, and to themselves last. They care for little, because they want but little; and the reason is, a little contents them. In this they are sufficiently revenged on us. If they are ignorant of our pleasures, they are also free from our pains.—We sweat and toil to live. Their *pleasure* feeds them; I mean their hunting, fishing, and fowling; and this table is spread every where.

In sickness they are very impatient, and use strange remedies, such as stewing themselves in a close cabin with hot steam from water thrown on red hot stones, until the sweat pours down from them, and in this state they will plunge into brooks of coldest water. If they die, they bury them in their apparel, the nearest of kin throwing into the grave with them something precious, as a token of their *love;* for dead or alive nothing is cared for by these people but love to and from their friends. They are very choice of the graves of their dead, and will sometimes go out of their way great distances to sit by them.

These poor people are under a dark night in things of religion, at least the tradition; yet they firmly believe in the Great Spirit or God, and the immortality of the soul; for they say there is a great king who made them, who dwells in a bright country to the southward of them; and that the souls of the good shall go thither where they shall live again. Their worship consists of two parts, SACRIFICE and CANTICO. Their SACRIFICE is their *first fruits*. The first and fullest buck they kill goes to the fire, where he is all burnt, with a mournful ditty of him who performeth the ceremony, but with such marvellous fervency and labour of body, that he will even sweat to a foam. The other part is their CANTICO, performed by round dances accompanied sometimes with words, sometimes songs, and then shouts, which are raised by two persons, standing in the middle, who begin, and by singing and drumming on a board, direct the chorus. Their postures in the dance are very antic and various, but all in exact measure. The whole is done with surprising earnestness and labour, and with strong expressions of joy. In the fall when the corn comes in, they begin to feast one another. There have been two great festivals already, to which all who choose can come. I was at one myself. Their entertainment was by a large spring under some shady trees, and twenty fat bucks with hot cakes made of the meal of new corn and beans baked in leaves in the ashes. After dinner they fell to dance. All who go carry a small present in their kind of money; it may be sixpence, made of the bone of a fish; the black is with them as gold; the white, silver; they call it wampum.

Their government is by kings, called sachems, who reign by succession; but always of the mother's side. The children of him who is now king will not succeed, but his brother by the same mother, or the sons of his sister, for no woman inherits. It is astonishing to see how piously and peaceably they all follow this ancient usage.

Every king has his COUNCIL, consisting of all the old and wise men of the nation. Nothing of moment is undertaken, be it war, peace, or selling of land, without advising with them; and which is more, with the young men too. It is admirable to consider how powerful the kings are, and yet how entirely the creatures of their people. And it is equally admirable to see the exquisite order and decorum that are always observed in their national councils. The king sits in the middle of a half moon, formed by the old and wise men, his counsellors, on the right and left. Behind them sit the younger fry in the same half moon figure. Every thing being ready for business, the king beckons to one of his old men to speak, which he does, rising with much solemnity, and begging it to be kept in mind that it is not he, but the KING who is speaking. While he is on the floor not a man among them, young or old, would be guilty of such rudeness as to whisper, smile, or move a foot, for the world.—Their speeches are short, but always vehement, and sometimes figurative and eloquent in the highest degree. And as to their natural sagacity and management of the business, especially such as they are familiar with, he must be a wit who gets the advantage of them.

As to the original of this extraordinary people, I cannot but believe they are of the Jewish race, I mean of the stock of the ten tribes so long lost; for the reasons following:—

Firstly. The ten tribes were to go to a land "*not planted nor known*," which certainly Asia, Africa, and Europe *were*. And God who pronounced that singular judgment upon them, might make the way passable to them as it is "*not impossible in itself from the eastermost parts of Asia to the westernmost parts of America.*"*

Secondly. I find the Indians of the like countenance with the Jews; and their children of so lively resem-

* The world laughed at William Penn for this bold conjecture. But captain Cook, and later navigators, have shown it to be very practicable and probable.

blance, that a man on looking at them, would think himself in DUKE'S PLACE, or Berry street, London.

Thirdly. They agree with the Jews in many of their *religious rites.*

Fourthly. They reckon time by *Moons*, like the Jew.

Fifthly. They offer their *first fruits*, as the Jews do.

Sixthly. They have a kind of *feast of tabernacles*, like them.

Seventhly. They are said to lay their altar upon *twelve stones.*

Eighthly. They have the same practice of *mourning a year.*

Ninthly. They have the same delicate *customs of women.*

Now all these things considered of them, and also taking into the account their many and grand cardinal virtues which they practise, such as,

1st. Their noble readiness to forgive any injuries done them by one who was drunk, saying, "*it was the drink and not the man who abused 'em.*"

2d. Their exceeding *hospitality to strangers.*

3d. Their never-ending esteem of those who only do *them justice*, (as in the case of William Penn.)

4th. Their *love stronger than death to their friends.*

5th. Their everlasting gratitude to benefactors.

Now on a people possessing so *distinct a knowledge of good and evil*, O what immortal fruits might not be grafted by persons of a still brighter light and love coming among them ; not in vain *words*, preaching up *notions* and *sacraments*, but in their own brotherly tempers and actions, showing the divine beauty and blessedness of men "*dwelling together in love.*"

CHAPTER XXI.

William Penn had now been in his colony near two years; and indeed, as is said, had serious thoughts of spending the rest of his days in it, with his family, whom he meant to send for. But alas, why should poor mortals talk of years to come, when the wisest among them cannot tell "*what a day may bring forth!*" For while this most virtuous of men, like a good angel descended from heaven, was thus diligently and delightfully employed in ameliorating the physical and moral condition of the red and white men of his great family, and to render his province the garden spot and glory of the earth, behold a ship arrived from England with packages of letters from his best friends, recommending it to him by all means to return without loss of time.—They stated that he was every where posted as a "PAPIST" and a "JESUIT," and that too in such terms of execration that there was no telling how it might affect the government against him, even to the taking away of his charter and province. And still worse, (for indeed he smiled at such baseless fabrications that affected only *himself*,) the letters informed him of things infinitely more painful to his feelings, viz. that the persecutions against his poor friends, the quakers, had broken out again, and with a malignity and fury far beyond any thing ever known before. The letters concluded with entreating that he would instantly return and use all his interest in their favour with the king, who, it was well known, was much his friend.

The effect of these letters on him, was an immediate determination to return to England, as soon as possible: so having empowered his COUNCIL to act in his place, and filled up all the various offices and departments of government with the fittest men, he took his leave, exceedingly to the regret of all, but of none more than of the Indians. To these poor people, the report that their "FATHER ONAS" was going away to leave them, was matter of deep heart-sinking and sorrow. Having found out the day on which he was to depart, they came in betimes into the city, in great crowds both men and women, and all of them with some present in their hands for "*father Onas.*" They followed him to the shore, like children crowding to the funeral of a beloved father, and in shaking hands with him, many of them shed tears.

Immediately on his arrival in England, (October 1684) he commenced his inquiries into the condition of the quakers, and the *persecutions against them*, which he found to be fully equal, in point of savage unfeelingness and barbarity, to the worst accounts he had received. I will detail a few of those cases, that our horror-struck readers, while they mark the blinding influence of an ancient priestcraft, and mourn the sufferings of its unfortunate victims, may raise their shouts of praise to God for the blessed time and country in which they live: and also do their part, in the way of a *good life*, to prevent disunion and civil war, which, by introducing a KING and an ESTABLISHED CHURCH, may revive those calamities upon our hapless posterity.

Extract of cruel persecutions of the poor quakers in England, in the days of king Charles II. viz.

"Only for attending a meeting in Leicestershire, *four* persons were sent *to prison*, and their *goods* of various kinds, with beds, working tools, &c. taken from them to the amount of two hundred and thirty six pounds sterling, equal now to *three thousand dollars!!* In clearing the meeting-house on this occasion, not only men but women were dragged out, some by the heels, and others by the hair of their heads!"

"In Nottinghamshire, James Nevil, Justice of the Peace, took from T. Samson, by *warrant* (on account of his attending *two meetings*,) nineteen head of cattle, and goods to the amount of sixty pounds sterling," equal now to seven or eight hundred dollars.

"In the county of Norfolk, John Patterson had two hundred fat sheep taken from him,—equal to three hundred dollars.

"William Borbu of Norfolk, had cows, carts, a plough, harrows, and hay, taken from him to the amount of fifty pounds sterling.

"William Brazier, a shoemaker at Cambridge, was fined by John Hunt, (Mayor) and John Spencer (Vice-chancellor,) twenty pounds, only for having a religious meeting in his own house."

N. B. The officers who distrained for this sum, took his leather, his lasts, the seat he worked upon, wearing clothes, bed and bedding!!!

"In Somersetshire, F. Pawlet, Justice of the Peace, fined *thirty-two persons* only for being at a burial! and seized for the fines, cows, corn, and other goods to the amount of eighty-two pounds sterling. No one appearing to buy the distrained cattle, the justice employed a person to buy them in *for himself!!*

"In Berkshire, Thomas Curtis was fined three pounds fifteen shillings by Justice Craven, who ordered his mare to be seized, which was worth seven pounds. Curtis put in an appeal against this proceeding, according to the act; but it was thrown out. The officers also offered the fine to Craven, but he would not take it; but had the mare valued at 4*l.* and then kept her himself!!

"In Cheshire, Justice Daniel took from T. Briggs the value of 116*l.* in corn, horses, and cattle; the latter he kept and worked for *his own use!*

"In the same county, Justice Manwaring took by warrant for fines which amounted to 87*l.* goods to the value of 101*l.* in cattle, bacon, brass, pewter, corn, cloth, shoes, and cheese. Some of the sufferers appealing, the Jury acquitted them; but the Justices would not receive the verdict, and at the next sessions gave judgment for *the informers*, with *treble costs!!!*"

Scores of other cases equally shocking might be quoted; but these are sufficient to show what man is capable of when under the dominion of bigotry and superstition; and how easy a thing it is, for a selfish Priest to persuade a poor sinner, that if he but mutters a few prayers *after him*, and *kneels* and *sings* as *he* directs, and gravely takes the *Sacrament*, he may fly like a wild Arab upon the most humble, and harmless, and industrious, and peaceable of his fellow creatures, and triumphantly carry off their carts and horses, and cows, and calves, and corn, and meal, thus breaking them up root and branch, and leaving their poor little children crying in vain to their mothers for their simple suppers of bread and milk.

With a heart bleeding for such cruelties of man to man, William Penn flew to the King, entreating him even with tears, that he would interpose his royal arm to the prevention of such hellish practices, dishonourable to his reign and disgraceful to the most benevolent religion in the world—THE GOSPEL. But to his equal astonishment and grief, all that he could obtain was "*a sort of promise from the King, that he would do something in the matter.*" But while he, Felix like, was waiting for that "*more convenient season,*" to do the good work to which William Penn so earnestly entreated him, hundreds of poor harmless and humble souls were suffering all the horrors of starving at home, or groaning in dungeons. But his time to act so inhuman a part, and to abuse the high trust confided to him of God, was not long. In about a quarter of a year after this, as he sat down one Sunday morning to be shaved, he was suddenly seized with violent spasms, or twitchings of his head to both sides, when, uttering a fearful shriek, he fell down as dead, and so remained for three hours. His physician, at hand, bled him, and fearing to lose the time necessary to blister him by flies, ordered his head to be shaved, and plied with red-hot frying pans. Being brought to his senses by such unheard of tortures, he showed himself humble as a whipped child—seemed deeply penitent—begged pardon of all, even the poorest he had ever wronged—prayed most fervently himself, and prayed that others would pray to God for him. And in this way he breathed on, till the following Saturday at noon, and then died—an awful lesson to the proud and great, how easy a thing it is for God to make such worms bow before him! His throne had not time to get cold, before it was filled up by his brother the Duke of York, who, at three o'clock that same day, was proclaimed King James the Second! The reader will remember that this was the same Duke of York, under whom, and next in command, William Penn's father had fought so gallantly against the Dutch fleet, in 1666; and who had sent word to that officer, on his death-bed, that he would be a *friend* to his son. And, indeed, in many respects he was as good as his word; for like Herod towards the holy Baptist, he had a most exalted opinion of William Penn; not only of his "*rare honesty*," but also of his "*rich mind and acquirements*," insomuch that he would often have William Penn with him, and allowed him such lengthy conversations as gave umbrage to his nobles, who, more than once, took the liberty to *tell* him, that *when he was with Penn he forgot them*."

Soon as decency would permit, William Penn waited upon his royal friend, with the grievous case of his poor afflicted subjects the quakers. The King, with a smile, clapped his hand upon his shoulder, and said, "Friend William, don't make thyself uneasy on that score, for it is not my desire that peaceable people should be disturbed for their religion." Finding the King in such good humour, Penn put in a word for his friend the celebrated John Locke, who it is known was almost if not altogether *a quaker*, and who had recently been deprived of his place and salary in the University of Oxford. "*Well*, William," replied the King, in the same gracious manner, "*for thy sake I do pardon John Locke, and thou mayest so tell him from me.*" Indeed so high did Penn stand in favour with the King, and so generally was this known, as also the exceeding pleasure which he took in improving it to the relief of the oppressed, that he was always surrounded by applicants. His firmness in the case of the Duke of Hamilton, while it shows exactly the character of Penn, affords a striking proof what important services a benevolent and brave man may sometimes render to the injured. Learning that Robert Stewart, of Coltness, a very worthy Scotchman, had been obliged, through the religious persecutions of the times, to fly his country, and that his estate had been given to the Earl of Arran, afterwards the Duke of Hamilton, William Penn called upon this nobleman, and with all the majesty of truth, thus gravely accosted him,—" Friend James, what is this I hear of thee? thou hast taken possession of Robert Coltness's estate. *Thou knowest it is not thine.*" The Duke, evidently self-condemned, but straining for an apology, replied, " Why, Mr. Penn, I received no other reward for my expensive and troublesome embassy to France, but this estate; so that I am sure I am very much out of pocket by the bargain."

" That may be," returned the intrepid quaker, " but let me assure thee now, that if thou do not immediately send for Coltness, who is in town, and pay him 200*l.* to carry him on his journey, and also 100*l.* a year to subsist on till matters are adjusted, *I will make it as many thousands out of thy way with the king.*"

The Duke was so struck with this manly pleading in favour of the injured, that he immediately sent for Coltness, and did by him exactly as Penn had advised. And behold! after the revolution which took place in some two or three years subsequent to this date, poor Coltness (with the rest of the fugitives for their *religion*) was restored; when the duke of Hamilton was obliged to return him not only his estate, but all the back rents, except the payments which he had made, as above, at the instance of William Penn.

But to be the most successful friend and protector of injured individuals, even on the large scale that he filled, seemed but a small thing to the boundless charity of Penn. Nay, to promote the tenderest love between his own followers the quakers, or between the church and the quakers *alone*, did not half satisfy him. He longed to see that sweet spirit of the gospel shining on the faces of all Christian societies towards each other, as the only thing that can ever bring glory upon the religion of Christ, and give it a universal spread among the nations. Hence his incessant and most vehement labours with the king and government, if not to do away all established churches, yet to do away all "*religious tests*, and *all penal statutes*, and *fines*, and *confiscations*, and *imprisonments*, and *murders for religion*," as being utterly *anti-christian*, and barbarous, and most fatal in their effects upon the tempers and morals of society, destroying that which is the very end of all Christ's preaching, that is, LOVE, which can seldom grow in men's hearts towards others, when agonizing under cruel treatment from them.

"What signifies," says he, "all this pomp and show of religion; these great cathedrals, and these ringings of bells, and noise of organs, with all this to do about sacraments, and baptisms, and parade of so many priests in their white robes and black? What is the end and design of all this, but, as these preachers themselves will confess, to promote religion and *brotherly love?* But what chance is there that all this outward noise and show of *one* sect, will promote the brotherly love of the rest, when their dearest rights (of religion) are not only denied them, but when they are robbed and ruined for only *claiming* them! When the poor presbyterian sees the rich churchman, (*made rich too out of his spoils*,) or when the half-starved catholic sees the fat protestant bishop rolling by him in his coach and four, set up out of the fines on the poor catholics! Ah, how hardly can love grow there! St. Paul would not "*as long as the world stood, taste a peice of meat*," though honestly come by, from making and selling his own tents, "*if it gave his weak brother offence!!*" There was a Christian bishop of the *right* sort! But what sort of Christian bishop must he be who can consent to ride in his coach and four, with his revenues of thousands, when it tends to stir up deadly hate and to destroy immortal souls for whom Christ died!

And for these cruel penal laws and tests, are they to be found among the *examples* of Christ? Did he "*call down fire from heaven upon those who dissented from him?*" Or, are they to be found any where in the genius and spirit of that blessed religion which is summed up in "*doing unto others as you would they should do unto you?*" Ah! who among us would like to be lying on the cold floor of a dungeon, with tears trickling down his cheeks, thinking of his poor wife and children starving at home, by Christian hands too; and all because he could not worship God as did the bishop! But indeed what *common honesty* is there in these penal laws and tests? Suppose that for fear of having his cows and calves taken from his children, a man should consent to go and kneel and pray by rote after the priest whose cold formalities he despised, what would this but make a hypocrite of him; and thus, instead of a *trophy to God, erect a monument to the devil!* And even suppose that your brother should stout it out, and in spite of all your penal laws and tests, still stick to his conscience, what glory could you win in so infamous a contest with your poor brother, as whether he should bear with most patience, or you inflict with most cruelty? Oh shame! shame!

shame upon our profession as Christians! Oh, when will come the time, the happy time that these practices shall no more be mentioned among us *as becometh saints!* nor indeed as becometh true patriots who know that the prosperity of their common country depends on the union of the citizens: and that again on their treating each other with such justice and kindness in all things that every man shall look on his neighbour as his brother, and by such union of fruitful *loves* and *interests*, and not of barren *forms* and *opinions* render old England the glory of the earth.

The effect of this address, on king James and his council, was but little short of miraculous. A royal proclamation was issued, the week following, for a general pardon of "*all who were then in prison for conscience sake!*" In consequence of this, *twelve hundred quakers alone* were restored to their families and business—many of whom had been in confinement *for years!* also of the *papists* and other sects, hundreds upon hundreds were let loose to enjoy the sweet air and light of day, with all the countless blessings of liberty and dear society.

CHAPTER XXII.

THE joy of William Penn for such services to his fellow men must have been very great; but they were somewhat dashed by certain wormwood advices, received at this time (1685,) from Pennsylvania. These advices turned upon the most unexpected and scandalous conduct of his colonists; not indeed of any of his own society, the *quakers;* for of them he learned, with exceeding joy, that they continued the same industrious, orderly and peaceable citizens he left them: but that his beloved COUNCIL, whom he had left to rule, had all fallen to discord and neglect of the public good—that many others preferred a life of sloth and extortion in town, to the independence and innocent delights of the country, were filling his virgin city of Philadelphia with taverns!—that even "THE CAVES," were converted into *tipling shops!*—that his surveyors, fond of collations and gin, had spread their tables for such uses in his land offices, making the purchasers of lots pay the *expense*, which in some cases amounted to one fourth of the prime cost of the lots, thus checking the sale of his land; retarding the population of his province; encouraging drunkenness and immorality, especially among his Indians; and bringing infamy and ruin both upon himself and his colony—and to render such news the more painful, with all his anxiety to hasten to America, he actually had not the means—he could get no remittances of his *quit rents*, although five hundred pounds sterling a year were due to him for *one million of acres* which he had sold, (the low quit rents of one shilling the hundred acres,) for twenty thousand pounds sterling—these twenty thousand pounds had been laid out in presents to the Indians—in various purchases of lands—in aiding his poor followers—in setting up and maintaining his government and governor—besides, sixteen thousand pounds which he had given up to king Charles, barely for his *good will*—also six thousand pounds which he had spent on this philanthropic enterprise, making in all, as money now values, at least *one half a million of dollars!* which, with maintenance of his own large family—much hospitality—costs for travelling and preaching; printing his numerous books, &c. had kept him low, and confined him to England. And even there it does not appear that he was allowed much peace, owing chiefly to the most unlucky state of public affairs at that time, on account of James's turn to popery, and the nation's dread of the dismal times of bloody Mary. Hence if William Penn waited on the king though but to beg, as usual, some kindness for the *injured*, he was branded as a *papist*, and *jesuit*. If petitioners, for favours, crowded his own door, the suspicious populace would have it, "*all these people did not come to him for nothing!*" of course a *gun-powder plot* or something *worse* was *a brewing;* and both himself and his poor quakers were often insulted in the streets, and the windows of their houses broken. If he preached a sermon though never so much like that of Christ on the mount—conjuring his hearers to do nothing "*to get praise of men;*" but every thing for the "*glory of God*," making his love and that of our neighbour, the sole end of our being; he was sure to stir up a hornet's nest of angry hard-visaged puritans, reviling him as a *false prophet* who would make the '*blood of Christ of none effect—by mixing it with man's good works.* But, for the sake of poor human nature, let us drop the recital of such unamiable truths, and bring our history towards a close. My readers will not, I hope, be offended. We are all born for pleasure; and the moment that pleasure ceases, the work we engaged in for pleasure ought to cease also. Writing a book should be like decanting wine for our friends; we ought never to pay them so ill a compliment as to disgust them with the dregs. Let others spin out the history of an individual to three or four large volumes; I, for my part, like the better example of the sacred biographers. These inspired penmen, in the life of any great personage they paint, whether it be good king Josiah or wicked king Ahab, after giving his characteristic features, and in colours never to fade, delicately add—"*as for the rest of the acts of Josiah, are they not written in the book of the Chronicles of the kings of Israel?*" So I must take the liberty to say to my readers concerning Penn; "I have given them the history of a "POLYCHRESTUS," i. e. *a man of many virtues*, the least of which have conferred immortality on saints of old; a man meek as

Moses; pure as Joseph; patient as Job; intrepid as Paul; and affectionate as St. John; and who, by the same spirit that made him all this, has been made a blessing to millions, and his name, engraved on their hearts in lines of moral beauty, never to be forgotten while goodness retains power to heave the throb of admiration and esteem—"*and as to the rest of the acts of William Penn, and what he did to break the power of antichrist, even religious persecutions; and to pull down the high places of priestcraft, that he might erect a pure spiritual worship for his God, are they not written in the book of the chronicles of the people called Quakers, by Joseph Proud, and Thomas Clarkson, and divers others?*"

But, passing by much of these thin histories of Penn, which, from this period, 1686, are little else than histories of the unceasing vexations which he suffered, alternately, from pontifical persecution in England, and from the blunders of his own provincial governors in America.

I will give my reader the few following facts of William Penn, and which are the only ones in the life of this great good man, that I think he would take much interest in.

Be it known unto thee, then, O most patient reader,

In the first place, that William Penn still continued, (such is the charm of honesty!) to be a great favourite with king James; and that he never *once* abused that favouritism to supplant rivals, or to fill his own house with gaudy carpets, and side-boards, but *often* improved it to the advantage of merit oppressed, and chiefly to promote religious toleration and love among Christians.

2d. That the English nation, getting alarmed about king James, for saying his prayers to the Almighty in Latin, a tongue they did not understand, compelled him, in 1689, to give up the throne to his son-in-law, the Prince of Orange, alias king William, a *stiff* PROTESTANT.

3d. That this prince, though no persecutor in heart, yet put up to it by his great ones in church and state, revived what his more honest predecessor, although a papist, had put to sleep, i. e. the persecution of the poor quakers, which in his reign was carried to such scandalous lengths, that, "*if a quaker* was seen on a horse worth five *guineas* or *upwards*, (no matter whether fifty or five hundred) any man of the *national church* might, *by law!* order him to *dismount* and give up his horse!"

4th. That king William, soon hurled by death from a throne which he had so disgraced, was succeeded by his consort queen Anne, whose Christian spirit, taking part, of course, with the oppressed quakers, quickly put a stop to measures so disgraceful to humanity.

5th. That, in 1693, William Penn was severed, by the consumption, from his wife Wilhelmina Maria; of whose rare piety the reader will ask no better eulogy than the following—feeling the icy hand of death gaining fast on her vitals, she begged that her children might be brought to her bed side.—Then giving them the last tender embrace with a dying mother's blessing, she lifted her eyes, beaming with reverence and hope, and said, "*Lord thou knowest I never asked grandeur for my children but only* GODLINESS." After this solemn duty performed, she desired them to be taken out of her sight; then sinking on her husband's bosom, she calmly breathed her last.

6th. That, in 1696, William Penn was honoured in his own family with another glorious triumph of piety over mortality, in the case of his eldest son Springett Penn; who in the article of dying, uttered shouts of victory over the grave, that drew tears of joy from every eye; and sufficient to make those blush who think that the Father of Mercies can save none but those who *sprinkle* or *plunge*, *take* the *bread* or the *wafer* exactly as they do.

7th. That, in consequence of much disorder in Pennsylvania, occasioned by his governors and councils, William Penn's charter was taken away by the king.

8th. That his majesty, fully convinced of the blamelessness of William Penn in those matters, restored his charter.

9th. That, in 1699, being stricken in years, and al most worn out with weighty cares and labours, William Penn, with his family, went over to North America, to spend his last days in peace and in the improvement of his province.

10th. That the following fact, almost the first after his landing, affords pleasing proof, that persecutions to those who "*walk with God*," instead of serving like water to extinguish, only act like oil to kindle higher their godlike affections. "Being told of a large slip of choice lands lying on the Neshaminy, and not included in his first purchase, William Penn caused it to be inquired of the sachems, whether they would sell it to him. They replied that they did not wish to part with that piece of ground, the bones of their fathers and mothers lying there ; but still to please "*their father Onas who was so good as to come to live with his red children again, they would sell him some of it.* In short, they agreed to sell him as much land as could be walked around in one day by one of his own young men, beginning at the great river above Coaquanoc (Kensington,) and ending at the great river just below Kallapingo, (Bristol.) The Indians were to be paid, as usual, in British goods. The bargain being made, a young Englishman was pitched on, who having been much exercised in his own country as a pedestrian, made a walk that equally astonished and mortified the Indians. Observing that their looks when they came to receive their pay, were not bright towards him as formerly, William Penn asked them the cause.

They replied, that *father Onas's young man had cheated them.*

Aye, how could that be, replied he, calmly; was it not of your own choosing that the ground should be measured in this way?

True, returned the Indians, but the *white brother* made *too big a walk!*

Here some of the commissioners getting warm, said that the bargain was a very fair one, and that the Indians ought to stand to it; and that if they did not, they ought to be compelled. At this William Penn looking exceedingly shocked, replied, *compelled!* how are they to be *compelled!* Don't you see that this points to *murder!* Then turning to the Indians with the kindliest smile on his countenance, he said, Well, if you think you have given too much land for the goods first agreed on, tell us now how much more will do? At this they appeared greatly pleased, and said, if father Onas would give them so many more yards of cloth and fishing hooks, they would be well satisfied. Soon as the Indians, having received their goods and shaken hands with him, were gone away smiling and happy, Penn looking very significantly on his friends, and lifting his hands and eyes, exclaimed, O what a SWEET and CHEAP thing is CHARITY! Here mention was made just now of *compelling* these poor creatures to stick to their bargain; that is in plain English, to fight and kill them, and all about a little piece of land! Don't you consider that the very *rum* which a regiment of soldiers would drink, would cost twice as much as those few yards of poor cloth which we have given them? and which has sent them away happy as little children, with their apples and cakes?"

O what is there in the universe that can so greaten the soul, and dispose it to every thing generous and godlike, as the simply sublime religion of Christ! For lack of the spirit of this most ennobling religion, several of his old enemies in England, sickening at his growing fame and fortunes in America, began to revive their former slanders, wherein they were so successful, that several of his best friends in England advised him to return and defend himself.

11th. I am sorry to add, that, yielding to the wishes of his friends, Penn embarked with his family in 1701, and bidding farewell to Pennsylvania, never to see it again, returned to England, where his presence, like a summer morning sun, quickly dispersed all the clouds which his enemies had gathered over him.

12th. That from this period, 1712, though now nearly threescore, he still enjoyed excellent health, which, as he had been wont from his youth, he continued to consecrate to the most delightful, because most useful purposes, such as writing masterly defences of the quaker construction of the gospel, which being, as he said, "*intended for the ignorant, must be simple; not requiring great learning in the head, but honesty in the heart, bravely to practice the arduous lessons of loving and doing good to all men.*" Also constantly corresponding with his governors and councils, and all others of influence in his province, but particularly his own followers the quakers: conjuring them to keep in mind, "what an honour was done them of God, in placing them on a field of action, where they might do so much for his pleasure, in *the world's good and their own temporal and eternal welfare;* to remember the divine philosophy of the Bible, that '*no man liveth for himself alone, but for all:*' and that he who, in all his dealings, tramples base self under foot, and acts justice and mercy to all, shall in the universal good find his particular and great reward." He begged them to remember too, that, though far retired beyond the sea, and in the wild woods of America, they were not beyond the eagle eye of malice, which was constantly watching the opportunity, through any wrong act of theirs, to pounce down and bear them aloft to the world's scorn : and that now was the time to vindicate before the universe, the excellency of their faith ; and to demonstrate, that while pride, extravagance, and base flesh-pleasing of all sorts, tend to poverty, and desperation, and wars that pull down the greatest nations, the opposite virtues of justice and mercy, manifested in all the blessed fruits of *honest, industrious*, and *peaceable lives*, will exalt the poorest families and nations to riches and honours."

13th. I have now to add, in the thirteenth place, that while engaged in these divine labours with a zeal too great for his advanced age, (near 70,) he was suddenly struck with two or three shocks of the apoplexy. This desirable messenger of mortality did not at once dissolve the ties between soul and body, but it left his memory and judgment so impaired, that he was never able afterwards to write or speak with his pristine perspicuity and vigour. But as a vessel early filled with choice wine, will, ever after it is empty, still refresh the sense with the precious odour of what it once contained, so the mind of Penn, though almost gone, still supported even to the last, the angel character which it had acted through life.

As all men take such an interest in the sun as to feel a strong curiosity to look at him, though under an eclipse, even so, many will wish to see Penn, though in the last stage of nature's decay. The following is from the journal of a learned and pious friend, who frequently visited him.

"In March, 1713, I was much with him at his own house, and always found him happy. And though he recollected a great number of his past actions, he was often at a loss for the names of persons. The finest sentiments, however, were often falling from his lips, rendering his company quite delightful, and abundantly proving, that his religious principles were founded on a rock that nothing could shake.

"In 1714, his faculties were by no means altered for the worse. I accompanied him in his coach to meeting. He could speak but little, but what he did say was very affecting. Every eye seemed to press forward upon him with the deepest interest. He put me in mind of what we are told of the Evangelist John, who in his extreme age and feebleness, placed by his disciples in his pulpit, and able only to whisper, "*little children love one another*," was yet listened to with a devotion, that none of his congregation would have exchanged for the eloquence of the world.

"In 1715, towards the end, his memory became sensibly altered for the worse; but his love of the Deity and his habitual rejoicings were the same; as also the peculiar lovingness in his manner of receiving and parting from his friends.

"In 1716, I went to see him, taking with me another friend of his acquaintance. He manifested great joy at seeing us; and although he could not recollect our names, his conversation proved that he knew us perfectly well. He was then in a state of great weakness both of body and mind, but still exhibited all the endearing sensibilities of the most affectionate spirit, which, happy in itself, thought of nothing but to make others so. Hence I could never look at him without fancying I saw *personified* in him, all those brilliant adornings which Solomon gives to his honoured "WISDOM," with *crowns of glory on her head, and chains of gold around her neck*. For while worldly-minded old men, suddenly stopped in their career by sickness, and no longer able to bustle and vapour, are low spirited, silent and sad; William Penn, on the contrary, was a *perfect model* of the most enviable serenity. He appeared to me like a soldier, who, after a long life of brilliant victories for his sovereign, and disabled through age for further duties, has now his armour thrown aside, and given himself up to welcome repose; but still ever smiling, at thought of what he has done, and of the reward that awaits him. Yes, such is the divinity of virtue like his, that I never looked on William Penn without feeling an affectionate reverence that I lack words to express. I shall never forget how I felt, when at our taking leave of him, he said—*my love is with you. May the Lord take care of you; and remember that I am bound to you by a friendship that is eternal.*

"In 1717 I visited him again, and for the last time His mind was so entirely gone, that he could not recollect me one instant; and his body so feeble, that he could not walk a step without support; and even his speech, now reduced to a whisper, was hardly intelligible. But still he was William Penn. I shed tears as I looked at him; but they were tears of joy to think what he *had been;* and my tears rose to rapture, when I remembered, as he tottered, that he tottered at the THRESHOLD OF HEAVEN."

Thus, after a gradual decay of six years, without suffering any of those pangs that often embitter the close of human life, his vital spark silently went out, and on the 30th of May, 1718, his happy spirit exchanged its coarse tenement of clay for *that glorious body not made with hands, eternal in the heavens."* His hallowed ashes slept at JORDAN, in the county of Buckingham, by the side of his first wife and many of his family.

Such was the end of a man whose life was a long exercise of patience and submission to the will of Heaven; who, by the faith of Christ, was enabled to overcome the vices of flesh and blood, and all the enemies of human nature; and to demonstrate a truth too little known, that to escape the miseries of life, man has but to *conquer himself;* and that to enjoy all its *pleasures*, he has but to obey the laws of God, and resolutely maintain an *unwounded conscience.*

Such were the achievements of William Penn, who had the rare wisdom to improve nobility of birth with the majesty of the virtues; and to sacrifice the illusions of false grandeur to the solid charms of moral feeling and of real goodness—humble in prosperity, superior in adversity, and sublimed to all the greatness of benevolence, he smiled on insult, and found a godlike satisfaction in forgiving injuries. He trampled under foot all the allurements of the senses, that he might labour unceasingly for the benefit of suffering humanity, and establish in the new world, as he had always wished, "*a government founded on the pure principles of the gospel;* a worship most simple, yet most sublime; a morality pure as that of angels; a toleration universal; laws perfectly equal; magistrates more anxious to prevent crimes than to punish them; thence, a country filling up with a new and vast population—cities springing up out of the wilderness—a people fond of peace, and enjoying it in the happy simplicity of patriarchal manners—abounding in the fruits of the earth—blessed with a flourishing trade—honoured by the sister colonies—beloved by the neighbouring savages, and under the sacred canopy of innocence and harmony, enjoying the sweetest calm, undisturbed by discord, and unstained by a drop of human blood. Such were, during the days of William Penn, and such during the rule of his quaker successors, even 70 years, have been the influences of the pure religion of Christ, whose sublime sweetness has rendered this people so happy, because it has for its object to adore the one true God; to love all men without distinction; never to harm any; and to fly, as monsters of nature, those persecuting homicides, who, in the name of the God of peace, can murder their fellow men only that they may plunder them.

CHARACTER OF WILLIAM PENN,

By Dr. Marsillac, Deputy Extraordinary from the Quakers in France, to the National Assembly, 1791.

"After so many acts of violence and oppression, so many robberies and murders committed by the Europeans in the new world, the heart finds some consolation in pausing over the part which William Penn acted there. In an age when savage Europe put to death so many innocent people merely because they could not embrace the faith of their sovereigns; and spread over so large a part of America those horrors of fire and sword at which nature revolts, William Penn, like an angel from heaven, presented the olive branch to those afflicted people, and by acts of godlike justice, not only restored tranquillity to their ravaged quarters, but laid the foundation of extensive liberty and happiness. He was perhaps the first who ever built one of the fairest empires of the world, on the sole basis of general good; and by assuring universal toleration and community of rights, offered a happy asylum to persecuted innocence throughout the earth.

"There are but few sections of the American continent that have not been drenched with human blood; and to their eternal shame, it was the enlightened and polished Europeans who did this; and who murdered by thousands, the poor harmless natives, who received them with hospitality! and then, to extenuate their guilt, they branded those as SAVAGES, whom they had so barbarously slaughtered. The arrival of William Penn put a stop to those frightful enormities. His godlike humanity to these oppressed people; treating them as brothers, buying their lands and heaping them with favours, melted their simple natures with gratitude and affection. Astonished to see a *white man* who was good, and who abhorred injustice and bloodshed, they revered him as something more than man, and gloried in calling him "FATHER."

"Of all the Europeans who have mitigated the ills of life and the fury of religious persecution, William Penn most deserves the gratitude of posterity. His first act in America held up a lovely presage of the prosperity that was to follow. And in his unyielding efforts to shield the oppressed, he looks like Moses, followed by a host of religious friends, whom he conducted across the wilderness of waves, to a new "*land of promise*," flowing with the *milk and honey* of freedom, peace and plenty.

"Abhorring persecution, as the direst reproach and scourge of mankind, he resolved effectually to bar the door against it. Hence that sublime charter of his, guaranteeing the most perfect liberty of conscience, to all the honest worshippers of God, no matter what their opinions and forms. Instantly crowds of persons, oppressed in their own country because of religion, embarked for the country of William Penn. Then shone forth that divine philosophy, "LOVE THY NEIGHBOUR AS THYSELF," in the blessed fruits resulting from it. For, while among the antichrists of Europe, the Popes and Bishops, nothing was heard but cries and groans from the inquisitions and dungeons; nothing talked of but sales of property belonging to heretics and dissenters; nothing seen but marks of deadly hate, between the oppressing and the oppressed churches, in good William Penn's country, glory to God, you met with no spectacles of this sort; but on the contrary, every thing to sparkle the eye of charity with pleasure—there you saw worshippers of an hundred different sects, moving along the streets to their several churches, in the most perfect peace and harmony—there, whether Jews or Christians, Catholics or Protestants, all adored God in the way they thought most rational; and meeting with no persecution themselves, they felt no temptation to persecute others. Every poor emigrant to Pennsylvania, was welcomed as an exile from his native land; and having neither country nor family of his own, he found in William Penn a tender and generous father. This most virtuous of men, was the honoured instrument of blessings to thousands of the unfortunate; and his institutions have laid the imperishable foundations of a new empire, which shines like a star in the west, and whose rays have already begun to open the eyes of Europe.

"Having held the reins of government no longer than was necessary for the good of his province, he mixed among his people, as only one of their number; and despising, on the one hand, all the pomps of the falsely great, and filling up life, on the other, with the most beneficent labours, he came to the grave in a good old age, eulogized by the greatest philosophers, honoured above the proudest kings; and to this day revered by the Indians, as a benevolent spirit, sent down from heaven to establish the reign of peace and happiness on the earth."

"POWER MAY COMMAND AWE; WISDOM MAY EXCITE ADMIRATION; BUT IT IS GOODNESS ALONE THAT CAN CAPTIVATE OUR HEARTS."

No man, perhaps, has ever had the honour, by a single act of his life, to confer such an obligation on mankind as William Penn has done by his treaty with the Indians. The greatest philosophers of the civilized world, no matter what their country, or what their religious opinions, have never ceased to gaze on it with an enthusiasm that shows the immortal charms which justice holds in the eyes of all men. And we should fill a volume were we to transcribe only one half of all the handsome eulogies that have been pronounced on it. But if this famous treaty has appeared so lovely in the eyes of all good men, who only beheld it as a distant star that shone on other times and people, then how must it have appeared to those people themselves, who beheld it near at hand as their own sun in all his full-orbed glory; at once delighting their eyes with its beauties, and showering on their heads its delicious fruits? Indeed the blessed fruits of this treaty both on the red and white men, are sufficient to convince us that he who created man in his own likeness, has implanted in him certain noble springs of action which may be far more advantageously wrought by justice and mercy, than by fraud and violence. And these springs, glory be to God, are implanted in all men, the wildest not excepted; as hath been seen in Penn's memorable treaty, wherein it would seem as though God, in order to show the "*universality of his grace*," had purposely called that heavenly-spirited man to the exceeding honour of demonstrating it, in the face of the whole world, by his extraordinary experiments on those North American Indians, generally thought the most lawless and savage of the human race. Indeed, from the unparalleled fierceness with which they carried on their wars, and the long and painful marches which they would make to surprise their enemies, and the lingering and cruel deaths which they inflicted on their wretched captives, many have doubted whether, as Charles II. said, the grace of God had ever appeared to them. At any rate it appears that the Europeans treated them as though they were beasts in human shape, and even worse; for while they would show kindness to a dog to win his friendship, they treated the Indians as if they thought that nothing but powder and ball could ever manage such cannibals, This was the line of march pursued by all the first English settlers in this country. Take that case which, having happened in Virginia, is best known to us, I mean the English colony settled at old James town, in 1607. When this devoted company sailed up James river, it appears that they never once dreamt of setting foot on shore until they should first have discovered some snug little peninsula which might easily be defended against the murderous natives. After much slow sailing and sharp looking out, they happened to light on just such a spot! Then thanking God as for a most lucky discovery, they landed their munitions of war, and heaving up a tremendous ditch, covered it over with their cannon with mouths of hideous red and black, threatening destruction to the "*blood-thirsty savages.*" The next thing they did was to build a church. But this was only another fort in disguise. with loop-holes all around; and while one half of the congregation, pale and quaking, were praying very devoutly, the other half, more bold, with their guns poked out at the loop-holes were drawing their sights towards the dark woods, as if they momently expected a host of brindled savages to burst out upon them.

Now, why had they all this fear and precaution, but because their hearts were not right towards these poor people. They who meditate injuries against others are always suspicious and fearful. These false Christians had an evil eye upon the country to make it *their own;* hence, feeling themselves enemies to the natives, they felt that the natives were enemies to them. All this was but honest instinct; or the voice of God himself, in their guilty consciences prophesying evil concerning them. And so it turned out; for, by making the above forcible lodgment in their country, and invading their hunting grounds, they virtually hurled defiance into the teeth of the natives. Powhatan, the old king of the country, and his people all felt it as such; and SHYNESS, and HATE, and FEAR, with all manner of ill offices, quickly appeared on both sides. If the Christians went out to trade with the Indians though but for a little corn, they always carried their muskets with them, and kept their matches lighted ready for battle. If they invited the Indians on board their ships, to dine with them, it was only to seize some royal hostage that might serve to keep their subjects from fighting them. If the Indian kings sent them a supper of barbacued venison and roasting ears, it was that they might take advantage of them while eating, and mingle their blood with their dishes. If an Indian approached their fort, though but to sell a raccoon, he was not suffered to enter until he had undergone a strict search both of his greasy bear-skin coat and mocassins, for fear the "*bloody wretch*," had some weapon or other about him to kill the good Christians withal. And so true is that voice which saith—"*the ungodly are in fear where no fear is*," that the English, even at *noon day*, still acted with as much circumspection as though they continually felt themselves in the country of an implacable enemy. And at night, so great was their dread of the Indians, that even in Jamestown they did not think of going to sleep until fully satisfied that every street and lane was well guarded by the soldiers, all ready to fire at a moment's warning. And even then it was no easy matter to fall into a doze, though easy enough to be started out of it, as they often were, by a frightened fancy, dreaming of the savages and their bloody tomahawks. If an Englishman ventured outside of the fort, he was way-laid and murdered even in broad day, if the Indian who fell in with him had but the strength to do it. And, indeed, so deadly was the hate of the Indians against the Christians, for wronging them out of their lands and driving them from the bones of their fathers, that they never lost sight of revenge. And ten years afterwards, while the English, suspecting no harm, were ploughing the soil which they had so unjustly acquired the Indians took them by surprise, and with their *own hoes and axes*, in one fatal hour, murdered near four hundred of these poor wretches; mingling, in many instances, the blood of the innocent children with that of their guilty parents.

See there, O horror-struck reader, see there the HELL which was introduced into Virginia by following the selfish policy of this poor blind world. But to raise our spirits from the depression occasioned by such horrible scenes, let us turn to Pennsylvania and contemplate that HEAVEN which is created among men who act up to the just and benevolent spirit of the gospel. And if we wish to see an angel in human shape, let us look at William Penn among the savages of North America—let us look at him as, with a countenance shining with the heavenliest charity, and a voice of music, he salutes them as BROTHERS—honours them as the proprietors of the country given unto them of the "GREAT SPIRIT," and expresses a modest petition that they would give unto him, their brother from beyond the Big water, a portion of their land in exchange for GOOD THINGS which the "GREAT SPIRIT" had given to him. Ye narrow bigots who can think that Christ has no sheep but those of *your own fold*, look at these Indians in the wilds of North America, and say whether eyes, thus bright with the admiration of eternal justice, and faces glowing with such affection for the honest stranger, do not bespeak the operation of that spirit who is "*no respecter of persons, but in every nation, and to every soul of man, imparts grace sufficient for salvation.*" And as that grace never displayed itself in smiles of more undissembled love, than in the countenances of these uneducated heathens, so never did it bring forth richer fruits of "PEACE and GOOD WILL," than were manifested in all the intercourse between them and William Penn.

Captain John Smith, after that he had invaded their rights in Virginia, was fain to seek his safety in his soldiers, and cannon, and stockade forts, and loophole churches. But honest William Penn saved *all that expense;* and proved in the face of the whole world, that a Philadelphia (a city of *brotherly love*) needs no soldiers nor cannon to defend it.—Captain Smith and his freebooters in James-town, could not sleep without their sentinels and guards constantly around them. Honest William Penn and his quakers, in their infant Philadelphia, though surrounded by thousands of savages, slept sweetly even without bars and bolts to their doors! At James-town, an Indian was never suffered to come in without strict search. At Philadelphia the Indians came in and out, just as familiarly as the large dogs in a tanner's yard, to which, if need was, they were a ready defence. In Virginia, Captain John Smith could not get a grain of corn for his starving colony at James-town, without pushing up the rivers in his boats, often at the risk of life from the arrows of the Indians, who were so desirous to drive these invaders out of their country, that they held back their provisions, whereby numbers of the little colony (only one hundred and twenty at first) were actually starved to death. But in Pennsylvania, in consequence of the godlike justice and humanity of William Penn, the hearts and souls of the Indians were so strongly knit to him like children to a father, as indeed they called him, that they brought him in provisions in such quantities as abundantly to supply his followers the quakers, near three thousand in number. And if any of these were so poor that they could not buy at the low prices set, they would give to them for nothing, as to the poor children of "*their father Onas*," as they called William Penn! Yes, and they would both show and assist them to make bark huts against the winter; and also freely and lovingly offer their services to unload their ships and bear their goods to their huts and houses. Captain Smith himself, only taking a solitary walk along the shore near James-town, was suddenly attacked by a single Indian, and but for superior address would certainly have been slain in spite of the broad-sword by his side. But honest William Penn, or any of his quakers, with only his broad-brimmed beaver, and staff in his hand, might have walked throughout the country, not only in safety, but even thronged by the Indians, eagerly running to shake hands, calling him *brother! brother!* and carrying him with joy to their cabins to feast him on the best provisions they had. Captain Smith and the Indians were always in "*hot water*," and often in bloody wars, which never ended but in the *extermination of the latter.* But honest William Penn and the Indians lived so perfectly in the spirit of brothers, that during all the time that he and his followers, the FRIENDS, had the rule in Pennsylvania, even seventy years, there was never known one single instance of murder. Captain Smith's city, (old James-town) built on violence and blood, is now swept from the face of the earth; scarcely a broken tomb-stone remaining to tell where it stood. But William Penn's city, Philadelphia, established in justice and brotherly kindness though founded a long time after the other, has grown up to be the glory of this western world—with lovely streets, extending from the Delaware to the Schuylkill, and noble wharves, warehouses, work-shops, arsenals, bridges, markets, aqueducts, hospitals, dispensaries, alms-houses, museums, academies, colleges, universities, and churches, with other buildings public and private, to an exceeding amount, both in number and elegance, and filled up with a crowded population of between one and two hundred thousand souls. Indeed no man can cast his eyes over this beauteous city, covering as it does, for many a mile, the lovely plains of silver-flooded Delaware and the winding Schuylkill—with its thousands of red shining edifices, and stately domes, and towering spires, without exclaiming, as did the prophet when from the tops of Pisgah he beheld the plains of Jericho covered over with the chosen seed, "*how goodly are thy tents, O*

Jacob, and thy tabernacles, O Israel! Happy are they who are in such a state; yea, blessed are the people who have the Lord for their God."

O when will mankind learn that "GOD IS LOVE"—that his plan embraces the happiness of ALL; and that none but those who seek their own consistently with the good of others, shall ever find it?

CHARACTER OF WILLIAM PENN,

FROM EDMUND BURKE.

"William Penn, as a legislator, deserves great honour among all mankind. He created a commonwealth, which, from a few hundreds of indigent refugees, have in seventy years grown to a numerous and flourishing people. A people who, from a wilderness, have brought their territory to a state of high cultivation; filled it with wealthy and populous towns; and who, in the midst of a fierce and lawless race of men have preserved themselves, with unarmed hands, by the rules of justice and moderation, better than any other have done by *policy* and *arms*. The way in which he did this, deserves eternal notice. Though brought up, as it were, in the corrupt courts of Charles the Second, who had endeavoured to carry the kingly prerogative to as high a pitch of aristocracy as possible, yet—O glorious! O all subduing power of religion! when he got *that*, he thought of nothing but to make every body happy. To take the lands from the Indians, he abhorred; he bought their lands.—To exact and starve the poor who followed him across the ocean for conscience and quiet sake, he could not brook. He put the lands at the low rate of forty shillings a hundred acres, and one shilling per hundred acres yearly quit rent.

"But what crowned all, was the noble charter of privileges by which he made them more free, perhaps, than any people on earth; and which, by securing both civil and religious liberty, caused the eyes of the oppressed from all parts of the world to look to his country for relief. This one act of godlike wisdom and goodness has settled Penn's country in a more strong and permanent manner than the wisest regulations could have done on any other plan. A man has but to believe that there *is a God;* that he is the inspector of our actions, and the future rewarder and punisher of our good and ill, and he is not only tolerated, but, if possessed of talents and integrity, is on the road to place.

"This great and good man lived to see an extensive country rescued from the wilderness and filled with a free and flourishing people — he lived to lay the foundation of a splendid and wealthy city — he lived to see it promise every thing from the situation which he himself had chosen, and from the encouragement which he himself had given it — he lived to see all this — but he died in the Fleet prison!

"'Tis pleasing to do honour to those great men whose virtues and generosity have contributed to the peopling of the earth, and to the freedom and happiness of mankind — who have preferred the interest of a remote posterity, and times unknown, to their own fortune, and to the quiet and security of their own lives. Now, both Britain and America reap great benefit from his labours and his losses. And his posterity have a vast estate out of the quit rents of that very province, whose establishment was the ruin of their predecessor's fortune."

MONTESQUIEU, ON PENN.

A character so extraordinary in the institutions of Greece, has shown itself lately in the dregs and corruption of modern times. A very honest legislator has formed a people, to whom probity seems as natural as bravery to the Spartans. William Penn is a real Lycurgus: and though the former made peace his principal aim, as the latter did war, yet they resemble one another in the singular way of living to which they reduced their people — in the ascendant they gained over freemen, in the prejudices they overcame, and in the passions which they snbdued.

THE END.

REFLECTIONS AND MAXIMS

OF

WILLIAM PENN.

IGNORANCE.

1. It is admirable to consider how many millions of people come into and go out of the world, ignorant of themselves, and of the world they have lived in.

2. If one went to see Windsor-castle, or Hampton-court, it would be strange not to observe and remember the situation, the building, the gardens, fountains, &c., that make up the beauty and pleasure of such a seat. And yet few people know themselves: no, not their own bodies, the houses of their minds, the most curious structure in the world; a living, walking tabernacle; nor the world of which it was made, and out of which it is fed; which would be so much our benefit, as well as our pleasure, to know. We cannot doubt of this when we are told that the "invisible things of God are brought to light by the things that are seen;" and consequently we read our duty in them, as often as we look upon them, to Him that is the great and wise author of them, if we look as we should do.

3. The world is certainly a great and stately volume of natural things, and may be not improperly styled the hieroglyphics of a better; but, alas, how very few leaves of it do we seriously turn over! This ought to be the subject of the education of our youth; who, at twenty, when they should be fit for business, know little or nothing of it.

EDUCATION.

4. We are in pain to make them scholars, but not men; to talk, rather than to know; which is true canting.

5. The first thing obvious to children is what is sensible; and that we make no part of their rudiments.

6. We press their memory too soon, and puzzle, strain,

and load them with words and rules to know grammar and rhetoric, and a strange tongue or two, that it is ten to one may never be useful to them; leaving their natural genius to mechanical, and physical or natural knowledge uncultivated and neglected; which would be of exceeding use and pleasure to them through the whole course of their lives.

7. To be sure languages are not to be despised or neglected; but, things are still to be preferred.

8. Children had rather be making tools and instruments of play: shaping, drawing, framing, and building, &c., than getting some rules of propriety of speech by heart: and those also would follow with more judgment, and less trouble and time.

9. It were happy if we studied nature more in natural things; and acted according to nature: whose rules are few, plain, and most reasonable.

10. Let us begin where she begins, go her pace, and close always where she ends, and we cannot miss of being good naturalists.

11. The creation would not be longer a riddle to us. The heavens, earth, and waters, with their respective, various, and numerous inhabitants, their productions, natures, seasons, sympathies, and antipathies, their use, benefit, and pleasure, would be better understood by us; and an eternal wisdom, power, majesty, and goodness, very conspicuous to us, through those sensible and passing forms: the world wearing the mark of its Maker, whose stamp is everywhere visible, and the characters very legible to the children of wisdom.

12. And it would go a great way to caution and direct people in their use of the world, that they were better studied and known in the creation of it.

13. For how could men find the confidence to abuse it, while they should see the great Creator stare them in the face, in all and every part thereof?

14. Their ignorance makes them insensible; and to that insensibility may be ascribed their hard usage of several parts of this noble creation: that has the stamp and voice of a Deity every where, and in everything, to the observing.

15. It is a pity therefore that books have not been composed for youth, by some curious and careful naturalists,

and also mechanics, in the Latin tongue, to be used in schools, that they might learn things with words; things obvious and familiar to them, and which would make the tongue easier to be obtained by them.

16. Many able gardeners and husbandmen are ignorant of the reason of their calling; as most artificers are of the reason of their own rules that govern their excellent workmanship. But a naturalist and mechanic of this sort is master of the reason of both; and might be of the practice too, if his industry kept pace with his speculation; which were very commendable; and without which he cannot be said to be a complete naturalist or mechanic.

17. Finally, if man be the index or epitome of the world, as philosophers tell us, we have only to read ourselves well, to be learned in it. But because there is nothing we less regard than the characters of the Power that made us, which are so clearly written upon us, and the world he has given us, and can best tell us what we are and should be, we are even strangers to our own genius: the glass in which we should see that true, instructing, and agreeable variety, which is to be observed in nature, to the admiration of that wisdom, and adoration of that Power, which made us all.

PRIDE.

18. And yet we are very apt to be full of ourselves, instead of him that made what we much value: and but for whom we can have no reason to value ourselves. For we have nothing that we can call our own; no, not ourselves; for we are all but tenants, at will too, of the great Lord of ourselves, and the rest of this great farm, the world that we live upon.

19. But, methinks, we cannot answer it to ourselves, as well as our Maker, that we should live and die ignorant of ourselves, and thereby of him, and the obligations we are under to him for ourselves.

20. If the worth of a gift sets the obligation, and directs the return of the party that receives it, he that is ignorant of it, will be at a loss to value it, and the giver for it.

21. Here is a man in his ignorance of himself: he knows not how to estimate his Creator, because he knows not how

to value his creation. If we consider his make, and lovely compositure, the several stories of his wonderful structure, his divers members, their order, function, and dependency; the instruments of food, the vessels of digestion, the several transmutations it passes, and how nourishment is carried and diffused throughout the whole body, by most intricate and imperceptible passages; how the animal spirit is thereby refreshed, and, with an unspeakable dexterity and motion, sets all parts at work to feed themselves; and, last of all, how the rational soul is seated in the animal, as its proper house, as is the animal in the body; I say, if this rare fabric alone were but considered by us, with all the rest by which it is fed and comforted, surely man would have a more reverent sense of the power, wisdom, and goodness of God, and of that duty he owes to him for it. But if he would be acquainted with his own soul, its noble faculties, its union with the body, its nature and end, and the providence by which the whole frame of humanity is preserved, he would admire and adore his good and great God. But man has become a strange contradiction to himself; but it is of himself; not being by constitution, but corruption, such.

22. He would have others obey him, even his own kind; but he will not obey God, that is so much above him, and who made him.

23. He will lose none of his authority; no, not abate an ace of it. He is humorsome to his wife, beats his children, is angry with his servants, strict with his neighbors, revenges all affronts to the extremity; but, alas! forgets all the while that he is the man; and is more in arrear to God that is so very patient with him than they are to him, with whom he is so strict and impatient.

24. He is curious to wash, dress, and perfume his body, but careless of his soul; the one shall have many hours, the other not so many minutes; this shall have three or four new suits a year, but that must wear its old clothes still.

25. If he be to receive or see a great man, how nice and anxious is he that all things be in order; and with what respect and address does he approach and make his court? But to God, how dry and formal, and constrained in his devotion.

26. In his prayers he says, "Thy will be done;" but means his own: at least acts so.

27. It is too frequent to begin with God, and end with the world. But he is the good man's beginning and end, he is Alpha and Omega.

LUXURY.

28. Such is now become our delicacy, that we will not eat ordinary meat, nor drink small, palled liquor; we must have the best, and the best cooked for our bodies, while our souls feed on empty or corrupted things.

29. In short, man is spending all upon a bare house, and hath little or no furniture within to recommend it; which is preferring the cabinet to the jewel, a lease of seven years before an inheritance. So absurd a thing is man, after all his proud pretences to wit and understanding.

INCONSIDERATION.

30. The want of due consideration is the cause of all the unhappiness man brings upon himself. For his second thoughts rarely agree with the first; which pass not without a considerable retrenchment or correction. And yet that sensible warning is, too frequently, not precaution enough for his future conduct.

31. Well may we say, "Our infelicity is of ourselves; since there is nothing we do that we should not do, but we know it, and yet do it.

DISAPPOINTMENT AND RESIGNATION.

32. For disappointments, that come not by our own folly, they are the trials or corrections of Heaven: and it is our own fault, if they prove not to our advantage.

33. To repine at them does not mend the matter: it is only to grumble at our Creator. But to see the hand of God in them, with an humble submission to his will, is the way to turn our water into wine, and engage the greatest love and mercy on our side.

34. We must needs disorder ourselves, if we only look at our losses. But if we consider how little we deserve

what is left, our passion will cool, and our murmurs will turn into thankfulness.

35. If our hairs fall not to the ground, less do we, or our substance, without God's providence.

36. Nor can we fall below the arms of God, how low soever it be we fall.

37. For though our Saviour's passion is over, his compassion is not. That never fails his humble, sincere disciples. In him they find more than all that they lose in the world.

MURMURING.

38. Is it reasonable to take it ill, that anybody desires of us that which is their own? All we have is the Almighty's: and shall not God have his own when he calls for it?

39. Discontentedness is not only in such a case ingratitude, but injustice: for we are both unthankful for the time we had it, and not honest enough to restore it, if we could keep it.

40. But it is hard for us to look on things in such a glass, and at such a distance from this low world; and yet it is our duty, and would be our wisdom and our glory, to do so.

CENSORIOUSNESS.

41. We are apt to be very pert at censuring others, where we will not endure advice ourselves. And nothing shows our weakness more, than to be so sharp-sighted at spying other men's faults, and so purblind about our own.

42. When the actions of a neighbor are upon the stage, we can have all our wits about us, are so quick and critical we can split a hair, and find out every failure and infirmity; but are without feeling, or have but very little sense, of our own.

43. Much of this comes from ill nature, as well as from an inordinate value of ourselves: for we love rambling better than home, and blaming the unhappy, rather than covering and relieving them.

44. In such occasions some show their malice, and are witty upon misfortunes; others their justice, they can reflect

apace; but few or none their charity, especially if it be about money matters.

45. You shall see an old miser come forth with a set gravity, and so much severity against the distressed, to excuse his purse, that he will, ere he has done, put it out of all question that riches is righteousness with him. 'This,' says he, 'is the fruit of your prodigality, (as if, poor man, covetousness were no fault,) or, of your projects, or grasping after a great trade;' while he himself would have done the same thing, but that he had not the courage to venture so much ready money out of his own trusty hands, though it had been to have brought him back the Indies in return. But the proverb is just, "Vice should not correct sin."

46. They have a right to censure, that have a heart to help: the rest is cruelty, not justice.

BONDS OF CHARITY.

47. Lend not beyond thy ability, nor refuse to lend out of thy ability; especially when it will help others more than it can hurt thee.

48. If thy debtor be honest and capable, thou hast thy money again, if not with increase, with praise. If he prove insolvent, do not ruin him to get that which it will not ruin thee to lose: for thou art but a steward, and another is thy owner, master, and judge.

49. The more merciful acts thou dost, the more mercy thou wilt receive: and if with a charitable employment of thy temporal riches, thou gainest eternal treasure, thy purchase is infinite: thou wilt have found the art of multiplying indeed.

FRUGALITY, OR BOUNTY.

50. Frugality is good, if liberality be joined with it. The first is leaving off superfluous expenses; the last bestowing them to the benefit of others that need. The first without the last begins covetousness; the last without the first begins prodigality. Both together make an excellent temper. Happy the place where that is found.

51. Were it universal, we should be cured of two extremes, want and excess: and the one would supply the

other, and so bring both nearer to a mean; the just degree of earthly happiness.

52. It is a reproach to religion and government, to suffer so much poverty and excess.

53. Were the superfluities of a nation valued, and made a perpetual tax for benevolence, there would be more alms houses than poor, schools than scholars, and enough to spare for government besides.

54. Hospitality is good, if the poorer sort are the subjects of our bounty; else too near a superfluity.

DISCIPLINE.

55. If thou wouldst be happy and easy in thy family, above all things observe discipline.

56. Every one in it should know their duty; and there should be a time and place for every thing; and, whatever else is done or omitted, be sure to begin and end with God.

INDUSTRY.

57. Love labor: for if thou dost not want it for food, thou mayest for physic. It is wholesome for thy body, and good for thy mind. It prevents the fruits of idleness, which many times come of nothing to do, and lead too many to do what is worse than nothing.

58. A garden, an elaboratory, a workhouse, improvements, and breeding, are pleasant and profitable diversions to the idle and ingenious; for here they miss ill company, and converse with nature and art; whose varieties are equally grateful and instructing, and preserve a good constitution of body and mind.

TEMPERANCE.

59. To this a spare diet contributes much. Eat therefore to live, and do not live to eat. That is like a man, but this below a beast.

60. Have wholesome, but not costly food: and be rather cleanly than dainty in ordering it.

61. The receipts of cookery are swelled to a volume, but a good stomach excels them all: to which nothing contributes more than industry and temperance.

62. It is a cruel folly to offer up to ostentation so many lives of creatures, as make up the state of our treats; as it is a prodigal one to spend more in sauce than in meat.

63. The proverb says, "That enough is as good as a feast;" but it is certainly better, if superfluity be a fault, which never fails to be at festivals.

64. If thou rise with an appetite, thou art sure never to sit down without one.

65. Rarely drink but when thou art dry; nor then, between meals, if it can be avoided.

66. The smaller the drink, the clearer the head, and the cooler the blood: which are great benefits in temper and business.

67. Strong liquors are good at some times, and in small proportions: being better for physic than food; for cordials than common use.

68. The most common things are the most useful; which shows both the wisdom and goodness of the great Lord of the family of the world.

69. What, therefore, he has made rare, do not use too commonly; least thou shouldst invert the use and order of things, become wanton and voluptuous, and thy blessings prove a curse.

70. "Let nothing be lost," said our Saviour; but that is lost that is misused.

71. Neither urge another to that thou wouldst be unwilling to do thyself: nor do thyself what looks to thee unseemly, and intemperate in another.

72. All excesses is ill; but drunkenness is of the worst sort. It spoils health, dismounts the mind, and unmans men. It reveals secrets, is quarrelsome, lascivious, impudent, dangerous, and mad. In fine, he that is drunk is not a man; because he is so long void of reason, that distinguishes a man from a beast.

APPAREL.

73. Excess in apparel is another costly folly. The very trimming of the vain world would clothe all the naked one.

74. Choose thy clothes by thine own eyes, not another's. The more plain and simple they are, the better; neither

unshapely nor fantastical; for use and decency, and not for pride.

75. If thou art clean and warm, it is sufficient, for more doth but rob the poor, and pleases the wanton.

76. It is said of the true church, "The King's daughter is all glorious within." Let our care, therefore, be of our minds, more than our bodies, if we would be of her communion.

77. We are told with truth, 'That meekness and modesty are the rich and charming attire of the soul;' and the plainer the dress, the more distinctly, and with greater lustre, their beauty shines.

78. It is a great pity such beauties are so rare, and those of Jezebel's forehead are so common; whose dresses are incentives to lust; but bars, instead of motives, to love or virtue.

RIGHT MARRIAGE.

79. Never marry but for love; but see that thou lovest what is lovely.

80. If love be not thy chiefest motive, thou wilt soon grow weary of a married state, and stray from thy promise, to search out thy pleasures in forbidden places.

81. Let not enjoyment lessen, but augment, affection: it being the basest of passions to like when we have not, what we slight when we possess.

82. It is the difference betwixt lust and love: this is fixed, that volatile. Love grows, lust wastes, by enjoyment: and the reason is, that one springs from an union of souls, and the other springs from an union of sense.

83. They have divers originals, and so are of different families: that, inward and deep; this, superficial: this, transient; and that permanent.

84. They that marry for money, cannot have the true satisfaction of marriage; the requisite means being wanting.

85. Men are generally more careful of the breed of their horses and dogs, than of their children.

86. Those must be of the best sort, for shape, strength, courage, and good condition; but as for these, their own posterity, money shall answer all things. With such, it

makes the crooked straight, sets squint eyes right, cures madness, covers folly, changes ill conditions, mends the skin, gives a sweet breath, repairs honor, makes young, works wonders.

87. O how sordid is man grown! man, the noblest creature of the world, as a God on earth, and the image of him that made it thus to mistake earth for heaven, and worship gold for God.

AVARICE.

88. Covetousness is the greatest of monsters, as well as the root of all evil. I have once seen the man who died to save charges! 'What! give ten shillings to a doctor, and have an apothecary's bill besides, that may come to I know not what!' No, not he: valuing life less than twenty shillings. But indeed, such a man could not well set too low a price upon himself; who, though he lived up to the chin in bags, had rather die, than find in his heart to open one of them, to help to save his life.

89. Such a man is 'felo de se,' and deserves not christian burial.

90. He is a common nuisance; a way across the stream, that stops the current; an obstruction, to be removed by a purge of the law. The only gratification he gives his neighbors, is to let them see that he himself is as little the better for what he has as they are. For he always looks like Lent: a sort of Lay-Minim. In some sense he may be compared to Pharaoh's lean kine; for all that he has does him no good. He commonly wears his clothes till they leave him, or that nobody else can wear them. He affects to be thought poor, to escape robbery and taxes; and by looking as if he wanted an alms, excuse himself from giving any. He ever goes late to markets to cover buying the worst; but does it because that is cheapest. He lives on the offal. His life were an insupportable punishment, to any temper but his own: and no greater torment to him on earth, than to live as other men do. But the misery of his pleasure is, that he is never satisfied with getting, and always in fear of losing what he cannot use.

91. How vilely he has lost himself, that becomes a slave to his servant, and exalts him to the dignity of his Maker! Gold is the God, the wife, the friend, of the money-monger of the world. But in

MARRIAGE

92. Do thou be wise: prefer the person before money, virtue before beauty, the mind before the body: then thou hast a wife, a friend, a companion, a second self, one that bears an equal share with thee, in all thy toils and troubles.

93. Choose one that measures her satisfaction, safety, and danger, by thine; and of whom thou art sure, as of thy most secret thoughts: a friend as well as a wife; which indeed, a wife implies; for she is but half a wife that is not, or is not capable of being such a friend.

94. Sexes make no difference; since in souls there is none: and they are the subjects of friendship.

95. He that minds a body and not a soul, has not the better part of that relation; and will consequently want the noblest comfort of a married life.

96. The satisfaction of our senses is low, short, and transient; but the mind gives a more raised and extended pleasure, and is capable of a happiness founded upon reason; not bounded and limited by the circumstances that bodies are confined to.

97. Here it is we ought to search out our pleasure, where the field is large and full of variety, and of an enduring nature: sickness, poverty, or disgrace, being not able to shake it, because it is not under the moving influences of worldly contingencies.

98. The satisfaction of those that do so is in well-doing, and in the assurance they have of a future reward; that they are best loved by those they love most; and that they enjoy and value the liberty of their minds above that of their bodies: having the whole creation for their prospect; the most noble and wonderful works and providences of God, the histories of the ancients, and in them the actions and examples of the virtuous: and lastly, themselves, their affairs and family, to exercise their minds, and friendship upon.

99. Nothing can be more entire and without reserve; nothing more zealous, affectionate, and sincere; nothing more contented and constant, than such a couple; nor no greater temporal felicity, than to be one of them.

100. Between a man and his wife, nothing ought to rule but love. Authority is for children and servants; yet not without sweetness.

101. As love ought to bring them together, so it is the best way to keep them well together.

102. Wherefore use her not as a servant, whom thou wouldst, perhaps, have served seven years to have obtained.

103. A husband and wife that love and value one another, show their children and servants that they should do so too. Others visibly lose their authority in their families by their contempt of one another; and teach their children to be unnatural by their own examples.

104. It is a general fault, not to be more careful to preserve nature in children; who, at least in the second descent, hardly have a feeling of their relation; which must be an unpleasant reflection to affectionate parents.

105. Frequent visits, presents, intimate correspondence, and intermarriages within allowed bounds, are means of keeping up the concern and affection that nature requires from relations.

FRIENDSHIP.

106. Friendship is the next pleasure we may hope for. and where we find it not at home, or have no home to find it in, we may seek it abroad. It is an union of spirits, a marriage of hearts, and the bond thereof virtue.

107. There can be no friendship where there is no freedom. Friendship loves a free air, and will not be penned up in straight and narrow inclosures. It will speak freely, and act so too; and take nothing ill where no ill is meant; nay, where it is, it will easily forgive, and forget too, upon small acknowledgments.

108. Friends are true twins in soul; they sympathize in everything, and have the same love and aversion.

109. One is not happy without the other; nor can either of them be miserable alone. As if they could change

bodies, they take their turns in pain as well as in pleasure; relieving one another in their most adverse conditions.

110. What one enjoys, the other cannot want. Like the primitive Christians, they have all things in common, and no property, but in one another.

QUALITIES OF A FRIEND.

111. A true friend unbosoms freely, advises justly, assists readily, adventures boldly, takes all patiently, defends courageously, and continues a friend unchangeably.

112. These being the qualities of a friend, we are to find them before we choose one.

113. The covetous, the angry, the proud, the jealous, the talkative, cannot but make ill friends, as well as false.

114. In short, choose a friend as thou dost a wife, till death separate you.

115. Yet be not a friend beyond the altar, but let virtue bound thy friendship; else it is not friendship, but an evil confederacy.

116. If my brother, or kinsman, will be my friend, I ought to prefer him before a stranger; or I show little duty or nature to my parents.

117. And as we ought to prefer our kindred in point of affection, so too in point of charity, if equally needing and deserving.

CAUTION AND CONDUCT.

118. Be not easily acquainted; lest, finding reason to cool, thou makest an enemy instead of a good neighbor.

119. Be reserved, but not sour; grave, but not formal; bold, but not rash; humble, but not servile; patient, not insensible; constant, not obstinate; cheerful, not light; rather sweet, than familiar; familiar, than intimate; and intimate with very few, and upon very good grounds.

120. Return the civilities thou receivest, and be ever grateful for favors.

REPARATION.

121. If thou hast done an injury to another, rather own it than defend it. One way thou gainest forgivness; the other, thou doublest the wrong and reckoning.

122. Some oppose honor to submission; but it can be no honor to maintain what it is dishonorable to do.

123. To confess a fault that is none, out of fear, is indeed mean; but not to be afraid of standing in one, is brutish.

124. We should make more haste to right our neighbour, than we do to wrong him; and instead of being vindictive, we should leave him to judge of his own satisfaction.

125. True honor will pay treble damages, rather than justify one wrong by another.

126. In such controversies, it is but too common for some to say, 'Both are to blame,' to excuse their own unconcernedness; which is a base neutrality. Others will cry, 'They are both alike;' thereby involving the injured with the guilty, to mince the matter for the faulty, or cover their own injustice to the wronged party.

127. Fear and gain are great perverters of mankind; and where either prevails, the judgment is violated.

RULES OF CONVERSATION.

128. Avoid company, where it is not profitable or necessary: and on these occasions, speak little, and last.

129. Silence is wisdom where speaking is folly, and always safe.

130. Some are so foolish, as to interrupt and anticipate, those that speak, instead of hearing and thinking before they answer; which is uncivil, as well as silly.

131. If thou thinkest twice before thou speakest once, thou wilt speak twice the better for it.

132, Better say nothing than not to the purpose. And to speak pertinently, consider both what is fit, and when it is fit, to speak.

133. In all debates, let truth be thy aim; not victory, or an unjust interest: and endeavor to gain, rather than to expose, thy antagonist.

134. Give no advantage in argument, nor lose any that is offered. This is a benefit which arises from temper.

135. Do not use thyself to dispute against thine own judgment, to show wit; lest it prepare thee to be too indifferent about what is right: nor against another man, to vex him, or for mere trial of skill; since to inform, or to be informed, ought to be the end of all conferences.

136. Men are too apt to be more concerned for their credit, than for the cause.

ELOQUENCE.

137. There is a truth and beauty in rhetoric; but it oftener serves ill turns than good ones.

138. Elegancy is a good mien and address given to matter, be it by proper, or by figurative speech: where the words are apt, and allusions very natural, certainly it has a moving grace; but it is too artificial for simplicity, and oftentimes, for truth. The danger is, lest it delude the weak; who, in such cases, may mistake the handmaid for the mistress, if not error for truth.

139. It is certain, truth is least indebted to it because she has least need of it, and least uses it.

140. But it is a reproveable delicacy in them that despise truth in plain clothes.

141. Such luxuriants have but false appetites; like those gluttons, that by sauce force them, where they have no stomach, and sacrifice to their palate, not their health: which cannot be without great vanity, nor that without some sin.

TEMPER.

142. Nothing does reason more right, than the coolness of those that offer it; for truth often suffers more by the heat of its defenders, than from the arguments of its opposers.

143. Zeal ever follows an appearance of truth, and the assured are too apt to be warm; but it is their weak side in argument; zeal being better shown against sin, than persons, or their mistakes.

TRUTH.

144. Where thou art obliged to speak, be sure to speak

the truth, for equivocation is half way to lying the whole way to hell.

JUSTICE.

145. Believe nothing against another, but upon good authority: nor report what may hurt another, unless it be a greater hurt to others to conceal it.

SECRECY.

146. It is wise not to seek a secret; and honest not to reveal one.

147. Only trust thyself, and another shall not betray thee.

148. Openness has the mischief, though not the malice of treachery.

COMPLACENCY.

149. Never assent merely to please others; for that is, besides flattery, oftentimes untruth, and discovers a mind to be servile and base: nor contradict to vex others: for that shows an ill temper, and provokes, but profits nobody.

SHIFTS.

150. Do not accuse others to excuse thyself; for that is neither generous nor just. But let sincerity and ingenuousness be thy refuge, rather than craft a falsehood; for cunning borders very near upon knavery.

151. Wisdom never uses nor wants it. Cunning to the wise, is as an ape to a man.

INTEREST.

152. Interest has the security, though not the virtue, of a principal. As the world goes, it is the surest side; for men daily leave both relations and religion to follow it.

153. It is an odd sight, but very evident, that families and nations of cross religions and humors, unite against those of their own, where they find an interest to do it.

154. We are tied down by our senses to this world;

and where that is in question, it can be none with worldly men, whether they should not forsake all other considerations for it.

INQUIRY.

155. Have a care of vulgar errors. Dislike as well as allow, reasonably.

156. Inquiry is human, blind obedience brutal. Truth never loses by the one, but often suffers by the other.

157. The most useful truths are plainest; and while we keep to them, our differences cannot rise high.

158. There may be a wantonness in search, as well as stupidity in trusting. It is great wisdom equally to avoid the extremes.

RIGHT TIMING.

159. Do nothing improperly. Some are witty, kind, cold, angry, easy, stiff, jealous, careless, cautious, confident, close, open, but all in the wrong place.

160. It is ill mistaking, where the matter is of importance.

161. It is not enough that a thing be right, if it be not fit to be done. If not prudent, though just, it is not adviseable. He that loses by getting, had better lose than get.

KNOWLEDGE.

162. Knowledge is the treasure, but judgment the treasurer, of a wise man.

163. He that has more knowledge than judgment, is made for another man's use more than his own.

164. It cannot be a good constitution, where the appetite is great, and the digestion weak.

165. There are some men, like dictionaries, to be looked into upon occasions; but have no connection, and are little entertaining.

166. Less knowledge than judgment, will always have the advantage upon the injudicious, knowing man.

167. A wise man makes what he learns his own; the other shews he is but a copy, or a collection at most.

WIT.

168. Wit is a happy and striking way of expressing a thought.

169. It is not often, though it be lively and mantling, that it carries a great body with it.

170. Wit, therefore, is fitter for diversion than business, being more grateful to fancy than judgment.

171. Less judgment than wit, is more sail than ballast.

172. Yet it must be confessed that wit gives an edge to sense, and recommends it extremely.

173. Where judgment has wit to express it, there is the best orator.

OBEDIENCE TO PARENTS.

174. If thou wouldst be obeyed being a father, being a son, be obedient.

175. He that begets thee owns thee, and as a natural right over thee.

176. Next to God, thy parents; next to them, the magistrate.

177. Remember that thou art not more indebted to thy parents for thy nature, than for their love and care.

178. Rebellion therefore, in children was made death by God's Law, and in the people, the next thing to idolatry which is renouncing God, the great parent of all.

179. Obedience to parents, is not only our duty; but our interest. If we received our life from them, we prolong it by obeying them; for obedience is the first commandment with promise.

180. The obligation is as indissoluble as the relation.

181. If we must not disobey God to obey them, at least we must let them see that there is nothing else in our refusal: for some unjust commands cannot excuse the general neglect of our duty. They will be our parents, and we must be their children still: and if we cannot act for them against God, neither can we act against them for ourselves, or any thing else.

BEARING.

182. A man in business must put up with many affronts, if he loves his own quiet.

183. We must not pretend to see all that we see, if we would be easy.

184. It were endless to dispute upon every thing that is disputable.

185. A vindictive temper is not only uneasy to others, but to them that have it.

PROMISING.

186. Rarely promise; but, if lawful, constantly perform.

187. Hasty resolutions are of the nature of vows; and to be equally avoided.

188. 'I will never do this,' says one, yet does it. 'I am resolved to do that,' says another; but flags upon second thoughts; or does it, though awkwardly for his word's sake; as if it were worse to break his word, than to do amiss in keeping it.

189. Wear none of thine own chains; but keep free, whilst thou art free.

190. It is an effect of passion that wisdom corrects, to lay thyself under resolutions that cannot be well made, and worse performed.

FIDELITY.

191. Avoid, all thou canst, being entrusted; but do thy utmost to discharge the trust thou undertakest; for carelessness is injurious if not unjust.

192. The glory of a servant is fidelity, which cannot be without diligence, as well as truth.

193. Fidelity has enfranchised slave and adopted servants to be sons.

194. Reward a good servant well: and rather quit, than disquiet thyself with an ill one.

MASTER.

195. Mix kindness with authority; and rule more by discretion than rigor.

196. If thy servant be faulty, strive rather to convince him of his error, than to discover thy passion; and when he is sensible, forgive him.

197. Remember he is thy fellow-creature; and that God's goodness, not thy merit, has made the difference betwixt thee and him.

198. Let not thy children domineer over thy servants; nor suffer them to slight thy children.

199. Suppress tales in the general; but where a matter requires notice, encourage the complaint, and right the aggrieved.

200. If a child, he ought to entreat, and not to command; and if a servant, to comply, where he does not obey.

201. Though there should be but one master and mistress in a family, yet servants should know that children have the reversion.

SERVANT.

202. Indulge not unseemly things in thy master's children, nor refuse them what is fitting; for one is the highest unfaithfulness, and the other indiscretion, as well as disrespect.

203. Do thine own work honestly and cheerfully; and when that is done, help thy fellow, that so another time he may help thee.

204. If thou wilt be a good servant, thou must be true; and thou canst not be true if thou defraudest thy master.

205. A master may be defrauded many ways by a servant: as in time, care, pains, money, trust.

206. But a true servant is the contrary; he is diligent, careful, trusty. He tells no tales, reveals no secrets, refuses no pains, is not to be tempted by gain or awed by fear, to unfaithfulness.

207. Such a servant serves God, in serving his master; and has double wages for his work, to wit, here and hereafter.

JEALOUSY.

208. Be not fancifully jealous, for that is foolish; as to be reasonably so is wise.

209. He that superfines upon other men's actions, cozens himself as well as injures them.

210. To be very subtle and scrupulous in business is as hurtful, as being over confident and secure.

211. In difficult cases such a temper is timorous, and in dispatch irresolute.

212. Experience is a safe guide; and a practical head is a great happiness in business.

POSTERITY.

213. We are too careless of posterity; not considering that as they are, so the next generation will be.

214. If we would amend the world, we should mend ourselves; and teach our children to be, not what we are, but what they should be.

215. We are too apt to awaken and tune up their passions by the example of our own; and to teach them to be pleased, not with what is best, but with what pleases best.

216. It is our duty, and ought to be our care, to ward against that passion in them, which is more especially our own weakness and affliction, for we are in great measure accountable for them, as well as for ourselves.

217. We are in this, also, true turners of the world upside down: for money is first, and virtue last, and least in our care.

218. It is not how we leave our children, but what we leave them.

219. To be sure, virtue is but a supplement, and not a principal, in their portion and character: and therefore we see little wisdom, or goodness, among the rich, in proportion to their wealth.

A COUNTRY LIFE.

220. The country life is to be preferred, for there we see the works of God; but in cities, little else but the works of men: and the one makes a better subject for our contemplation than the other.

221. As puppets are to men, and babies to children; so is man's workmanship to God's: we are the picture, he the reality.

222. God's works declare his power, wisdom, and goodness: but man's works, for the most part, his pride, folly, and excess. The one is for use, the other, chiefly, for ostentation and lust.

223. The country is both the philosopher's garden and library, in which he reads and contemplates the power, wisdom, and goodness of God.

224. It is his food, as well as study: and gives him life, as well as learning.

225. A sweet and natural retreat from noise and talk, and allows opportunity for reflection, and gives the best subjects for it.

226. In short, it is an original, and the knowledge and improvement of it man's oldest business and trade, and the best he can be of.

ART AND PROJECT.

227. Art is good, where it is beneficial. Socrates wisely bounded his knowledge and instruction by practice.

228. Have a care, therefore, of projects; and yet despise nothing rashly, or in the lump.

229. Ingenuity, as well as religion, sometimes suffers between two thieves: pretenders and despisers.

230. Though injudicious and dishonest projectors often discredit art; yet the most useful and extraordinary inventions have not, at first, escaped the scorn of ignorance; as their authors rarely have cracking of their heads, or breaking of their backs.

231. Undertake no experiment in speculation, that appears not true in art; nor then at thine own cost, if costly or hazardous in making.

232. As many hands make light work, so several purses make cheap experiments.

INDUSTRY.

233. Industry is certainly very commendable, and supplies the want of parts.

234. Patience and diligence, like faith, remove mountains.

235. Never give out while there is hope; but hope not beyond reason; for that shows more desire than judgment.

236. It is profitable wisdom to know when we have done enough: much time and pains are spared, in not flattering ourselves against probabilities.

TEMPORAL HAPPINESS.

237. Do good with what thou hast, or it will do thee no good.

238. Seek not to be rich, but happy. The one lies in bags, the other in content, which wealth can never give.

239. We are apt to call things by wrong names. We will have prosperity to be happiness, and adversity to be misery; though that is the school of wisdom, and oftentimes the way to eternal happiness.

240. If thou wouldst be happy, bring thy mind to thy condition, and have an indifference for more than what is sufficient.

241. Have but little to do, and do it thyself; and do to others as thou wouldst have them do to thee: so thou canst not fail of temporal felicity.

242. The generality are the worse for their plenty. The voluptuous consumes it, the miser hides it; it is the good man that uses it, and to good purposes. But such are hardly found among the prosperous.

243. Be rather bountiful, than expensive.

244. Neither make nor go to feasts; but let the laborious poor bless thee at home in their solitary cottages.

245. Never voluntarily want what thou hast in possession; nor so spend it as to involve thyself in want unavoidable.

246. Be not tempted to presume by success: for many,

that have got largely, have lost all by coveting to get more.

247. To hazard much to get much, has more of avarice than wisdom.

248. It is great prudence, both to bound and use prosperity.

249. Too few know when they have enough ; and fewer know how to employ it.

250. It is equally adviseable not to part lightly with what is hardly gotten, and not to shut up closely what flows in freely.

251. Act not the shark upon thy neighbor; nor take advantage of the ignorance, prodigality, or necessity of any one, for that is next door to a fraud, and, at best, makes but an unblessed gain.

252. It is oftentimes the judgment of God upon greedy rich men, that he suffers them to push on their desires of wealth to the excess of over-reaching, grinding, or oppression ; which poisons all they have gotten : so that it commonly runs away as fast, and by as bad ways, as it was heaped up together.

RESPECT.

253. Never esteem any man, or thyself, the more for money ; nor think the meaner of thyself, or another, for want of it : virtue being the just reason of respecting, and the want of it of slighting any one.

254. A man, like a watch, is to be valued for his goings.

255. He that prefers him upon other accounts, bows to an idol.

256. Unless virtue guide us, our choice must be wrong.

257. An able bad man is an ill instrument, and to be shunned as the plague.

258. Be not decieved with the first appearance of things, but give thyself time to be in the right.

259. Show it not substance: realities govern wise men.

260. Have a care therefore, where there is more sail than ballast.

HAZARD.

261. In all buisness, it is best to put nothing to hazard: but where it is unavoidable, be not rash, but firm and resigned.

262. We should not be troubled for what we cannot help; but if it was our fault, let it be so no more. Amendment is repentance if not reparation.

263. As a desparate game needs an able gamester, so consideration often would prevent, what the best skill in the world cannot recover.

264. Where the probability of advantage exceeds not that of loss, wisdom never adventures.

265. To shoot well flying, is well; but to choose it, has more of vanity than judgment.

266. To be dexterous in danger, is a virtue; but to court danger, to show it, is weakness.

DETRACTION.

267. Have a care of that base evil, detraction. It is the fruit of envy, as that is of pride, the immediate offspring of the Devil; who, of an angel, a Lucifer, a son of the morning, made himself a serpent, a Devil, a Beelzebub, and all that is noxious to the eternal Goodness.

268. Virtue is not secure against envy. Men will lessen what they will not imitate.

269. Dislike what deserves it; but never hate, for that is of the nature of malice; which is almost ever to persons, not things; and is one of the blackest qualities sin begets in the soul.

MODERATION.

270. It were a happy day if men could bound and qualify their resentments with charity to the offender: for then our anger would be without sin, and better convict and edify the guilty: which alone can make it lawful.

271. Not to be provoked is best; but if moved, never

correct till the fume is spent; for every stroke our fury strikes, is sure to hit ourselves at last.

272. If we did but observe the allowances our reason makes upon reflection, when our passion is over, we could not want a rule how to behave ourselves again on the like occasion.

273. We are more prone to complain than redress, and to censure than excuse.

274. It is next to unpardonable, that we can so often blame what we will not once mend. It shows that we know, but will not do, our Master's will.

275. They that censure, should practise; or else, let them have the first stone, and the last too.

TRICK.

276. Nothing needs a trick, but a trick; sincerity loathes one.

277. We must take care to do things rightly; for a just sentence may be unjustly executed.

278. Circumstances give great light to true judgment, if well weighed.

PASSION.

279. Passion is a sort of fever in the mind, which ever leaves us weaker than it found us.

289. But, being intermitting, to be sure it is curable with care.

281. It, more than any thing, deprives us of the use of our judgment; for it raises a dust very hard to see through.

282. Like wine, whose lees fly up, being jogged, it is too muddy to drink.

283. It may not unfitly be termed the mob of the man, that commits a riot upon his reason.

284. I have oftentimes thought, that a passionate man is like a weak spring that cannot stand long locked.

285. And it is as true, that those things, are unfit for use, that cannot bear small knocks without breaking.

286. He that will not hear, cannot judge; and he that,

cannot bear contradiction, may with all his wit, miss the mark.

287. Objection and debate sift our truth; which needs temper as well as judgment.

288. But above all, observe it in resentments; for there passion is most extravagant.

289. Never chide for anger, but instruction.

290. He that corrects out of passion, raises revenge sooner than repentance.

291. It has more of wantonness than wisdom; and resembles those that eat to please their palate, rather than their appetite.

292. It is the difference between a wise and weak man; this judges by the lump, that by parts and their connexion.

293. The Greeks used to say, 'All cases are governed by their circumstances.' The same thing may be well and ill, as they change or vary the matter.

294. A man's strength is shown by his bearing. 'Bonum agere, and mala pati, regis est.'

PERSONAL CAUTION.

295. Reflect without malice, but never without need.

296. Despise nobody, nor any condition; lest it come to be thy own.

297. Never rail nor taunt. The one is rude, the other is scornful, and both evil.

298. Be not provoked by injuries to commit them.

299. Upbraid only ingratitude.

300. Haste makes work, which caution prevents.

301. Tempt no man, lest thou fall for it.

302. Have a care of persuming upon after games, for if that miss, all is gone.

303. Opportunities should never be lost, because they can hardly be gained.

394. It is well to cure, but better to prevent a distemper. The first shows more skill, but the last more wisdom.

305. Never make a trial of skill in difficult or hazardous cases.

306. Refuse not to be informed, for that shows pride or stupidity.

307. Humility and knowledge in poor clothes, excel pride and ignorance in costly attire.

308. Neither despise, nor oppose, what thou dost not understand.

BALANCE.

309. We must not be concerned above the value of the thing that engages us; nor raised above reason, in maintaining what we think reasonable.

310. It is too common an error, to invert the order of things, by making an end of that which is a means, and a means of that which is an end.

311. Religion and government escape not this misehief; the first is too often made a means instead of an end: the other an end, instead of a means.

312. Thus men seek wealth, rather than subsistence; and the end of clothes is the least reason of their use. Nor is the satisfying of our appetite our end in eating, so much as the pleasing of our palate. The like may be also said of building, furniture, &c., where the man rules not the beast, and appetite submits not to reason.

313. It is great wisdom to proportion our esteem to the nature of the thing: for as that way, things will not be undervalued, so neither will they engage us above their intrinsic worth.

314. If we suffer little things to have great hold upon us, we shall be as much transported for them, as if they deserved it.

315. It is an old proverb, 'Maxima bella ex lavissimis causis;' The greatest feuds have had the smallest beginnings.

316. No matter what the subject of the dispute be, but what place we give it in our minds; for that governs our concern and resentment.

317. It is one of the most fatal errors of our lives, when

we spoil a good cause by an ill management: and it is not impossible but we may mean well in an ill buisness; but that will not defend it.

318. If we are but sure the end is right, we are too apt to gallop over all bounds to compass it; not considering, that lawful ends, may be very unlawfully attained.

319. Let us be careful to take just ways to compass just things; that they may last in their benefits to us.

320. There is a troublesome humor some men have, that if they may not lead, they will not follow; but had rather a thing were never done, than not done their own way, though otherwise very desirable.

321. This comes of an over-fullness of ourselves, and shows we are more concerned for praise, than the success of what we think a good thing.

POPULARITY.

322. Affect not to be seen, and men will less see thy weakness.

323. They that show more than they are, raise an expectation they cannot answer; and so loose their credit, as soon as they are found out.

324. Avoid popularity. It has many snares, and no real benefit to thyself; and uncertainty to others.

PRIVACY.

325. Remember the proverb, 'Bene qui latuit, bene vixit;' They are happy, that live retiredly.

326. If this be true, princes and their grandees, of all men are the unhappiest; for they live least alone: and they that must be enjoyed by every body, can never enjoy themselves as they should.

327. It is the advantage little men have upon them; they can be private, and have leisure for family comforts, which are the greatest worldly contents men can enjoy.

328. But they that place pleasure in greatness, seek it there: and we see, rule is as much the ambition of some natures, as privacy is the choice of others.

GOVERNMENT.

329. Government has many shapes; but it is sovereignty, though not freedom, in all of them.

330. Rex and Tyrannus, are very different characters: one rules his people by laws, to which they consent; the other by his absolute will and power. That is called freedom; this, tyranny.

331. The first is endangered by the ambition of the populace, which shakes the constitution; the other by an ill administration, which hazards the tyrant and his family.

332. It is great wisdom, in princes of both sorts, not to strain points too high with their people; for whether the people have a right to oppose them or not, they are ever sure to attempt it when things are carried too far: though the remedy oftentimes proves worse than the disease.

333. Happy that king who is great by justice, and the people who are free by obedience.

334. Where the ruler is just, he may be strict; else it is two to one it turns upon him: and though he should prevail, he can be no gainer, where his people are the losers.

335. Princes must not have passions in government, nor resent beyond interest and religion.

336. Where example keeps pace with authority, power hardly fails to be obeyed, and magistrates to be honored.

337. Let all the people think they govern, and they will be governed.

338. This cannot fail, if those they trust are trusted.

339. That prince who is just to them in great things, and humours them oftentimes in small ones, is sure to have and keep them from all the world.

340. For the people are the politic wife of the prince, that may be better managed by wisdom, than ruled by force.

341. But where the magistrate is partial, and serves ill turns, he loses his authority with the people, and gives the populace opportunity to gratify their ambition: and so lays a stumbling-block for his people to fall.

342. It is true, that where a subject is more popular than the prince, the prince is in danger; but it is as true, that it is his own fault: for nobody has the like means, interest, or reason, to be as popular, as he.

343. It is an unaccountable thing, that some princes incline rather to be feared than loved; when they see, that fear does not oftener secure a prince against the dissatisfaction of his people, than love makes a subject too many for such a prince.

344. Certainly service upon inclination is like to go farther, than obedienee upon compulsion.

345. The Romans had a just sense of this, when they placed Optimus before Maximus, to their most illustrious captains and Cæsars.

346. Besides, experience tells us, that goodness raises a nobler passion in the soul, and gives a better sense of duty, than severity.

347. What did Pharaoh get by increasing the Israelites' task? Ruin to himself in the end.

348. Kings, chiefly in this, should imitate God; their mercy should be above all their works.

349. The difference between the prince and the peasant is in this world; but a temper ought to be observed by him that has the advantage here, because of the judgment of the next.

350. The end of every thing should direct the means: now that of government being the good of the whole, nothing less should be the aim of the prince.

351. As often as rulers endeavor to attain just ends by just mediums, they are sure of a quiet and easy government; and as sure of convulsions, where the nature of things are violated, and the order over ruled.

352. It is certain, princes ought to have great allowances made them for faults in government, since they see by other people's eyes, and hear by their ears: but ministers of state, their immediate confidants and instruments, have much to answer for, if, to gratify private passions, they misguide the prince to do public injury.

353. Ministers of state should undertake their posts at their peril. If princes overrule them, let them shew the

law, and humbly resign; if fear, gain, or flattery prevail, let them answer it to the law.

354. The prince cannot be preserved, but where the minister is punishable; for people as well as princes, will not endure 'imperium in imperio.'

355. If ministers are weak or ill men, and so spoil their places, it is the prince's fault that chose them; but if their places spoil them, it is their own fault to be made worse by them.

356. It is but just, that those that reign by their princes, should suffer for their princes: for it is a safe and necessary maxim, not to shift heads in government, while the hands are in being that should answer for them.

357. And yet it were intolerable to be a minister of state, if every body may be accuser and judge.

358. Let, therefore, the false accuser no more escape an exemplary punishment, than the guilty minister.

359. For it profanes government to have the credit of the leading men in it subject to vulgar censure, which is often ill-grounded.

360. The safety of a prince, therefore, consists in a well chosen council: and that only can be said to be so, where the persons that compose it are qualified for the business that comes before them.

361. Who would send to a tailor to make a lock, or to a smith to make a suit of clothes?

362. Let there be merchants for trade, seamen for the admiralty, travellers for foreign affairs, some of the leading men of the country for home-business, and common and civil lawyers to advise of legality and right, who should always keep to the strict rules of law.

363. Three things contribute much to ruin government; looseness, oppression, and envy.

364. Where the reins of government are too slack, there the manners of the people are corrupted: and that destroys industry, begets effeminacy, and provokes Heaven against it.

365. Oppression makes a poor country, and a desperate people, who always wait an opportunity to change.

~~366. "He that ruleth over men, must be just, ruling in~~

366. "He that ruleth over men, must be just, ruling in the fear of God;" said an old and wise king.

367. Envy disturbs and distracts government, clogs the wheels, and perplexes the administration: and nothing contributes more to this disorder, than a partial distribution of rewards and punishments in the sovereign.

368. As it is not reasonable that men should be compelled to serve; so those that have employments should not be endured to leave them humorsomely.

369. Where the state intends a man no affront, he should not affront the state.

A PRIVATE LIFE.

370. A private life is to be preferred; the honor and gain of public posts bearing no proportion with the comfort of it. The one is free and quiet, the other servile and noisy.

371. It was a great answer of the Shunamite woman, "I dwell among my own people."

372. They that live of their own, neither need, nor often list, to wear the livery of the public.

373. Their subsistence is not during pleasure, nor have they patrons to please or present.

374. If they are not advanced, neither can they be disgraced; and as they know not the smiles of majesty, so they feel not the frowns of greatness, nor the effects of envy.

375. If they want the pleasures of a court, they also escape the temptations of it.

376. Private men, in fine, are so much their own, that, paying common dues, they are sovereigns of all the rest.

A PUBLIC LIFE.

377. Yet the public must and will be served; and they that do it well, deserve public marks of honor and profit.

378. To do so, men must have public minds, as well as salaries; or they will serve private ends at public cost.

379. Government can never be well administered, but where those entrusted make conscience of well discharging their places.

QUALIFICATIONS.

380. Five things are requisite to a good officer; ability, clean hands, despatch, patience, and impartiality.

CAPACITY.

381. He that understands not his employment, whatever else he knows, must be unfit for it; and the public suffer by his inexpertness.

382. They that are able should be just too; or the government may be the worst for their capacity.

CLEAN HANDS.

383. Covetousness in such men, prompts them to prostitute the public for gain.

384. The taking of a bribe, or gratuity, should be punished with as severe penalties as the defrauding of the state.

385. Let men have sufficient salaries, and exceed them at their peril.

386. It is a dishonor to government, that its officers should live on benevolence; as it ought to be infamous for officers to dishonor the public, by being twice paid for the same business.

387. But to be paid and not do business, is rank oppression.

DESPATCH.

388. Despatch is a great and good quality in an officer, where duty, not gain, excites it. But of this too many make their private market, and overplus to their wages. Thus the salary is for doing and the bribe for despatching the business; as if business could be done before it was despatched; or they were to be paid apart, one by the government, the other by the party.

389. Despatch is as much the duty of an officer, as doing; and very much the honor of the government he serves.

390. Delays have been more injurious than direct injustice.

391. They too often starve those they dare not deny.

392. The very winner is made a loser, because he pays twice for his own; like those that purchase estates, mortgaged before to the full value.

393. Our law says well, 'To delay justice, is injustice.

394. Not to have a right, and not to come at it, differ little.

395. Refusal, or despatch, is the duty and wisdom of a good officer.

PATIENCE.

396. Patience is a virtue every where; but it shines with greatest lustre in the men of government.

397. Some are so proud or testy, they will not hear what they should redress.

398. Others are so weak, they sink or burst, under the weight of their office; though they can lightly run away with the salary of it.

399. Business can never be well done, that is not well understood; which cannot be without patience.

400. It is cruelty, indeed, not to give the unhappy a hearing, when we ought to help; but it is the top of oppression to brow beat the humble and modest miserable, when they seek relief.

401. Some, it is true, are unreasonable in their desires and hopes; but then we should inform, not rail at and reject them.

402. It is, therefore, as great an instance of wisdom as a man in business can give, to be patient under the impertinences and contradictions that attend it.

403. Method goes far to prevent trouble in business; for it makes the task easy, hinders confusion, saves abundance of time, and instructs those that have business depending, what to do, and what to hope.

IMPARTIALITY.

404. Impartiality, though it be the last, is not the least part of the character of a good magistrate.

405. It is noted as fault in holy writ, even to regard the poor in judgment; how much more the rich?

406. If our compassion must not sway us: less should our fears, profits, or prejudices.

407. Justice is justly represented blind, because she sees no difference in the parties concerned.

408. She has but one scale and weight, for rich and poor, great and small.

409. Her sentence is not guided by the person, but the cause.

410. The impartial judge, in judgment, knows nothing but the law; the prince, no more than the peasant; his kindred, than a stranger. Nay, his enemy is sure to be on equal terms with his friend, when he is upon the bench.

411. Impartiality is the life of justice, as that is of government.

412. Nor is it only a benefit to the state: for private families cannot subsist comfortably without it.

413. Parents that are partial, are ill obeyed by their children; and partial masters not better served by their servants.

414. Partiality is always indirect, if not dishonest: for it shows a bias, where reason would have none; if not an injury, which justice every where forbids.

415. As it makes favorites without reason, so it uses no reason in judging of actions: confirming the proverb, 'The crow thinks her own bird the fairest.'

416. What some sees to be no fault in one, they will have criminal in another.

417. Nay, how ugly do our failings look to us in the persons of others; which yet we see not in ourselves.

418. And but too common it is, for some people not to know their own maxims and principles in the mouths of other men, when they give occasion to use them.

419. Partiality corrupts our judgment of persons and things, of ourselves and others.

420. It contributes more than any thing, to factions in the government, and feuds in families.

421. It is a prodigal passion, that seldom returns till it is hunger-bit, and disappointments bring it within bounds.

422. And yet we may be indifferent to a fault.

INDIFFERENCE.

423. Indifference is good in judgment, but bad in relation, and stark naught in religion.

424. And even in judgment, our indifference must be to the persons, not causes; for one, to be sure, is right.

NEUTRALITY.

425. Neutrality is something else than indifference; and yet of kin to it too.

426. A judge ought, to be indifferent; and yet he cannot be said to be neutral.

427. The one being, to be even in judgment, and the other not to meddle at all.

428. And where it is lawful, to be sure, it is best to be neutral.

429. He that espouses parties, can hardly divorce himself from their fate; and more fall with their party than rise with it.

430. A wise neuter joins with neither, but uses both, as his honest interest leads him.

431. A neuter only has room to be a peace maker; for being of neither side, he has the means of meditating a reconciliation of both.

A PARTY.

432. And yet where right or religion gives a call, a neuter must be a coward or a hypocrite.

433. In such cases we should never be backward; nor yet mistaken.

434. When our right or religion is in question, then is the fittest time to assert it.

435. Nor must we always be neutral, where our neighbor is concerned: for though meddling is a fault, helping is a duty.

436. We have a call to do good, as often as we have the power and occasion.

437. If Heathens could say, 'We are not born for ourselves;' surely Christians should practise it.

438. They are taught so by his example, as well as doctrine, from whom they have borrowed their name.

OSTENTATION.

439. Do what good thou canst unknown; and be not vain of what ought rather to be felt than seen.

440. The humble, in the parable of the day of judgment, forgot their good works, "Lord when we did so and so?"

441. He that does good for good's sake, seeks neither praise nor reward, though sure of both at last.

COMPLETE VIRTUE.

442. Content not thyself that thou art virtuous in the general; for one link being wanting, the chain is defective.

443. Perhaps thou art rather innocent than virtuous, and owest more to thy constitution than to thy religion.

444. To be innocent is to be not guilty; but to be virtuous is to overcome our evil inclinations.

445. If thou hast not conquered thyself in that which is thy own particular weakness, thou hast no title to virtue, though thou art free of other men's.

446. For a covetous man to inveigh against prodigality, an atheist against idolatry, a tyrant against rebellion, or a liar against forgery, and a drunkard against intemperance, is vice reproving viciousness.

447. Such a reproof would have but little success, because it would carry but little authority with it.

448. If thou wouldst conquer thy weakness, thou must never gratify it.

449. No man is compelled to evil; his consent only makes it his.

450. It is no sin to be tempted, but to be overcome.

451. What man, in his right mind, would conspire his own hurt? Men are beside themselves, when they transgress against their convictions.

452. If thou wouldst not sin, do not desire: and if thou wouldst not lust, do not embrace the temptation: no, not look at it, nor think of it.

453. Thou wouldst take much pains to save thy body: take some, prithee, to save thy soul.

RELIGION.

454. Religion is the fear of God, and its demonstration good works; and faith is the root of both: "For without faith we cannot please God;" nor can we fear what we do not believe.

455. The devils also believe and know abundance; but in this is the difference, their faith works not by love, nor their knowledge by obedience; and therefore they are never the better for them. And if ours be such, we shall be of their church, not of Christ's; for as the head is, so must the body be.

456. He was holy, humble, harmless, meek, merciful, &c., when among us; to teach us what we should be when he was gone; and yet he is among us still, and in us too, a living and perpetual preacher of the same grace, by his spirit in our consciences.

457. A minister of the gospel ought to be one of Christ's making, if he would pass for one of Christ's ministers.

458. And if he be one of his making, he knows and does, as well as believes.

459. That, minister, whose life is not the model of his doctrine, is a babbler rather than a preacher, a quack rather than a physician of value.

460. Of old time, they were made ministers by the Holy Ghost: and the more that is an ingredient now, the fitter they are for that work.

461. Running streams are not so apt to corrupt as stagnant waters; nor itinerant, as settled preachers; but they are not to run before they are sent.

462. As they freely receive from Christ, so they give.

463. They will not make that a trade, which they know ought not, in conscience, to be one.

464. Yet there is no fear of their living, that design not to live by it.

465. The humble and true teacher meets with more than he expects.

466. He accounts content with godliness great gain, and therefore seeks not to make a gain of godliness.

467. As the ministers of Christ are made by him, and are like him, so they beget people into the same likeness.

468. To be like Christ, then, is to be a christian. And regeneration is the only way to the kingdom of God, which we pray for.

469. Let us to day, therefore, hear his voice, and not harden our hearts who speaks to us many ways: in the scriptures, in our hearts, by his servants and providences; and the sum of all his holiness, and charity.

470. St. James gives a short draught of the matter, but very full and teaching: "Pure religion, and undefiled before God the Father, is this, to visit the fatherless and the widows in their afflictions, and to keep ourselves unspotted from the world;" which is comprised in these two words, charity and piety.

471. They that truly make these their aim, will find them their attainment; and, with them, the peace that follows so excellent a condition.

472. Amuse not thyself, therefore, with the numerous opinions of the world; nor value thyself upon verbal orthodoxy, philosophy, or thy skill in tongues, or knowledge of the fathers; (too much the business and vanity of the world) but in this rejoice, "That thou knowest God, that is the Lord, who exerciseth loving kindness, and judgment, and righteousness in the earth."

473. Public worship is very commendable, if well performed. We owe it to God and good example. But we must know, that God is not tied to time or place, who is every where at the same time; and this we shall know as far as we are capable, if, wherever we are, our desires are to be with him.

474. Serving God, people generally confine to the acts of public and private worship; and those the more zealous do often repent, in hopes of acceptance.

475. But if we consider that God is an infinite spirit, and as such, everywhere; and that our Saviour has taught us, that he will be worshipped in spirit and in truth, we shall see the shortness of such a notion.

476. For serving God concerns the frame of our spirits,

in the whole course of our lives; in every occasion we have, in which we may show our love to his law.

477. For as men in battle are continually in the way of shot, so we in this world, are ever within the reach of temptation; and herein do we serve God, if we avoid what we are forbid, as well as do what he commands.

478. God is better served in resisting a temptation to evil, than in many formal prayers.

479. This is but twice or thrice a day; but that every hour and moment of the day. So much more is our continual watch, than our evening and morning devotion.

480. Wouldst thou then serve God? Do not that alone, which thou wouldst not that another should see thee do.

481. Do not take God's name in vain, nor disobey thy parents, nor wrong thy neighbor, nor commit adultery, even in thy heart.

482. Neither be vain, lascivious, proud, drunken, revengeful, or angry· nor lie, detract, backbite, overreach oppress, deceive, or betray; but watch vigorously against all temptation to these things, as knowing that God is present, the overseer of all thy ways and most inward thoughts, and the avenger of his own law upon the disobedient; and thou wilt acceptably serve God.

483 Is it not reason, if we expect the acknowledgments of those to whom we are bountiful, that we should reverently pay ours to God, our most munificent and constant benefactor?

484. The world represents a rare and sumptuous palace; mankind the great family in it; and God, the mighty Lord and Master of it.

485. We are all sensible what a stately seat it is; the heavens adorned with so many glorious luminaries; and the earth with groves, plains, valleys, hills, fountains, ponds, lakes, and rivers; and variety of fruits and creatures for food, pleasure and profit; in short, how noble a house he keeps, and the plenty, and variety, and excellency of his table; his orders, seasons, and suitableness of every time and thing. But we must be as sensible, or at least ought to be, what careless and idle servants we are, and how short and disproportionable our behaviour is to

his bounty and goodness; how long he bears, how often he reprieves, and forgives us; who, notwithstanding our breach of promises, and repeated neglects, has not yet been provoked to break up house, and send us to shift for ourselves. Should not this great goodness raise a due sense in us of our undutifulness, and a resolution to alter our course, and mend our manners; that we may be for the future more worthy communicants at our Maker's good and great table? Especially, since it is not more certain that we deserve his displeasure, than that we shall feel it, if we continue to be unprofitable servants.

486. But though God has replenished this world with abundance of good things for man's life and comfort, yet they are all but imperfect goods. He only is the perfect good to whom they point. But alas! men cannot see him for them; though they should always see him in them.

487. I have often wondered at the unaccountableness of man in this, among other things; that, though he loves changes so well, he should care so little to hear or think of his last, great, and, if he pleases, his best, change.

488. Being, as to our bodies composed of changeable elements, we, with the world, are made up of, and subsist by revolution; but our souls being of another and nobler nature, we should seek our rest in a more enduring habitation.

489. The truest end of life is to know the life that never ends.

490. He that makes this his care will find it his crown at last.

491. Life else were a misery, rather than a pleasure; a judgment not a blessing.

492. For, to know, regret, and resent, to desire, hope, and fear, more than a beast, and not live beyond him, is to make a man less than a beast.

493. It is the amends of a short and troublesome life, that doing good, and suffering ill, entitle man to one longer and better.

494. This ever raises the good man's hope, and gives him tastes beyond this world.

495. As it is his aim, so none else can hit the mark.

496. Many make it their speculation, but it is the good man's practice.

497. His work keeps pace with his life, and so leaves nothing to be done when he dies.

498. And he that lives to live for ever, never fears dying.

499. Nor can the means be terrible to him that heartily believes the end.

500. For though death be a dark passage, it leads to immortaliy ; and that is recompense enough for suffering of it.

501. And yet faith lights us, even through the grave; being the evidence of things not seen.

502. And this is the comfort of the good, that the grave cannot hold them and that they live as soon as they die.

503. For death is no more than a turning of us over from time to eternity.

504. Nor can there be a revolution without it; for it supposes the dissolution of one form in order to the succession of another.

505. Death, then, being the way and condition of life, we cannot love to live, if we cannot bear to die.

506. Let us, then, not cozen ourselves with the shells and husks of things; nor prefer form to power, nor shadows to substance : pictures of bread will not satisfy hunger, nor those of devotion please God.

507. This world is a form ; our bodies are forms ; and no visible acts of devotion can be without forms. But yet the less form in religion the better, since God is a spirit ; for the more mental our worship, the more adequate to the nature of God ; the more silent, the more suitable to the language of a spirit.

508. Words are for others, not for ourselves : nor for God, who hears not as bodies do, but as spirits should.

509. If we would know this dialect, we must learn of the divine principle in us. As we hear the dictates of that, so God hears us.

510. There we may see him too in all his attributes ; though but in little, yet as much as we can apprehend or bear : for as he is in himself, he is incomprehensible, and

"dwelleth in that light no eye can approach." But in his image we may behold his glory: enough to exalt our apprehensions of God, and to instruct us in that worship which pleaseth him.

511. Men may tire themselves in a labyrinth of search, and talk of God; but if we would know him indeed, it must be from the impressions we receive of him: and the softer our hearts are, the deeper and livelier those will be upon us.

512. If he has made us sensible of his justice, by his reproof; of his patience, by his forbearance; of his mercy, by his forgiveness; of his holiness, by the sanctification of our hearts through his spirit; we have a grounded knowledge of God. This is experience, that speculation; this enjoyment, that report. In short, this is undeniable evidence, with the realities of religion, and will stand all winds and weathers.

513. As our faith, so our devotion, should be lively. Cold meat will not serve at those repasts.

514. It is a coal from God's altar must kindle our fire: and without fire, true fire, no acceptable sacrifice.

515. "Open thou my lips, and then" said the royal prophet, "my mouth shall praise God." But not till then.

516. The preparation of the heart, as well as the answer of the tongue, is of the Lord: and to have it, our prayers must be powerful, and our worship grateful.

517. Let us choose, therefore, to commune, where there is the warmest sense of religion; where devotion exceeds formality, and practice most corresponds with profession; and where there is, at least, as much charity as zeal: for where this society is to be found, there shall we find the church of God.

518. As good, so ill men, are all of a church: and every body knows who must be head of it.

519. The humble, meek, merciful, just, pious, and devout souls, are every where of one religion; and when death has taken off the mask, they will know one another, though the diverse liveries they wear here make them strangers.

520. Great allowances are made for education and per-

sonal weaknesses; but it is a rule with me, 'That man is truly religious, that loves the persuasion he is of for the piety, rather than the ceremony of it.'

521. They that have one end, can hardly disagree when they meet. At least their concern in the greater, moderates their value for, and difference about, the lesser things.

522. It is a sad reflection, that many men hardly have any religion at all, and most men have none of their own; for that which is the religion of their education, and not of their judgment, is the religion of another, and not theirs.

523. To have religion upon authority, and not upon conviction, is like a finger-watch, to be set forwards or backwards, as he pleases that has it in keeping.

524. It is a preposterous thing, that men can venture their souls, where they will not venture their money: for they will take their religion upon trust, but not trust a synod about the goodness of half a crown.

525. They will follow their own judgment when their money is concerned, whatever they do for their souls.

526. But, to be sure, that religion cannot be right, that a man is the worse for having.

527. No religion, is better than an unnatural one.

528. Grace perfects, but never sours or spoils, nature.

529. To be unnatural in defence of grace is a contradiction.

530. Hardly any thing looks worse than to defend religion by ways that show it has no credit with us.

531. A devout man is one thing, a stickler is quite another.

532. When our minds exceed their just bounds, we must not discredit what we would recommend.

533. To be furious in religion is to be irreligiously religious.

534. If he that is without bowels is not a man; how, then, can he be a Christian?

535. It were better to be of no church, than to be bitter for any.

536. Bitterness comes very near to enmity, and that is Beelzebub; because the perfection of wickedness.

537. A good end cannot sanctify evil means ; nor must we ever do evil that good may come of it.

538. Some folks think they may scold, rail, hate, rob, and kill too ; so it be but for God's sake.

539. But nothing in us unlike him can please him.

540. It is a great presumption to send onr passions upon God's errands, as it is to palliate them with God's name.

541. Zeal dropt in charity, is good ; without it, good for nothing : for it devours all it comes near.

542. They may first judge themselves, that presume to censure others ; and such will not be apt to over-shoot the mark.

543. We are too ready to retaliate, rather than forgive, or gain by love and information.

544. And yet we could hurt no man that we believe loves us.

545. Let us, then, try what love will do ; for if men do once see that we love them, we should soon find they would not harm us.

546. Force may subdue, but love gains ; and he that forgives first, wins the laurel.

547. If I am even with my enemy, the debt is paid ; but if I forgive it, I oblige him for ever.

548. Love is the hardest lesson in christianity ; but, for that reason, it should be most our care to learn it. 'Difficilia quæ pulchra.'

549. It is a severe rebuke upon us, that God makes us so many allowances, and we make so few to our neighbor : as if charity had nothing to do with religion ; or love with faith, that ought to work by it.

550. I find all sorts of people agree, whatsoever were their animosities, when humbled by the approaches of death ; then they forgive, then they pray for, and love one another : which shows us, that it is not our reason, but our passion, that makes and holds up the feuds that reign among men in their health and fullness. They, therefore, that live nearest to that state in which they should die, must certainly live the best.

551. Did we believe a final reckoning and judgment,

or did we think enough of what we do believe, we should allow more love in religion than we do: since religion itself is nothing else but love to God and man.

552. "He that lives in love, lives in God." says the beloved disciple: and, to be sure, a man can live no where better.

553. It is most reasonable men should value that benefit which is most durable. Now tongues shall cease, and prophecy fail, and faith shall be consummated in sight, and hope in enjoyment; but love remains.

554. Love is indeed heaven upon earth; since heaven above would not be heaven without it; for where there is not love, there is fear; but, "Perfect love casts out fear." And yet we naturally fear most to offend what we most love.

555. What we love, we will hear; what we love, we will trust: and what we love, we will serve, aye, and suffer for too. "If you love me," says our blessed Redeemer, "keep my commandments." Why? Why then, he will love us: then we shall be his friends; then he will send us the Comforter; then whatever we ask we shall receive; and then, where he is we shall be also, and that for ever. Behold, the fruits of love; the power, virtue, benefit, and beauty of love!

556. Love is above all; and when it prevails in us all, we shall all be lovely, and in love with God, and one with another. Amen.

THE RIGHT MORALIST.

557. A right moralist is a great and good man; but for that reason, he is rarely to be found.

558. There are a sort of people that are fond of the character, who, in my opinion, have but little title to it.

559. They think it enough, not to defraud a man of his pay, or betray his friend; but never consider, that the law forbids the one at his peril, and that virtue is seldom the reason of the other.

560. But certainly, he that covets can no more be a moral man, than he that steals; since he does it so in his mind. Nor can he be one that robs his neighbor of his credit, or that craftily undermines him of his trade or office.

561. If a man pays his tailor, but debauches his wife, is he a current moralist?

562. But what shall we say of the man that rebels against his father, is an ill husband, or an abusive neighbor; one that is lavish of his time, of his health, and of his estate, in which his family is so nearly concerned? Must he go for a right moralist, because he pays his rent well?

563. I would ask some of those men of morals, whether he that robs God, and himself too, though he should not defraud his neighbor, be the moral man?

564. Do I owe myself nothing? And do I not owe all to God? And if paying what we owe makes the moral man, is it not fit we should begin to render our dues where we owe our very beginning; aye, our all?

565. The complete moralist begins with God; he gives him his due, his heart, his love, his service: the bountiful giver of his well being, as well as being.

566. He that lives without a sense of this dependence and obligation, cannot be a moral man, because he does not know his returns of love and obedience, as becomes an honest and sensible creature: which very term implies he is not his own; and it cannot be very honest to misemploy another's goods.

567. But now! can there be no debt to a fellow creature? Or, will our exactness in paying those trifling ones, while we neglect our weightier obligations, cancel the bonds we lie under, and render us right and thorough moralists?

568. As judgments are paid before bonds, and bonds before bills or book-debts; so the moralist considers his obligations according to their several dignities. In the first place, him to whom he owes himself. Next, himself, in his health and livelihood. Lastly, his other obligations, whether rational or pecuniary; doing to others, to the extent of his ability, as he would have them do unto him.

569. In short, the moral man is he that loves God above all, and his neighbor as himself; which fulfils both tables at once.

THE WORLD'S ABLE MAN.

570. It is by some thought the character of an able man, to be dark, and not understood. But I am sure that is not fair play.

571. If he be so by silence, it is better; but if by disguises, it is insincere and hateful.

572. Secrecy is one thing, false lights are another.

573. The honest man that is rather free than open, is ever to be preferred: especially when sense is at the helm.

574. The glorying of the other humor is in a vice: for it is not human to be cold, dark, and unconversable. I was going to say, they are like pickpockets in a crowd, where a man must ever have his hand on his purse: or as spies in a garrison, that, if not prevented, betray it.

575. They are the reverse of human nature; and yet this is the present world's wise man and politician.

576. Like highwaymen, that rarely rob without vizards, or in the same wigs and clothes, but have a dress for every enterprise.

577. At best, he may be a cunning man, which is a sort of lurcher in politics.

578. He is never too hard for the wise man upon the square; for that is out of his element, and puts him quite by his skill. Nor are wise men ever catched by him, but when they trust him.

579. But as cold and close as he seems, he can and will please all, if he gets by it; though it should neither please God nor himself at bottom.

580. He is for every cause that brings him gain; but implacable, if disappointed of success.

581. And what he cannot hinder, he will be sure to spoil by over-doing it.

582. None are so zealous then as he, for that which he cannot abide.

583. What is it he will not, or cannot do, to hide his true sentiments?

584. For his interest he refuses no side or party; and will take the wrong by the hand, when the other will not do, with as good a grace as the right.

585. Nay, he commonly chooses the worst, because that brings the best bribe; his cause being ever money.

586. He sails with all winds, and is never out of his way, where any thing is to be had.

587. A privateer, indeed, and every where a bird of prey.

588. True to nothing but himself: and false to all persons and parties, to serve his own turn.

589. Talk with him as often as you please, he will never pay you in good coin; for it is either false or clipped.

590. But to give a false reason for any thing, let my reader never learn of him, no more than to give a brass half crown for a good one: not only because it is not true, but because it deceives the person to whom it is given: which I take to be an immorality.

591. Silence is much preferable; for it saves the secret, as well as the person's honor.

592. Such as give themselves the latitude of saying what they do not mean, come to be arrant jockeys at more things than one: but in religion and politics it is pernicious.

593. To hear two men talk the reverse of their own sentiments, with all the good breeding and appearance of friendship imaginable, on purpose to cozen or pump each other, is, to a man of virtue and honor, one of the most melancholy, as well as most nauseous things in the world.

594. But that it should be the character of an able man, is to disinherit wisdom, and paint out our degeneracy to the life, by setting up fraud, an arrant impostor, in her room.

595. The trial of skill between these two is, who shall believe least of what the other says; and he that has the weakness or good nature, to give out first, (viz. to believe any thing the other says) is looked upon to be tricked.

596. I cannot see the policy, any more than the necessity, of a man's mind giving the lie to his mouth; or his mouth giving false alarms of his mind: for no man can be long believed, that teachss all men to distrust him; and since the ablest have sometimes need of credit, where lies the advantage of their politic cant or banter upon mankind?

597. I remember a passage of one of queen Elizabeth's great men, as advice to his friend: 'The advantage,' says, he, 'I had upon others at court, was, that I always spoke as I thought; which being not believed by them, I both preserved a good conscience, and suffered no damage from that freedom:' which, as it shows the vice to be older than our times, so does it that gallant man's integrity to be the best way of avoiding it.

598. To be sure it is wise, as well as honest, neither to flatter other men's sentiments, nor dissemble, and less to contradict, our own.

599. To hold one's tongue, or to speak truth, or talk only of indifferent things, is the fairest conversation.

600. Women that rarely go abroad without vizard masks, have none of the best reputation. But when we consider what all this art and disguise are for, it equally heightens the wise man's wonder and aversion; perhaps it is to betray a father, a brother, a master, a friend, a neighbor, or one's own party.

601. A fine conquest! what noble Grecians and Romans abhorred; as if government could not subsist without knavery, and that knaves were the most useful props to it; though the basest, as well as greatest, perversions of the ends of it.

602. But that it should become a maxim, shows but too grossly the corruptions of the times.

603. I confess I have heard the stile of 'An useful knave,' but ever took it to be a silly or a knavish saying; at least, an excuse of knavery.

604. It is as reasonable to think a loose woman makes the best wife, as a knave the best officer.

605. Beside, employing knaves encourages knavery, instead of punishing it, and alienates the reward of virtue; or at least, must make the world believe the country yields not honest men enough, able to serve her.

606. Art thou a magistrate? Prefer such as have clean characters where they live; and men of estates to secure a just discharge of their trusts, that are under no temptation to strain points for a fortune: for sometimes such may be found sooner than they are employed.

607. Art thou a private man? Contract thy acquaintance in a narrow compass, and choose those for the subjects of it that are men of principle; such as will make full stops, where honor will not lead them on: and that had rather bear the disgrace of not being thorough-paced men, than forfeit their peace and reputation by a base compliance.

THE WISE MAN.

608. The wise man governs himself by the reason of his case, and because what he does is best: best, in a moral and prudent, not a sinister sense.

609. He proposes just ends, and employs the fairest and most probable means and methods to attain them.

610. Though you cannot always penetrate his design, or his reasons for it, yet you shall ever see his actions of a piece, and his performance like a workman: they will bear the touch of wisdom and honor, as often as they are tried.

611. He scorns to serve himself by indirect means, or to be an interloper in government; since just enterprises never want any unjust ways to make them succeed.

612. To do evil that good may come of it, is for bunglers, in politics as well as morals.

613. Like those surgeons that will cut off an arm that they cannot cure, to hide their ignorance and save their credit.

614. The wise man is cautious, but not cunning; judicious, but not crafty; making virtue the measure of using his excellent understanding in the conduct of his life.

615. The wise man is equal, ready, but not officious; has in every thing an eye to surefooting; he offends no body, nor is easily offended; and is always willing to compound for wrongs, if not forgive them.

616. He is never captious nor critical; hates banter and jests; he may be pleasant but not light; he never deals but in substantial ware, and leaves the rest for the toy-pates, (or shops) of the world; which are so far from being his business, that they are not so much as his diversion.

617. He is always for some solid good, civil or moral:

as to make his country more virtuous, preserve her peace and liberty, employ her poor, improve land, advance trade, suppress vice, encourage industry, and all mechanical knowledge; and that they should be the care of the government, and the blessing and praise of the people.

618. To conclude, he is just, and fears God, hates covetousness, and eschews evil, and loves his neighbor as himself.

OF THE GOVERNMENT OF THOUGHTS.

619. Man being made a reasonable, and so a thinking creature, there is nothing more worthy of his being, than the right direction and employment of his thoughts: since upon this depends both his usefulness to the public, and his own present and future benefit in all respects.

620. The consideration of this has often obliged me to lament the unhappiness of mankind, that, through too great a mixture and confusion of thoughts, have hardly been able to make a right or mature judgment of things.

621. To this is owing the various uncertainty and confusion we see in the world, and the intemperate zeal that occasions them.

622. To this, also is to be attributed the imperfect knowledge we have of things, and the slow progress we make in attaining to a better; like the children of Israel, that were forty years upon their journey from Egypt to Canaan, which might have been performed in less than one.

623. In fine, it is to this we ought to ascribe, if not all, at least most of the infelicities we labor under.

624. Clear, therefore, thy head, and rally and manage thy thoughts rightly, and thou wilt save time, and see and do thy business well: for thy judgment will be distinct, thy mind free, and thy faculties strong and regular.

625. Always remember to bound thy thoughts to the present occasion.

626. If it be thy religious duty, suffer nothing else to share in them. And if any civil or temporal affair, observe the same caution, and, thou wilt be a whole man to every thing, and do twice the business in the same time.

627. If any point over-labors thy mind, divert and re-

lieve it by some other subject, of a more sensible or manual nature, rather than what may affect the understanding: for this were to write one thing upon another, which blots out our former impressions, or renders them illegible.

628. They that are least divided in their care, always give the best account of their business.

629. As, therefore, thou art always to pursue the present subject till thou hast mastered it, so if it fall out that thou hast more affairs than one upon thy hands, be sure to prefer that which is of most moment, and will least wait thy leisure.

630. He that judges not well of the importance of his affairs, though he may be always busy, must make but a small progress.

631. But make not more business necessary than is so; rather lessen than augment work for thyself.

632. Nor yet be over eager in the pursuit of any thing; for the mercurial too often happen to leave judgment behind them, and sometimes make work for repentance.

633. He that over-runs his business, leaves it for him that follows more leisurely to take it up: which has often proved a profitable harvest to them that never sowed.

634. It is the advantage that slower tempers have upon the men of lively parts, that though they do not lead, they will follow well, and glean clean.

635. Upon the whole matter, employ thy thoughts as thy business requires, and let that have place according to merit and urgency, giving every thing a review and due digestion; and thou wilt prevent many errors and vexations, as well as save much time to thyself in the course of thy life.

OF ENVY.

636. It is the mark of ill nature, to lessen good actions, and aggravate ill ones.

637. Some men do as much begrudge others a good name, as they want one themselves: and perhaps that is the reason of it.

638. But certainly they are in the wrong that can think they are lessened, because others have their due.

639. Such people generally have less merit than ambition, that covet the reward of other men's; and, to be sure, a very ill nature, that will rather rob others of their due, than allow them their praise.

640. It is more an error of our will than our judgment: for we know it to be an effect of our passion, not our reason; and therefore we are the more culpable in our partial estimates.

641. It is as envious as unjust, to underrate another's actions, where their intrinsic worth recommends them to disengaged minds.

642. Nothing shews more the folly, as well as fraud of man, than clipping merit and reputation.

643. And as some men think it an alloy to themselves, that others have their right; so they know no end of pilfering, to raise their own credit.

644. This envy is the child of pride; and mis-gives rather than mis-takes.

645. It will have charity to be ostentation; sobriety, covetousness; humility, craft; bounty, popularity. In short, virtue must be design, and religion only interest. Nay, the best of qualities must not pass without a 'but' to alloy their merit, and abate their praise. Basest of tempers! and they that have it, the worst of men.

646. But just and noble minds rejoice in other men's success, and help to augment their praise.

647. And, indeed they are not without a love to virtue, that take a satisfaction in seeing her rewarded; and such deserve to share her character, that do abhor to lessen it.

OF MAN'S LIFE.

648. Why is man less durable than the works of his hands, but because this is not the place of his rest.

649. And it is a great and just reproach upon him, that he should fix his mind where he cannot stay himself.

650. Were it not more his wisdom to be concerned about those works that will go with him, and erect a mansion for him, where time has power neither over him nor it?

651. It is a sad thing for a man so often to miss his way to his best, as well as most lasting home.

OF AMBITION.

652. They that soar too high, often fall hard; which makes a low and level dwelling preferable.

653. The tallest trees are most in the power of the winds; and ambitious men of the blasts of fortune.

654. They are most seen and observed, and most envied; least quiet, but most talked of, and not often to their advantage.

655. Those buildings had need of a good foundation, that lie so much exposed to weather.

656. Good works are a rock that will support their credit; but ill ones, a sandy foundation that yields to calamities.

657. And truly they ought to expect no pity in their fall, who, when in power, had no bowels for the unhappy.

658. The worst of distempers; always craving and thirsty, restless and hated; a perfect delirium in the mind; insufferable in success, and in disappointments most revengeful.

OF PRAISE OR APPLAUSE.

659. We are apt to love praise, but not to deserve it.

660. But if we would deserve it, we must love virtue more than that.

661. As there is no passion in us sooner moved, or more deceivable, so, for that reason, there is none over which we ought to be more watchful, whether we give or receive it: for if we give it, we must be sure to mean it, and measure it too.

662. If we are penurious it shews emulation; if we exceed, flattery.

663. Good measure belongs to good actions; more, looks nauseous, as well as insincere: besides, it is persecuting the meritorious, who is out of countenance to hear what he deserves.

664. It is much easier for him to merit applause, than hear of it: and he never doubts himself more, or the person that gives it, than when he hears so much of it.

665. But, to say true, there need not many cautions on

this hand; since the world is rarely just enough to the deserving.

666. However, we cannot be too circumspect how we receive praise: for if we contemplate ourselves in a false glass, we are sure to be mistaken about our dues: and because we are too apt to believe what is pleasing, rather than what is true, we may be too easily swelled beyond our just proportion, by the windy compliments of men.

667. Make ever, therefore, allowances for what is said on such occasions; or thou exposest, as well as deceivest thyself.

668. For an over value of ourselves, gives us but a dangerous security in many respects.

669. We expect more than belongs to us; take all that is given us, though never meant us; and fall out with those that are not so full of us as we are of ourselves.

670. In short, it is a passion that abuses our judgment, and makes us both unsafe and ridiculous.

671. Be not fond, therefore, of praise; but seek virtue that leads to it.

672. And yet no more lessen or dissemble thy merit, than over-rate it; for, though humility be a virtue, an affected one is none.

OF CONDUCT IN SPEECH.

673. Inquire often, but judge rarely, and thou wilt not often be mistaken.

674. It is safer to learn than to teach; and he who conceals his opinion has nothing to answer for.

675. Vanity or resentment often engages us, and it is two to one but we come off losers; for one shews a want of judgment and humility, as the other does of temper and discretion.

676. Not that I admire the reserved; for they are next to unnatural that are not communicable. But if reservedness be at any time a virtue, it is in throngs, or ill company.

677. Beware also of affectation in speech: it often wrongs matter, and ever shows a blind side.

678. Speak properly, and in as few words as you can,

but always plainly: for the end of speech is not ostentation, but to be understood.

679. They that affect words more than matter will dry up that little they have.

680. Sense never fails to give them that have it, words enough to make themselves understood.

681. But it too often happens in some conversations, as in apothecaries shops, that those pots that are empty, or have things of small value in them, are as gaudily dressed and flourished as those that are full of precious drugs.

682. This laboring of slight matter with flourished turns of expression is fulsome; and worse than the modern imitation of tapestry, and East-India goods, in stuffs and linens. In short, it is but tawdry talk, and next to very trash.

UNION OF FRIENDS.

683. They that love beyond the world cannot be separated by it.

684. Death cannot kill what never dies.

685. Nor can spirits ever be divided, that love and live in the same divine principle, the root and record, of their friendship.

686. If absence be not death, neither is theirs.

687. Death is but crossing the world, as friends do the seas; they live in one another still.

688. For they must needs be present that love and live in that which is omnipresent.

689. In this divine glass they see face to face; and their converse is free as well as pure.

690. This is the comfort of friends, that though they may be said to die, yet their friendship and society are, in the best sense, ever present, because immortal.

ON BEING EASY IN LIVING.

691. It is a happiness to be delivered from a curious mind, as well as from a dainty palate.

692. For it is not only a troublesome but slavish thing to be nice.

693. They narrow their own freedom and comforts, that make so much requisite to enjoy them.

694. To be easy in living is much of the pleasure of life; but difficult tempers will always want it.

695. A careless and homely breeding is therefore preferable to one nice and delicate.

696. And he that is taught to live upon little, owes more to his father's wisdom, than he that has a great deal left him, does to his father's care.

697. Children cannot well be too hardily bred: for besides that it fits them to bear the roughest providences, it is more active and healthy.

698. Nay, it is certain, that the liberty of the mind is mightily preserved by it; for so it is served, instead of being a servant, indeed a slave, to sensual delicacies.

699. As nature is soon answered, so are such satisfied.

700. The memory of the ancients is hardly in any thing more to be celebrated, than in a strict and useful instruction of youth.

701. By labor they prevented luxury in their young people, till wisdom and philosophy had taught them to resist and despise it.

702. It must be therefore a gross fault to strive so hard for the pleasure of our bodies, and be so insensible and careless of the freedom of our souls.

OF MAN'S INCONSIDERATENESS AND PARTIALITY.

703. It is very observable, if our civil rights are invaded or encroached upon, we are mightily touched, and fill every place with our resentment and complaint; while we suffer ourselves, our better and nobler selves, to be the property and vassals of sin, the worst of invaders.

704. In vain do we expect to be delivered from such troubles, till we are delivered from the cause of them, our disobedience to God.

705. When he has his dues from us, it will be time enough for him to give us ours out of one another.

706. It is our great happiness if we could understand it, that we meet with such checks in the career of our worldly enjoyments: lest we should forget the giver, adore

the gift, and terminate our felicity here, which is not man's ultimate bliss.

707. Our losses are often made judgments by our guilt, and mercies by our repentance.

708. Besides, it argues great folly in men to let their satisfaction exceed the true value of any temporal matter: for disappointments are not always to be measured by the loss of the thing, but the over-value we put upon it.

709. And thus men improve their own miseries, for want of an equal and just estimate of what they enjoy or lose.

710. There lies a proviso upon every thing in this world, and we must observe it at our own peril, viz. to love God above all, and act for judgment; the last I mean.

OF THE RULE OF JUDGING:

711. In all things reason should prevail: it is quite another thing to be stiff, than steady in an opinion.

712. This may be reasonable, but that is ever wilful.

713. In such cases, it always happens, that the clearer the argument, the greater the obstinacy, where the design is not to be convinced.

714. This is to value humor more than truth, and prefer a sullen pride to a reasonable submission.

715. It is the glory of a man to vail to truth; as it is the mark of a good nature to be easily entreated.

716. Beasts act by sense, man should act by reason; else he is a greater beast than ever God made: and the proverb is verified, 'The corruption of the best things is the worst and most offensive.'

717. A reasonable opinion must ever be in danger where reason is not judge.

718. Though there is a regard due to education, and the tradition of our fathers, truth will ever deserve, as well as claim the preference.

719. If, like Theophilus and Timothy, we have been brought up in the knowledge of the best thing, it is our advantage; but neither they nor we lose by trying the truth; for so we learn their, as well as its, intrinsic worth.

720. Truth never lost ground by inquiry, because she is, most of all, reasonable.

721. Nor can that need another authority that is self-evident.

722. If my own reason be on the side of a principle, with what can I dispute or withstand it?

723. And if men would once consider one another reasonably, they would either reconcile their differences, or mantain them more amicably.

724. Let that, therefore, be the standard, that has most to say for itself: though of that let every man be judge for himself.

725. Reason, like the sun, is common to all: and it is for want of examining all by the same light and measure, that we are not all of the same mind: for all have it to that end, though all do not use it so.

OF FORMALITY.

726. Form is good, but not formality.

727. In the use of the best of forms there is too much of that I fear.

728. It is absolutely necessary, that this distinction should go along with people in their devotion; for too many are apter to rest upon what they do, than how they do their duty.

729. If it were considered, that it is the frame of the mind that gives our performances acceptance, we would lay more stress on our inward preparation than our outward action.

OF THE MEAN NOTIONS WE HAVE OF GOD.

730. Nothing more shows the low condition man is fallen into, than the unsuitable notion we must have of God, by the ways we take to please him.

731. As if it availed any thing to him, that we performed so many ceremonies and external forms of devotion; who never meant more by them than to try our obedience and through them, to show us something more excellent and durable beyond them.

732. Doing, while we are undoing, is good for nothing.

733. Of what benefit is it to say our prayers regularly, go to church, receive the sacrament, and, may be, go to confessions too; aye, feast the priest, and give alms to the poor; and yet lie, swear, curse, be drunk covetous, unclean, proud, revengeful, vain, or idle, at the same time.

734. Can one excuse or balance the other? Or will God think himself well served, where his law is violated? Or well used where there is so much more show than substance?

735. It is a most dangerous error, for a man to think to excuse himself in the breach of a moral duty, by a formal performance of positive worship; and less, when of human invention.

736. Our blessed Saviour most rightly and clearly distinguished and determined this case, when he told the Jews, "That they were his mother, his brethren, and sisters, who did the will of his Father."

OF THE BENEFIT OF JUSTICE.

737. Justice is a great support of society, because an insurance to all men of their property: this violated, there is no security; which throws all into confusion to recover it.

738. An honest man is a fast pledge in dealing. A man is sure to have it, if it be to be had.

739. Many are so, merely of necessity; others not so only for the same reason; but such an honest man is not to be thanked; and such a dishonest man is to be pitied.

740. But he that is dishonest for gain, is next to a robber, and to be punished for example.

741. And, indeed, there are few dealers but what are faulty; which makes trade difficult, and a great temptation to men of virtue.

742. It is not what they should, but what they can get: faults or decays must be concealed, big words given where they are not deserved, and the ignorance or necessity of the buyer imposed upon, for unjust profit.

743. These are the men that keep their words for their own ends; and are only just for fear of the magistrate.

744. A politic rather than a moral honesty; a con-

strained, not a chosen justice; according to the proverb, 'Patience *per force*, and thank you for nothing.'

745. But of all injustice, that is the greatest that passes under the name of law. A cut-purse in Westminster-Hall exceeds; for that advances injustice to oppression, where law is alleged for that which it should punish.

OF JEALOUSY.

746. The jealous are troublesome to others, but a torment to themselves.

747. Jealousy is a kind of civil war in the soul, where judgment and imagination are at perpetual jars.

748. This civil dissension in the mind, like that of the body politic, commits great disorders, and lays all waste.

749. Nothing stands safe in its way: nature, interest, religion, must yield to its fury.

750. It violates contracts, dissolves society, breaks wedlock, betrays friends and neighbors: no body is good, and every one is either doing or designing them a mischief.

751. It has a venom that more or less rankles whereever it bites: and as it reports fancies for facts, so it disturbs its own house, as often as other folks.

752. Its rise is guilt or ill-nature; and by reflection it thinks its own faults to be other men's; as he that is overrun with the jaundice takes others to be yellow.

753. A jealous man only sees his own spectrum when he looks upon other men, and gives his character in theirs.

OF STATE.

754. I love service, but not state: one is useful, the other superfluous.

755. The trouble of this, as well as charge, is real; but the advantage only imaginary.

756. Besides, it helps to set us up above ourselves, and augments our temptation to disorder.

757. The least thing out of joint, or omitted, makes us uneasy; and we are ready to think ourselves ill served about that which is of no real service at all; or so much better than other men, as we have the means of greater state.

758. But this is all for want of wisdom, which carries the truest and most forcible state along with it.

759. He that makes not himself cheap by indiscreet conversation, puts value enough upon himself every where.

760. The other is rather pageantry than state.

OF A GOOD SERVANT.

761. A true, and a good servant, are the same thing.

762. But no servant is true to his master that defrauds him.

763. Now there are many ways of defrauding a master, as, of time, care, pains, respect, and reputation, as well as money.

764. He that neglects his work, robs his master, since he is fed and paid as if he did his best: and he that is not as diligent in the absence as in the presence of his master, cannot be a true servant.

765. Nor is he a true servant that buys dear to share in the profit with the seller.

766. Nor yet he that tells tales without doors; or deals basely, in his master's name, with other people; or connives at other's loiterings, wastings, or dishonorable reflections.

767. So that a true servant is diligent, secret, and respectful; more tender of his master's honor and interest, than of his own profit.

768. Such a servant deserves well; and, if modest under his merit, should liberally feel it at his master's hand.

OF AN IMMODERATE PURSUIT OF THE WORLD.

769. It shows a depraved state of mind, to cark and care for that which one does not need.

770. Some are as eager to be rich, as ever they were to live; for superfluity, as for subsistence.

771. But that plenty should augment covetousness, is a perversion of providence; and yet the generality are the worse for their riches.

772. But it is strange that old men should excel; for generally money lies nearest them, that are the nearest their graves; as if they would augment their love, in pro-

portion to the little time they have left to enjoy it: and yet their pleasure is without enjoyment, since none enjoy what they do not use.

773. So that instead of learning to leave their great wealth easily, they hold it the faster, because they must leave it: so sordid is the temper of some men.

774. Where charity keeps pace with gain, industry is blessed: but to slave to get, and keep it sordidly, is a sin, against providence, a vice in government, and an injury to their neighbors.

775. Such as they, spend not one fifth of their income; and, it may be, give not one tenth of what they spend to the needy.

776. This is the worst sort of idolatry, because there can be no religion in it, nor ignorance pleaded in excuse of it; and that it wrongs other folks that ought to share therein.

OF THE INTEREST OF THE PUBLIC IN OUR ESTATES.

777. Hardly any thing is given us for ourselves, but the public may claim a share with us. But of all we call ours, we are most accountable to God, and the public, for our estates: in this we are but stewards: and to hoard up all to ourselves is great injustice, as well as ingratitude.

778. If all men were so far tenants to the public, that the superfluities of gain and expense were applied to the exigences thereof, it would put an end to taxes, leave not a beggar, and make the greatest bank for national trade in Europe.

779. It is a judgment upon us, as well as weakness, though we will not see it, to begin at the wrong end.

780. If the taxes we give are not to maintain pride, I am sure there would be less, if pride were made a tax to the government.

781. I confess I have wondered that so many lawful and useful things are exercised by laws, and pride left to reign free over them and the public.

782. But, since people are more afraid of the laws of man than of God, because their punishment seems to be

nearest, I know not how magistrates can be excused in their suffering such excess with impunity.

783. Our noble English patriarchs as well as patriots, were so sensible of this evil, that they made several excellent laws, commonly called sumptuary, to forbid, at least limit, the pride of the people; and, because the execution of them would be our interest and honor, their neglect must be our just reproach and loss.

784. It is but reasonable that the punishment of pride and excess should help to support the government; since it must otherwise inevitably be ruined by them.

785. But some say, 'It ruins trade, and will make the poor burdensome to the public:' but if such trade, in consequence, ruins the kingdom, is it not time to ruin that trade? Is moderation no part of our duty; and is temperance an enemy to government.

786. He is a Judas, that will get money by any thing.

787. To wink at a trade that effeminates the people, and invades the ancient discipline of the kingdom, is a crime capital, and to be severely punished, instead of being excused by the magistrate.

788. Is there no better employment for the poor than luxury? Miserable nation!

789. What did they before they fell into these forbidden methods? Is there not land enough in England to cultivate, and more and better manufactories to be made?

790. Have we no room for them in our plantations, about things that may augment trade, without luxury?

791. In short, let pride pay, and excess be well excised; and if that will not cure the people, it will help to keep the kingdom.

THE VAIN MAN.

792. But a vain man is a nauseous creature: he is so full of himself, that he has no room for anything else, be it ever so good or deserving.

793. It is I, at every turn, that does this, or can do that. And as he abounds in his comparisons, so he is sure to give himself the better of every body else: according to the proverb, 'All his geese are swans.'

794. They are certainly to be pitied that can be so much mistaken at home.

795. And yet I have sometimes thought, that such people are, in a sort, happy, that nothing can put out of countenance with themselves, though they neither have nor merit other people's.

796. But, at the same time, one would wonder they should not feel the blows they give themselves, or get from others, for this intolerable and ridiculous temper; nor show any concern at that, which makes others blush for, as well as at them; viz. their unreasonable assurance.

797. To be a man's own fool is bad enough; but the vain man is every body's.

798. This silly disposition comes of a mixture of ignorance, confidence and pride; and as there is more or less of the last, so it is more or less offensive, or entertaining.

799. And yet, perhaps the worst part of this vanity is its unteachableness. Tell it any thing, and it has known it long ago; and outruns information and instruction, or else proudly puffs at it.

800. Whereas the greatest understandings doubt most, are readiest to learn, and least pleased with themselves; this, with nobody else.

801. For though they stand on higher ground, and so see farther than their neighbors, they are yet humbled by their prospect, since it shows them something so much higher, and above their reach.

802. And truly then it is that sense shines with the greatest beauty, when it is set in humility.

803. An humble able man is a jewel worth a kingdom; it is often saved by him, as Solomon's poor wise man did the city.

804. May we have more of them or less need of them.

THE CONFORMIST.

805. It is reasonable to concur, where conscience does not forbid compliance; for conformity is at least a civil virtue.

806. But we should only press it in necessaries; the rest may prove a snare or temptation to break society.

807. But, above all, it is a weakness in religion and government, where it is carried to things of an indifferent nature; since, besides that it makes way for scruples, liberty is always the price of it.

808. Such conformists have little to boast of, and, therefore, the less reason to reproach others that have more latitude.

809. And yet the latitudinarian that I love, is one that is only so in charity: for the freedom I recommend is no skepticism in judgment, and much less so in practice.

THE OBLIGATIONS OF GREAT MEN TO ALMIGHTY GOD.

810. It seems but reasonable that those whom God has distinguished from others by his goodness, should distinguish themselves to him by their gratitude.

811. For though he has made of one blood all nations, he has not ranged or dignified them upon the level, but in a sort of subordination and dependency.

812. If we look upwards, we find it in the heavens, where the planets have their several degrees of glory; and so the other stars, of magnitude and lustre.

813. If we look upon the earth, we see it among the trees of the wood, from the cedar to the bramble; among the fishes, from the leviathan to the sprat; in the air, among the birds, from the eagle to the sparrow; among the beasts, from the lion to the cat; and among mankind, from the king to the scavenger.

814. Our great men, doubtless, were designed, by the wise framer of the world, for our religious, moral, and politic planets; for lights and directions to the lower ranks of the numerous company of their own kind, both in precepts and examples; and they are well paid for their pains too, who have the honor and service of their fellow creatures, and the marrow and fat of the earth for their share.

815. But is it not a most unaccountable folly, that men should be proud of the providences that should humble them? or think the better of themselves, instead of him who raised them so much above the level; or of being so in their lives, in return for his extraordinary favors?

816. But it is but too near akin to us, to think no further than ourselves either in the acquisition, or use, of our wealth and greatness: when, alas! they are the preferments of Heaven, to try our wisdom, bounty and gratitude.

817. It is a dangerous perversion of the end of providence, to consume the time, power, and wealth, he has given us above other men, to gratify our sordid passions, instead of playing the good stewards, to the honor of our great benefactor, and the good of our fellow creatures.

818. But it is an injustice too; since those higher ranks of men are but the trustees of Heaven, for the benefit of lesser mortals: who as minors, are entitled to all their care and provision.

819. For though God has dignified some men above their brethren, it never was to serve their pleasures; but that they might take pleasure to serve the public.

820. For this cause, doubtless, it was that they were raised above necessity, or any trouble to live, that they might have more time and ability to care for others: and it is certain, where that use is not made of the bounties of providence, they are embezzled and wasted.

821. It has often struck me with a serious reflection, when I have observed the great inequality of the world; that one man should have such numbers of his fellow creatures to wait upon him, who have souls to be saved as well as he; and this not for business, but state. Certainly a poor employment of his money, and a worse of their time.

822. But that any one man should make work for so many, or rather keep them from work to make up a train, has a levity of luxury in it very reprovable, both in religion and government.

823. But even in allowable services, it has an humbling consideration, and what should raise the thankfulness of the great men to him who so much bettered their circumstances; and moderate the use of their dominion over those of their own kind.

824. When the poor Indians hear us call any of our family by the name of servants, they cry out, 'What! call brethren servants! we call our dogs servants, but never men.' The moral certainly can do us no harm, but may

instruct us to abate our height and narrow our state and attendance.

825. And what has been said of their excess may, in some measure, be applied to other branches of luxury, that set ill examples to the lesser world, and rob the needy of their pensions.

826. God Almighty touch the hearts of our grandees with a sense of his distinguished goodness, and the true end of it; that they may better distinguish themselves in their conduct, to the glory of Him that has thus liberally preferred them, and to the benefit of their fellow creatures!

OF REFINING UPON OTHER MEN'S ACTIONS OR INTERESTS.

827. This seems to be the master piece of our politicians; but no body shoots more at randon than those refiners.

828. A perfect lottery, and mere hazard! since the true spring of the actions of men is as invisible as their hearts; and so are the thoughts too, of their several interests.

829. He that judges of other men by himself, does not always hit the mark: because all men have not the same capacity, nor passions in interest.

830. If an able man refines upon the proceedings of an ordinary capacity, according to his own, he must ever miss it: but much more the ordinary man, when he shall pretend to speculate the motives to the able man's actions; for the able man deceives himself by making the other wiser than he is in the reason of his conduct; and the ordinary man makes himself so, in presuming to judge of the reasons of the abler man's actions.

831. It is, in short, a word, a maze; and of nothing are we more uncertain, nor in any thing do we oftener befool ourselves.

832. The mischiefs are many that follow this humor, and dangerous: for men misguide themselves, act upon false measures, and meet frequently with mischievous disappointments.

833. It excludes all confidence in commerce, allows of no such thing as a principle in practice; supposes every

man to act upon other reasons that what appear; and that there is no such thing as uprightness or sincerity among mankind: a trick, instead of truth.

834. Neither allowing nature, or religion, but some worldly turn or advantage, to be the true, the hidden motive of all men.

835. It is hard to express its uncharitableness, as well as uncertainty; and has more of vanity than benefit in it.

836. This foolish quality gives a large field; but let what I have said serve, for this time.

OF CHARITY.

837. Charity has various senses, but is excellent in all of them.

838. It imparts, first, the commiseration of the poor and unhappy of mankind, and extends a helping hand to mend their condition.

839. They that feel nothing of this are, at best, not above half of kin to the human race; since they must have no bowels, which make such an essential part thereof, who have no more nature.

840. A man! and yet not have the feeling of the wants or needs of his own flesh and blood! a monster rather! and may he never be suffered to propagate such an unnatural stock in the world!

841. Such an uncharitableness spoils the best gains; and two to one but it entails a curse upon the possessors.

842. Nor can we expect to be heard of God in our prayers, that turn the deaf ear to the petitions of the distressed among our fellow creatures.

843. God sends the poor to try us; as well as he tries them by being such: and he that refuses them a little, out of the great deal that God has given him, lays up poverty in store for his own posterity.

844. I will not say these works are meritorious, but I dare say they are acceptable, and go not without their reward; though, to humble us in our fullness, and liberality too, we only give what is given us to give, as well as to use: for if we ourselves are not our own, less is that so which God has intrusted us with.

845. Next, charity makes the best construction of things and persons; and is so far from being an evil spy, a back-biter, or a detractor, that it excuses weakness, extenuates miscarriages, makes the best of every thing, forgives every body, serves all, and hopes to the end.

846. It moderates extremes, is always for expedients, labors to accommodate differences, and had rather suffer than revenge; and is so far from exacting the utmost farthing, that it had rather lose, than seek its own violently.

847. As it acts freely, so zealously too; but it is always to do good, for it hurts nobody.

848. An universal enemy against discord, and a holy cement for mankind.

849. And lastly, it is love to God and the brethren, which raises the soul above all worldly considerations; and as it gives a taste of heaven upon earth, so it is heaven, in the fullness of it, to the truly charitable here.

850. This is the noblest sense charity has: after which all should press, as that " more excellent way."

851. Nay, most excellent; for as faith, hope, and charity, were the more excellent way that the great apostle discovered to the Christians; (too apt to stick in outward gifts and church performances) so, of that better way, he preferred charity as the best part, because it would outlast the rest and abide forever.

852. Wherefore a man can never be a true and good Christian without charity, even in the lowest sense of it; and yet he may have that part thereof, and still be none of the apostle's true Christian: since he tells us, " That though we should give all our goods to the poor, and want charity, (in her other and higher senses) it would profit us nothing."

853. Nay, " Though we had all tongues, all knowledge, and even gifts of prophecy, and were preachers to others, aye, and had zeal enough to give our bodies to be burned; yet if we wanted charity, it would not avail us for salvation.

854. It seems it was his (and indeed ought to be our) " Unum necessarium," or the " One thing needful;" which our Saviour attributed to Mary, in preference to her sister

Martha, that seems not to have wanted the lesser parts of charity.

855. Would to God this divine virtue were more implanted and diffused among mankind, the pretenders to Christianity especially; and we should certainly mind piety more than controversy; and exercise love and compassion, instead of censuring and persecuting one another, in any manner whatsoever.

BAXTER'S CALL TO THE UNCONVERTED

Bound in neat cloth. 18mo, 240 pp.

GOULD'S SYSTEM OF STENOGRAPHY; or, THE ART OF SHORT-HAND WRITING. 18mo, 260 pp.

HAZEN'S PANORAMA OF TRADES AND PROFESSIONS; or, EVERY MAN'S BOOK. Embellished with eighty-two engravings. 12mo, 320 pp.

The object of this book is to give the history of the ordinary trades and professions of men, with a description of the mode of working or manufacture used in producing the various articles used in common life. It is calculated to add much to the intelligence of all, particularly the young, and increase their desire to know and capacity to learn. The use of books like this and the Book of Commerce, as reading books in classes, while at the same time they afford good reading exercises, will impart a great amount of knowledge concerning the affairs of common life, which is of inestimable value.

THE BOOK OF COMMERCE BY SEA AND LAND, exhibiting its connection with Agriculture, the Arts, and Manufactures. 12mo, 185 pp.

In this work the learner is made acquainted with the origin, mode of manufacture, and history of all the articles used in daily life. It treats of the articles of food, furs, woods, metals, minerals, fisheries, glass-ware, China, pottery, drugs, banks, customs, tariff, history of commerce, &c. It is used in the best schools in New England, the city of Philadelphia, and other parts of the Union.

SUPER ROYAL OXFORD OCTAVO BIBLE.

Bound in sheep. The most beautiful edition of the Bible published.

This edition of the Bible is printed on a beautiful large type, incomparably more convenient for family use than the cumbrous quartos. The utmost care has been used to have it free from typographical errors. It is believed to approach nearer to perfection than any Bible extant and sold at a low price.

SCHOOL EDITIONS OF MILTON'S PARADISE LOST, POLLOK'S COURSE OF TIME, YOUNG'S NIGHT THOUGHTS, COWPER'S TASK, and THOMSON'S SEASONS. 18 mo.

These will be found the cheapest and best school editions of those authors published.

THE UNIVERSAL CLASS-BOOK. By T. Hughs.

This work contains a selection of the best specimens of the best English and American authors, and is offered at a price considerably less than that of any similar book in the market.

RANDOLPH'S ARITHMETIC ; or, THE PRACTICAL TEACHER ; being an easy and rational introduction to arithmetic, designed for beginners of every age. 12mo, 192 pp.

The following is an extract from a notice received from a number of teachers of Baltimore :—

We have examined, with attention, Mr. Randolph's system of arithmetic, and take pleasure in stating that, in our estimation, it is greatly superior, as an elementary work, to any thing of the kind that has fallen under our notice, &c.

Recommendation from Philadelphia teachers :—

The undersigned consider Mr. Randolph's Arithmetic one of the best productions of the kind which has fallen under their notice. It is what it pretends to be, "An Easy and Rational Introduction to Arithmetic." His definitions are clear and determinate. His rules are expressed in language so plain as to be intelligible to the youngest learner; their application is ample and judicious, and the whole is well calculated to sharpen and invigorate the intellect of youth, to lighten the labour of teaching, and render the study of this important branch of education pleasant and interesting.

Though this system is well calculated for general use, yet it seems to be particularly adapted to female seminaries, as it affords ample means for overcoming that disgust which females too often feel for this study, and for inspiring them with an attachment for this most useful science.

R. W. Cushman,	W. E. Ashton,	S. W. Crawford,
C. B. Trego,	William Mann,	D. R. Ashton.

GREEN'S INDUCTIVE GRAMMAR ; designed to give young pupils a knowledge of the first principles of language, accompanied by progressive parsing lessons: the whole intended to inculcate habits of thinking, reasoning, and expressing thought. By Richard W. Green. 18mo, 180 pp.

VALPY'S PALEY'S MORAL AND POLITICAL PHILOSOPHY ; with questions adapted to the use of schools, by R. W. Green ; to which are added notes from popular authors, embracing present opinions in ethical science, and an exposition of our own political institutions; the whole carefully adapted to the use of schools of both sexes. 12mo, 298 pp.

Paley's Moral Philosophy is a standard book. It is found in every gentleman's library, and is made use of as a text-book in many of our schools and colleges. It is a treatise above all others the best adapted to general use, both on account of its clearness of method and aptness of illustration, and also because it contains a code of ethics more universal in its application than any other. In the language of an English reviewer, "it is a masterly and inimitable work." He had many points of resemblance to Socrates ; the philosophy of both was common sense, and their study human nature.

www.ingramcontent.com/pod-product-compliance
Lightning Source LLC
LaVergne TN
LVHW010228110826
845151LV00004B/1217